7.95

6/93
STRAND PRICE
$20.00

6 23
STRAND PRICE
5.00

D1376763

# FOUNTAINS and POOLS

# FOUNTAINS and POOLS

## Construction Guidelines and Specifications

### Second Edition

## C. DOUGLAS AURAND

VNR VAN NOSTRAND REINHOLD
New York

Copyright ©1991 by Van Nostrand Reinhold

Library of Congress Catalog Card Number 90-49701
ISBN 0-442-00696-9

All rights reserved. No part of this work covered by the
copyright hereon may be reproduced or used in any form or
by any means — graphic, electronic, or mechanical, including
photocopying, recording, taping, or information storage and
retrieval systems — without written permission of the
publisher.

Manufactured in the United States of America

Published by Van Nostrand Reinhold
115 Fifth Avenue
New York, New York 10003

Chapman and Hall
2-6 Boundary Row
London, SE1 8HN

Thomas Nelson Australia
102 Dodds Street
South Melbourne 3205
Victoria, Australia

Nelson Canada
1120 Birchmount Road
Scarborough, Ontario M1K 5G4, Canada

16   15   14   13   12   11   10   9   8   7   6   5   4   3   2   1

**Library of Congress Cataloging-in-Publication Data**
Aurand, C. Douglas, 1956-
    Fountains and pools : construction guidelines and specifications /
C. Douglas Aurand. — 2nd ed.
        p.   cm.
    Includes bibliographical references and index.
    ISBN 0-442-00696-9
    1. Fountains — Design and construction.   I. Title.
TH4977.A87   1991
627 — dc20                                              90-49701
                                                          CIP

# CONTENTS

# PREFACE

In 1983 the author was contacted by the Landscape Architecture Foundation to expand on several curriculum handouts and to write a technical article pertaining to fountain implementation. This article was intended to be a condensed chapter in a handbook of construction.

After compiling the technical data required to write this article, the following observations were made:

1. The texts that had been published on water features were primarily devoted to the explanation of design principles and implications.
2. Technical data which existed were not comprehensive in nature. No text existed which elaborated on material selection, mechanical systems, electrical systems, basin sizing and construction detailing.
3. Technical data that were available assumed that the reader had substantial knowledge of the subject and did not require in depth explanation of the systems involved in implementing the fountain.

In light of these observations an expanded text in an independent publication was proposed.

Deep-felt appreciation goes out to the Foundation. Without their insight, encouragement and editorial comments, this text would never have been written.

At this time you may be asking yourself the following questions: Is this book for me? Should I buy it? If I buy this book will I be able to produce a complete set of construction drawings? Why should I produce construction documents when I can get this service free from certain fountain component manufacturers?

This book is intended for all designers involved with implementing a fountain design. The reader needs no previous knowledge of fountains prior to reading this text. Although the title specifically pertains to fountains, the contents is far more reaching than just implementation of a fountain. By all means buy the book, it is intended to be a reference book for all libraries.

Although comprehensive in nature, this book will not solve every problem or answer every question. Asking an author to write a book which would allow a designer to prepare a complete set of construction drawings would be as ludicrous as asking a physician to diagnose a rare disease over the phone. In both cases the "patient" must be studied before the antidote is prescribed. Construction detailing is more involved than tracing a detail out of a book or detail file. Each detail must be studied and revised accordingly to fit your site specific condition. Working out each construction detail is as much of a design problem as the actual aesthetics. Before you tell the contractor how, know why.

When receiving free construction drawings from product manufacturer, the designer should be aware of the old saying, "TANSTAAFL." Be aware that this service is free because you have committed yourself to using products from only one manufacturer.

Before committing to one manufacturer the designer should mentally answer the following questions:

1. By specifying products from only one manufacturer, will I receive a competitive bid proposal? Specifying several product options may lead to competitive prices.
2. Do other manufacturers supply a similar quality component at a cheaper price?
3. Are the components specified by the manufacturer the best-suited products for my specific application? Can a superior individual product be found?
4. Does the manufacturer produce a wide selection of components that will fulfill my needs? Some manufacturers have limited product lines.
5. Will the design intention of the fountain be modified by the component manufacturer so they can utilize their product line?
6. Who assumes the liability for omissions and errors in the construction documents?

Even if you decide to obtain free consulting work, this book will make you more knowledgeable about the subject and enable you to talk intelligently with the owner and consultant.

# 1

# INTRODUCTION

Various texts explain the many facets and implementations of fountain design. The main thrust of this book is to elaborate on the literature and provide information for the specification and construction of the fountain elements. After developing a strong concept for a fountain, the designer must determine the feasibility of beginning the design implementation phase of the project. Before proceeding into this phase, one should consider location, purpose, maintenance and feasibility of the fountain.[1]

Fountains will be affected by various environmental factors. High winds, dust, sun, and temperature extremes all affect water quality and longevity of fountain equipment. Specific site locations should consider these environmental factors.

Of equal importance is the purpose of the fountain. The fountain could be utilized to fulfill the following site considerations or program elements: 1) recreation and wading, 2) alteration of environmental factors to increase human comfort, 3) project image, 4) focal point, and 5) an organizing element for the site, or 6) enframing or captivating views.

Fountains in which people can interact with water will need additional precautions to ensure user safety. Protection of young children is imperative. Many local authorities will consider your fountain a swimming pool and require filtration and water sterilization.

Fountains are not different than fast cars, plush homes, and show dogs. They all require continual maintenance to ensure their long lasting beauty. The project owner should be aware of the maintenance requirements necessary to maintain good water quality and prevent clogging of fountain nozzles. Larger fountains may require one person whose specific responsibility is fountain maintenance. Consequently an appropriate maintenance budget must be considered as part of the overall project costs.

Fountains frequently become vehicles for a designer's ego. However, budget, purpose, and practicality must be considered by the designer to establish feasibility of fountain construction. If these factors are all favorable, the designer should proceed into the design implementation phase of the fountain. To assist the designer in the process, this book is divided into six areas: material selection and specification, mechanical systems, electrical systems, basin sizing and hydraulic calculations, construction detailing, and specialty items.

Appropriate material selection is important to create a durable and beautiful fountain that requires little maintenance. McCulley, in *The Handbook of Landscape Architectural Construction,* briefly describes the various qualities of fountain construction materials. This book elaborates on the material qualities and gives general guidelines for installation and specifications for them.

To select construction materials suitable for fountain construction, the designer must consider: durability, weight, longevity, resistance to weathering and cracking, and cost. All of these factors should be thoroughly understood early in the detail design and phase.

## PUBLIC WATER FEATURES

Throughout history, water features have been used for utilitarian purposes such as irrigation channels or public water supplies (See Figures 1.3 to 1.6). Examples of this are best represented by the Court of Oranges in Cordoba, Spain. In other periods of history, water features were used as methods of entertainment for royal families and their guests (See Figures 1.7 to 1.10). Just imagine life without television, movies, radio, discos or hot tubs. All kinds of games, visual effects, art, and items of conversation had to be created to occupy the idle minds of the royalty. During this period of history, the various royal water features must have provided similar environmental stimulation as our modern day surround-a-sound movies, 3-D glasses or compact disc players.

Visual interest, surprise, noise, changing images, and reflected light, were all provided for the guests. The foun-

**Figure 1.1** *Design concept destroyed by the insertion of a down spout into the fountain basin. Tulsa, Oklahoma.*

**Figure 1.2** *Ashes to ashes, dust to dust.*

**Figure 1.4** *Decorative drinking fountain. Enid, Oklahoma.*

**Figure 1.3** *Water source and wall mask. Great Britain.*

**Figure 1.5** *Decorative drinking fountain. Washington, District of Columbia.*

**Figure 1.6** *Decorative drinking fountain. London, England.*

**Figure 1.7** *Formal fountain. Castle Howard, England.*

**Figure 1.8** *Formal fountain. Castle Howard, England.*

**Figure 1.9** *Italian water garden. Hyde Park, London, England.*

tains provided all of the elements of nature which modern day electronics try to simulate.

Although these fountains were mainly intended for private use by royalty and their guests, their current day enjoyment has shifted to the general public. Much of the current day infatuation with water features revolves around vacation visits to the gardens of European kings and queens. These images have been modified and altered to comply with site conditions, budget and design theme to create our modern day fountains.

In most current day applications, water features are being used to fulfill one or more of the following design program requirements.

1. Create a setting, project image or backdrop for development (See Figures 1.11 and 1.12).
2. Develop a focal point or point of interest (See Figures 1.13 and 1.14).
3. Alter the perception of environmental conditions through:
   a. Masking of site noise;
   b. Altering the perception of extreme heat and humidity.
4. Provide a point of conversation or entertainment (See Figures 1.15 to 1.19).
5. Connect site elements or order and unite a series of spaces or design elements (See Figure 1.20).

## THE CITY OF FOUNTAINS

Several cities have tried to create urban fabric and identity by structuring their city around spaces graced with fountains.

3

**Figure 1.10** *Italian water garden. Hyde Park, London, England.*

**Figure 1.11** *Fountain used as a setting for buildings. Kew Gardens, England.*

**Figure 1.12** *Project image created by fountain and building. Chesapeake, Virginia.*

**Figure 1.13** *A fountain as a focal point of a park. Royal Leamington Spa, England.*

These fountains range in size from small garden scaled fountains, to water channels and large urban participatory fountains. In concept, this idea creates a wonderful atmosphere of beauty and solice.

Location of the fountains becomes critical for this purpose. Typically a group of fountains is located at key vistas to create a visual connection or axial relationship between major roads and urban open spaces. In some cities these fountains may even be memorials or reflecting pools.

Smaller fountains are located in city parks, and small urban spaces. These fountains serve as focal points for urban space and are intended to be enjoyed by people looking into or sitting in the urban space. Generally these fountains are sculptural in nature and may be constructed from carved stone or cast iron.

In addition to the two other types of fountains, these cities typically have one large major fountain. This fountain may consist of water channels, water gardens and/or participatory fountains in an urban space. These urban spaces are gathering places for people, encouraging them to come downtown and enjoy the city. In come cities these fountains are located close to municipal centers and create a sense of presence or importance to the governmental offices.

The overall image of the city is enhanced by the urban public spaces required for construction of these fountains. The fountains, parks and or planting provide a much needed visual break in the sea of asphalt, buildings and parking facilities. It is commendable that these cities realize the splendor and psychological benefits of providing quality urban open spaces.

The success of this fountain concept is directly related to the quality of each individual fountain. In an attempt to provide numerous fountains, some municipalities have set unrealistic construction or maintenance budgets. Use of improper construction techniques and deletion of filtration equipment are measures taken to reduce construction

**Figure 1.14** *A fountain as a point of interest. Boston, Massachusetts.*

**Figure 1.16** *Rotating granite sphere fountain. Wilmington, Delaware.*

Photo by R. John Summers

**Figure 1.15** *Cast bronze willow tree and fountain. Chatsworth, England.*

**Figure 1.17** *Dog swimming in fountain. Boston, Massachusetts.*

**Figure 1.18** *Children playing in fountain. Portsmouth, Virginia.*

**Figure 1.19** *Children playing in fountain. Portsmouth, Virginia.*

**Figure 1.22** *Gunite and stone lake edge. Virginia Beach, Virginia.*

**Figure 1.20** *Axis of garden defined with fountain. Compton Acres, England.*

**Figure 1.23** *Timber lake edge. Newport News, Virginia.*

**Figure 1.21** *Lawn Lake Edge. Newport News, Virginia.*

**Figure 1.24** *River rock lake edge with automatic fill device. Tulsa, Oklahoma.*

budgets. These shortcomings typically plague installations and create a negative attitude toward fountains. Like other types of construction, a poorly maintained and vandalized facility creates such a negative impression that the community would be better off without the faciltity.

## LAKE FOUNTAINS

Lakes and lake-related fountains are the newest trend in office complexes. These lakes are used for decorative purposes or as retention basins for paving run-off. In both instances, a well designed lake should include the following items:

1. Edge treatment
2. Water source
3. Water effects
4. Overflow
5. Filter or chemical treatment of water.

## EDGE TREATMENT

Evaporation and rainstorms can cause fluctuation of the lake level. This fluctuation can lead to overwatering of grass or plantings. If the lake edge abutts the lawn, swampy conditions will exist at the waterline. This makes grass mowing almost impossible. In addition, periods of drought can expose the dirt sides of the lake thus creating an unsightly view.

To alleviate these problems, edging material such as gravel, rock, gunite, or wetland plantings should be utilized. These materials allow for a variety of aesthetics effects (See Figures 1.21 to 1.24).

## LAKE WATER SOURCES

A supply of fresh water should be used to replenish lake water lost through evaporation. A properly designed system requires an automatic fill device, fill valve and water source.

Under certain conditions, automatic fill devices typically used on fountains can be easily clogged by lake dirt. A mercury float switch which is employed as a switch to control an electric solenoid valve will provide the best service with the least maintenance. As the lake level drops, the float valve drops and the circuit between the float switch and the solenoid valve is completed. When energized with current, the valve is opened and water is supplied to the lake until the float valve is raised.

In most instances the fresh water supply line can be located under water or connected to a decorative outlet along the lake edge (See Figure 1.24). This line is connected to a well or the city water line. In well applications the mercury float switch should also be used to start the well pump. If city water is used, a backflow preventor should be employed between the outfall device and the connection to city water.

**Figure 1.25** *Floating fountain. Virginia Beach, Virginia.*

**Figure 1.26** *Sewage lagoon pump.*

**Figure 1.27** *On shore pump vault.*

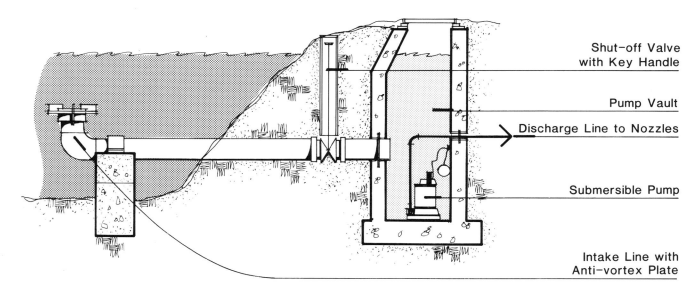

Shut-off Valve
with Key Handle

Pump Vault

Discharge Line to Nozzles

Submersible Pump

Intake Line with
Anti-vortex Plate

## Submersible Pump Vault on Shore

**Figure 1.28**

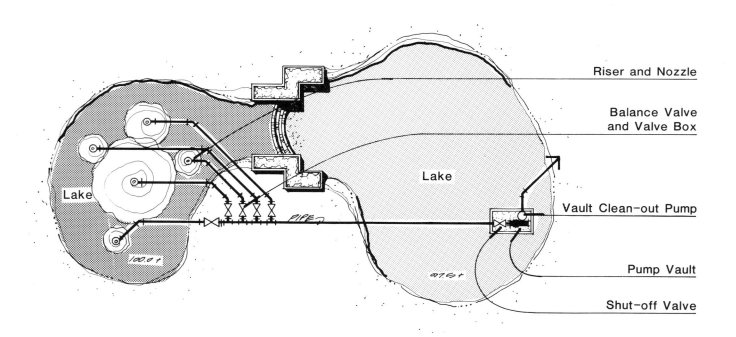

Riser and Nozzle

Balance Valve
and Valve Box

Lake

Vault Clean-out Pump

Pump Vault

Shut-off Valve

Lake

## Balancing Valves on Shore

**Figure 1.29**

## LAKE WATER EFFECTS

Water effects in lakes can be created through floating fountain units, sewage lagoon pumps connected to nozzles or permanent submersible pumps, vault and nozzle supports. In addition to creating visual interest, the introduction of aerated water reduces the potential of algae build-up in the lake.

## FLOATING FOUNTAINS

A floating fountain is by far the cheapest method of creating water effects in lakes. These units are pre-manufactured and are somewhat limited by the nozzle-displays which the manufacturers supply. They are anchored to the lake floor with cable and three weighted anchors. Underwater electrical cable supplies current to the unit from a control panel located onshore. In addition, units are supplied with various options and factory supplied lighting. Most manufacturers recommend removal of the floating fountain from the lake during winter. This allows the motor to be oiled and stored out of freezing water.

Care should be taken in designing the lake depth to accommodate the actual height of the float and submersible pump. If the lake is too shallow, the motor will sit in muddy water and be damaged by the dirt which moves through the submersible pump (See Figure 1.25).

## SEWAGE LAGOON PUMPS

Sewage lagoon pumps are suitable for lake applications. These pumps are set on a concrete slab located on the lake floor. They are designed to pump dirty water and are not impacted by the dirt on the lake floor. In this setting these pumps are located at low elevations in the lake and are connected to nozzles or waterfalls with poly piping or schedule 80 P.V.C. piping (See Figure 1.26).

## PERMANENT SUBMERSIBLE PUMP VAULTS AND NOZZLES

The most permanent approach to design of lake water effect systems is to include a permanent pump vault and nozzle riser system. Pump vaults can be located onshore or in the lake bottom. Onshore pump vaults are connected to the lake with a connection pipe which floods the vault and provides an onshore access to the pump and piping (See Figures 1.27 and 1.28).

Water located pump vaults are located at a low elevation in the lake. These vaults are supplied with submersible pumps. Typically they are constructed of concrete and covered with a suction screen on top of the the vault to prevent pump damage. Piping is run from the vault to a concrete post which encases the pipe riser and creates stability to the nozzle. Piping can be diverted to land located balancing valves which aid in nozzle adjustment (See Figure 1.29).

Several precautions should be taken to ensure proper operation of the submersed pump vault. The vault should be provided with a low-water cut-off which will not be influenced by too much water turbulence in the vault. In addition, a method of vault drainage should be provided so that pumps can be accessed for service. Drain down valves and/or sump pumps are suited for draining of the vault once the lake level has been reduced. In this application, the lake must be drained to service the equipment.

Pump vault location, lake depth and profile of the lake all impact the potential of algae build-up and damage to the submersible pumps located in the vault. The pump vault should be located and designed to create a horizontal water flow to the vault instead of a vertical flow. This will remove the potential for algae collecting in the vault and damaging the pumps. In addition, the pump vault top should be raised to an elevation so that lake floor dirt is not drawn into the vault.

**Figure 1.30** *Lake fountain using centrifugal pump. Newport News, Virginia.*

**Figure 1.31** *Lake fountain using centrifugal pump. Newport News, Virginia.*

9

## ADDITIONAL LAKE EFFECTS

When submersible pump vaults or sewage lagoon pumps are used in a lake, waterfalls or cascades can be introduced into the lake. In both instances, the pumps are located at the lower elevation of the lake and pumped to raised elements (See Figure 1.32). These elements create additional interest for apartment or office complexes. Extensive water effects are created with minimum expense when compared to traditional fountain construction (See Figure 1.33).

## LAKE OVERFLOW DEVICES

A lake overflow device should be used to control high lake levels during periods of heavy rains. Large vertical pipes or horizontal flow channels are typically used to control high water conditions. Both devices connect the lake to a drainage channel or storm sewer. In applications where vertical overflows are used, anti-vortex plates are required to prevent vortexing of excess run-off. In most uses, a vertical overflow pipe tends to ruin the aesthetics associated with a lake. The size of the pipe and the vortex-plates are very visible and ugly when water levels drop.

## FILTER OR CHEMICAL TREATMENT OF LAKE WATER

As mentioned previously, lake depth, lake size, profile and/or percent slopes of lake bottom and walls greatly impact lake temperature, lake stratification and natural circulation. Improper consideration of these items will lead to the development of algae blooms in the lake. Algae blooms typically are unsightly, odoriferous and can clog-up pumps. Prevention of algae is critical to the aesthetics of any installation.

In the past, algae has been treated in lakes by aeration and by chemicals. Algae treatment chemicals range from algaecide to water-tinting chemicals. Water-tinting chemicals typically create an undetectable oily film on the water which prevents UV penetration into the water and thus discourages algae growth. These chemicals prevent algae growth through blockage of light. Unlike algaecides, these chemicals are fairly stable and are effective for long periods of time. In addition, aeration of water does not disseminate the chemical. The only drawback to water tinting is the unnatural blue clolor that the tinting gives to the water. Water color can be controlled by adjusting the volume of tinting applied to the lake.

**Figure 1.32** *Lake water effects in storm retention pond. Tulsa, Oklahoma.*

**Figure 1.33** *Waterfall incorporated into lake fountain. See Figure 1.32. Tulsa, Oklahoma.*

**Figure 1.34** *Lake overflow and weirs. Richmond, Virginia.*

**Figure 1.35** *Swimming pool fountain. Virginia Beach, Virginia.*

**Figure 1.37** *Water flowing from fountain to swimming pool. See Figure 1.31.*

**Figure 1.36** *Water flowing from fountain to swimming pool. See Figure 1.31.*

## COMBINING FOUNTAINS WITH SWIMMING POOLS

Fountains can be combined with swimming pools to achieve the following design features in residential applications:

1. Backdrop
2. Setting
3. Alteration of Climate
4. Introduction of Sound.

Combining the swimming pool with the fountain makes economic sense in that the pool filtration system can service both bodies of water. Filter pumps or a separate pump can be used to create the water effects. Thus the client can be provided with both a fountain and swimming pool at a reduced cost (See Figures 1.35 to 1.38).

Along with catching splash from the fountain, the swimming pool serves as a reflection pool or collection basin for the fountain. When this combination is well designed, the swimming pool appears as an attractive water feature. This allows the owner to enjoy his investment during winter and fall months. Under typical conditions, the pool would be covered and closed for this period of time.

Several minor problems may be encountered when fountains are combined with swimming pools and should be considered on a case by case basis. They are:

1. Heat loss
2. Lighting
3. Expansion joints
4. Dissimilar metals
5. Increased need for water purification chemicals.

Figure 1.38 *Water flowing from fountain to swimming pool. See Figure 1.31.*

Figure 1.39 *Garden fountain. Manteo, North Carolina.*

Figure 1.40 *Flowers in small garden fountain. Manteo, North Carolina.*

Figure 1.41 *Garden fountain. Manteo, North Carolina.*

Figure 1.42 *Drip fountain. Washington, District of Columbia.*

## HEAT LOSS IN SWIMMING POOL FOUNTAINS

Long channels or tall waterfalls which empty into swimming pools act as air conditioners or cooling towers. When pool heaters are used, a substantial loss in heat may occur, requiring an oversized pool heater to accommodate the additional heat loss. To enhance overall aesthetics, waterfall height and water volume can be adjusted to optimize heat retention. In this application, the heater should be shut off in early fall to prevent substantial heat loss.

In water channel settings, an implied connection in conjunction with separate filter systems will allow the pool and fountain to look as an integrated element. A hidden collection sump is located at the connection of the swimming pool and fountain. Each system is independent of each other and allows the owner to economically heat the pool without heating the fountain.

## LARGE SWIMMING POOL FOUNTAINS

In large applications, expansion and control joints should be used to prevent uneven settlement or material damage caused by expansion and contraction. In most cases proper detailing between channels, fountain elements and/or swimming pool should be studied to prevent cracking of the gunite shell.

## GARDEN FOUNTAINS

Throughout history small intimate fountains have been used in residential gardens and public spaces.

Initially, these water features were spouts or overflows which were used as discharge devices for springs or water sources in public squares. Through time, these design elements were used in palace and estate planning to accomplish the following goals:

1. Develop a focal point
2. Create sound and interest
3. Alter the perception of heat and humidity
4. Create tranquility associated with streams and babbling brooks in nature
5. Provide sculpture to encourage conversation.

Although these fountains are relatively small in size, they generally leave a lasting impact on their visitors. In some applications these fountains can be as small as 30 inches square and include 2-foot high sculptural elements. Rather than being massive and impressive in effect and size, the charm of these water features is created by their intimate scale and gentle nature (See Figures 1.39 to 1.44).

Some of the most memorable garden fountains are incorporated into plantings and include small pieces of bronze sculpture. In some gardens it is traditional to float flowers in the fountain, thus giving color and fragrance to the water (See Figure 1.40).

The mechanical systems for these features are relatively simple and employ small submersible pumps which supply

**Figure 1.43** *Bird fountain. Williamsburg, Virginia.*

**Figure 1.44** *Jug fountain. Longwood Gardens, Pennsylvania.*

water at low volumes. It is important to note that in some applications, bigger is not necessarily better. When fountain scale is appropriate, the sound of a water trickle from pipe as small as ¼ inch diameter can be very impressive.

It is important to note that a genuine atmosphere will not always be created by introducing fountains into every public space and garden. Poorly designed gardens and spaces will not be corrected through inclusion of a fountain. Truly well-designed intimate garden spaces incorporate level changes, paving, planting, and fountains and are designed as a total concept.

An overall design concept which considers setting and spacial sequences is also important to garden fountains. Back lighting of the water effect will enhance the overall perception and appearance of the water. The fountain should be located in the garden to take advantage of the lighting. In some settings the inclusion of water-related plantings along the border of the fountain further enhances the atmosphere of the water and water-related setting (See Figures 1.45 and 1.46).

**Figure 1.45** *Compton Acres, England.*

**Figure 1.46** *Compton Acres, England.*

**Figure 1.47** *Brick fish pool and fountain. Norfolk, Virginia.*

## FISH PONDS OR POOLS

In recent years, residential pools and fountains for the display of fish and aquatic plants have become increasingly popular. Much of the current interest in these water features has been generated by the numerous water features gracing our public spaces and a fascination with the oriental culture.

Fish ponds are most successful when located close to patios or terraces and designed as small intimate site features. The basin holding the fish should be located at a lower elevation so that you can look down into the water. This make the fish visible against the bottom of the pool. Sunken pools or elevated viewing terraces or rooms create ideal viewing situations. In addition to viewing, introduction of morning and afternoon sun produces a shimmer on the water and the fish.

Many fish enthusiasts enjoy feeding their pets at poolside. With time, some fish can be trained to eat from your hand. To accommodate feeding, a seating wall of approximately 12 to 16 inches should be incorporated into the fish pool.

Traditionally, fish ponds have consisted of unimaginative basins constructed of vinyl liners and edging. However, when combined with classic fountain features and water effects, these ponds can be imaginative, attractive and functional (See Figures 1.47 to 1.50).

## WATER EFFECTS FOR FISH

The introduction of nozzles or trickling water helps maintain fish and adds interest to a pond (See Figure 1.47). Aerating type nozzles or falling water induce air into the water. This replenishes the oxygen consumed by the fish. Without oxygen, the fish will die.

The sound of a water trickle in a fish pond can enhance its beauty. This sound is reminiscent of a "babbling brook" and creates a cooling, pleasant nature experience. Care should be taken so that extensive water turbulence is not produced in the pool. Excessive turbulence makes it difficult for the fish to navigate and can place undo stress on them.

## FISH POND SIZE

A pool depth of 16 to 18 inches is a sufficient depth for small fish species. In conjunction with this, a live well should be incorporated into the pond.

When water lilies, iris or other boxed aquatic plants are intended for use in the pool, additional water depth is required. This allows coverage of the tub and blocking which holds the plant and soil. In some situations the live well can also be used as a deep well to cover the plant and tub.

Overall pool size should be dictated by the available space and the number of fish one wishes to display. One old wives' tale states that when 'KOI' are introduced into small pools, they will adjust to their environment and maintain a small body size through their life span.

## SIZING LIVE WELLS

Live wells are generally 3 feet square with a depth of 3 feet. In colder climates, sufficient water depth should be provided so that fish are not frozen solid into the ice. In pond applications where floor drains are used, be sure not to locate the primary drain in the live well. In a properly designed pool, the basin should drain, leaving fish and water in the live well. This provides a small wet area in which to net the fish and transfer them to a temporary facility during pool cleaning (See Figure 1.50).

It is best to locate the live well away from major viewing areas as additional depth is visually distracting and will cause accumulation of dirt.

## FISH POND COLOR

Most fish ponds are painted black or constructed from a black material. This makes gold and white fish contrast with the floor, thus enhancing viewing. Care should be taken when using black fish with a black pool. When viewed in the pool, they are almost invisible until they swim to the surface. Black fish are best viewed against a beige or off-white pool.

In climatic zones with intense summer sun, shallow black pools will act as a solar collector and retain solar energy. In this situation an alternative pool color, pool shading or additional pool depth should be considered to maintain lower water temperatures. This will alleviate stress on the fish.

## WATER FEATURES AND ANIMAL EXHIBITS

Water features are currently being used to enhance animal exhibits and to provide natural barriers to animals. Proper depths and widths of water can be used in lieu of tall fencing to restrain certain animals. These dimensions are dictated by physical animal characteristics such as jumping distance, wading capability, reaching height and swimming abilities.

Natural ponds or stream features allow the designer to reduce the fencing height so that the visitor's view is unobstructed. However, the cost of water features usually limits their use to observation areas (See Figure 1.51).

## EXHIBIT FILTER SYSTEMS

Animal exhibit filter systems should be designed to partially filter water in the event of equipment failure. The total filter capacity can be split in half and handled by two separate filter systems. These two systems operate at the same time to provide the total filtration. Double pipe runs are eliminated by use of pipe manifolds and valves. When equipment fails, the other half of the system provides partial water cleaning until the equipment is repaired (See Figure 1.52).

**Figure 1.48** *Fish pool and fountain. Norfolk, Virginia.*

**Figure 1.49** *Granite cobble fish pond and fountain. Norfolk, Virginia.*

**Figure 1.50** *Fish live well. See Figure 1.49.*

15

**Figure 1.51** *Water used as a natural barrier. Newport News, Virginia.*

**Figure 1.52** *Dual filter tanks for animal exhibits. Newport News, Virginia.*

**Figure 1.53** *Interior fountain. Norfolk, Virginia.*

In the case of animal exhibits, clear, clean water is critical for the health and display of aquatics and swimming mammals. Back-up or temporary filtration capabilities are critical maintenance considerations.

## INTERIOR FOUNTAINS

Fountains are often located in building interiors to create low level background noise, a point of interest and/or a setting or theme for an interior space. These fountains vary in size from huge multi-story waterfalls to small trickling fountains which occupy areas as small as 50 square feet (See Figures 1.53 to 1.56).

When designing interior fountains, locations and context are critical. Ample space should be provided around the water feature for proper circulation. This space will allow normal circulation to continue around persons stopping to view the fountain. In tight circulation areas, sharp corners at heights between 12 and 18 inches can become a liability and should be avoided.

Treatment of basin depth and the height of the basin wall above the floor should be carefully studied to prevent people from accidentally falling into the water feature. In some applications, providing ample floor space around the water feature is an appropriate safety measure. This may allow the designer to install the fountain at floor level or in a recessed level within the floor (See Figure 1.53).

**Figure 1.54** *Interior fountain. Virginia Beach, Virginia.*

**Figure 1.55** *Interior fountain. Virginia Beach, Virginia.*

**Figure 1.56** *Interior fountain. Norfolk, Virginia.*

Views to and from the water feature are critical and are often overlooked in multi-story spaces. The fountain should look attractive from both the ground and above. Small or clear water effects such as smooth-bore nozzles are hard to see from above and should be avoided. Bolder effects such as aerating nozzles, waterfalls and watersteps are attractive looking from above and at ground level.

In addition to these design issues, it is vital that the following technical items be discussed and considered during the design phase:

1. Provide acoustical materials such as wall coverings, curtains and/or carpets in small spaces containing a fountain. This will reduce echo and soften noise of the fountain.
2. Provide mechanical systems to deal with the additional humidity created by the fountain.
3. Design the basin to prevent splash. Water on an interior floor can be a liability problem.
4. Provide filtration and sanitation of the fountain water. Super chlorination of the interior fountain water can cause an objectionable smell.
5. Provide proper space for the electrical and mechanical requirements of the fountain. In most cases a 3 foot by 3 foot room is insufficient for pumps, filter and electrical panel clearance.
6. Provide waterproof membranes when the fountain is located over an inhabited space.
7. Provide proper overflows and venting of the overflow and floor drain.

## REFLECTING POOLS

Reflecting pools are large fountains normally devoid of visible water effects. These water features are usually painted black or another dark color so that the water reflects buildings or sculpture which are located in the fountain or around the perimeter of the basin. In most situations water depths of 10 inches to 16 inches are satisfactory to deter algae and provide the proper reflective qualities. Clean, clear water is critical to maximizing the water's reflective quality.

Filter use is mandatory and requires over-sizing of suction and discharge devices so that detection of water flow can be kept to a minimum. In most applications, the water appears almost motionless and pumps or filters are hidden from sight. In hotter climates, providing additional water depth will reduce water temperature and thus prevent algae growth (See Figures 1.57 to 1.59).

**Figure 1.57** *Reflecting pool with plantings and bird fountains. See Figure 1.43. Williamsburg, Virginia.*

**Figure 1.58** *Reflecting pool with granite disk bottom. Washington, District of Columbia.*

**Figure 1.59** *Reflecting pool with granite disk bottom. Washington, District of Columbia.*

2

# MATERIAL SELECTION AND SPECIFICATIONS

## *IN SITU* CONCRETE

*In situ* concrete is a term given to any concrete that is poured in place at a job site. Concrete which is to be used for submersed situations should be high in strength, workable in the plastic stage, low in absorption, resistant to freeze-thaw cycles, durable, and crack resistant.

### Strength and Absorption

Many sources recommend 3000 psi concrete for use in swimming pools and fountains;[2] this would have sufficient strength for fountain use, but is semi-porous. By lowering the water-cement ratio, the compressive strength and water tightness of the concrete is increased (See Table 2.1). Consequently when selecting concrete psi, the higher the strength the more watertight the concrete will be.

### Durability and Workability

Of major concern is the potentially damaging osmotic pressure developed within the concrete when the water trapped in its small pores freezes. Air-entrained admixes in concrete create small air bubbles within the concrete and prevent the development of osmotic pressure.[3] The air in the bubbles keeps the pore from filling with ice and solution. If enough air bubbles are present and they are .006 inches apart, osmotic pressure will be prevented, and a more durable concrete created. In addition, these bubbles act like ball bearings in the mix thereby increasing its workability even when the water cement ratio is lowered.

When using air-entrained concrete, it is important to reduce the water-cement ratio. Lower than normal concrete

**Table 2.1 Effect of Water Content on Compressive Strength of Concrete (Non Air Entrained)**

| Water cement ratio* | Probable compressive strength (At 28 days) |
|---|---|
| 9 | 2000 psi |
| 8 | 2500 psi |
| 7 | 3200 psi |
| 6 | 4000 psi |
| 5 | 5000 psi |
| 4 | 6000 psi |

* Water-cement ratio = Gals. of water per bag of cement. From ACI 6l3: ACI Recommended practice for selecting proportions for concrete.

strengths will result if the ratio is not reduced (See Table 2.2). Water-cement ratio should be specified to attain the desired strength.

For a constant water-cement ratio, the strength of the concrete is reduced as the air content is increased. For air contents higher than those listed in Table 2.3, the strengths will be proportionately less than those shown. Strengths are based on 6 x 12 inch cylinders moist-cured under standard conditions for 28 days. (See "Method of Making and Curing Compression and Flexure Test Specimens in the Field" [ASTM Designation C31].)

19

## Cracking

Plastic cracking and thermal cracking of concrete produces small hairline cracks which may lead to seepage. Plastic cracking of concrete results from:

1. Too rapid evaporation of water from the surface of concrete.[4]
2. Settlement of the plastic concrete as it stiffens.[5]

Shrinkage cracking, a form of plastic cracking, is the result of too rapid a rate of water evaporation from the surface of the concrete. This rapid evaporation can be attributed to concrete mix conditions and environmental factors.

Grading and absorption rate of the aggregate used, mix water, slab thickness, admix characteristics, degree of compaction, and wetness of forms and subgrade all influence plastic cracking.[6] As well, relative humidity, concrete temperature, wind velocity, and degree of exposure to sun and wind all determine the amount and rate of plastic cracking.[7]

By following these recommendations plastic cracking can be reduced:

1. Pour concrete in cooler temperatures to reduce evaporation.
2. Protect concrete from the drying effects of the sun.
3. Wet forms and subgrade. Dry forms and subgrade tend to draw moisture from the concrete.
4. Reduce the temperature of concrete to be poured. This can be achieved by cooling aggregates in chilled water or by adding crushed ice as part of the mix water. Water requirements of concrete increases as mix temperature increases.[8]
5. Specify air-entrained concrete with a total air content of 4½ to 1½ percent.[9]
6. Cure concrete with proper techniques.

Plastic settlement cracking occurs because of the resistance of the form work surface to the downward settlement of the concrete, and the concrete becoming "hung up" on other reinforcing or spacers. With air entrainment and proper compaction, the probability of plastic settlement cracking is reduced.

**Figure 2.1a** *Flexibility of design form using concrete construction. Tulsa, Oklahoma.*

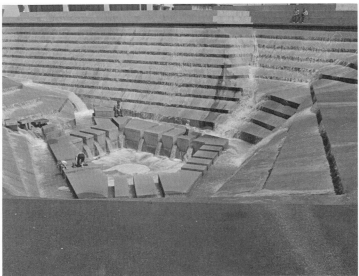

Photo by Theodore D. Walker

**Figure 2.1b** *Concrete construction. Fort Worth, Texas.*

**Table 2.2 Standard Recommended Practice for Selecting Proportions For Concrete. Compressive Strength of Concrete for Various Water-Cement Ratios***

| Water-cement ratio | Probable compressive strength at 28 days, psi | |
|---|---|---|
| gal. per bag of cement | Non-air-entrained concrete | Air-entrained concrete |
| 4 | 6000 psi | 4800 psi |
| 5 | 5000 psi | 4000 psi |
| 6 | 4000 psi | 3200 psi |
| 7 | 3200 psi | 2600 psi |
| 8 | 2500 psi | 2000 psi |
| 9 | 2000 psi | 1600 psi |

*\* These average strengths are for concrete containing not more than the percentages of entrained and/or entrapped air shown in Table 2.3*

**Table 2.3 Approximate Mixing Water Requirements for Different Slumps and Maximum Sizes of Aggregates***

| | Slump, inches | Aggregate size, inches | | | | | |
|---|---|---|---|---|---|---|---|
| | | 3/8" | 1/2" | 3/4" | 1" | 1 1/2" | |
| Non air-entrained concrete | 1 to 2 | 42 | 40 | 37 | 36 | 33 | gallons of water per cubic yard of concrete |
| | 3 to 4 | 46 | 44 | 41 | 39 | 36 | |
| Approximate amount of entrapped air in non air-entrained concrete, percent | | 3 | 2.5 | 2 | 1.5 | 1 | |
| Air-entrained concrete | 1 to 2 | 37 | 36 | 33 | 31 | 29 | gallons of water per cubic yard of concrete |
| | 3 to 4 | 41 | 39 | 36 | 34 | 32 | |
| Recommended average of total air content, percent | | 8 | 7 | 6 | 5 | 4.5 | |

*\* These quantities of mixing water are for use in computing cement factors for trial batches. They are maximum for reasonable well-shaped, angular, coarse aggregates graded within limits of accepted specifications. If more water is required than shown, the cement factor, estimated from these quantities should be increased to maintain desired water-cement ratio, except as otherwise indicated by laboratory tests for strength. If less water is required than shown, the cement factor, estimated from these quantities, should not be decreased except as indicated by laboratory tests for strength.*

## Semi-porous Concrete

Concrete for use in fountains and swimming pools should conform to the following standards:

1. Cement should be portland cement or sulphate-resistant cement if sulphates are present in the subsoil.
2. The maximum cement content of a compacted concrete should be 600 lbs. per cubic yard.
3. The maximum water/cement ratio should be 0.50 by weight.
4. Concrete slump should be 1 to 2½ inches maximum.
5. Aggregates should not exceed ¾ of an inch.
6. Admixture can be used, but must be chloride-free.
7. Minimum compressive strength at 28 days should be 3000 psi.[10]

## Waterproof Concrete

Waterproof concrete is often used in water tanks and hydraulic structures. This concrete is similar to that recommended for pools (semi-porous concrete) except for:

1. Minimum compressive strength at 28 days should be 4000 psi.[11]
2. The water-cement ratio of the mix should not exceed 6 gallons per sack of cement. As water content of the mix increases, the permeability of the concrete increases.[12]
3. The mix should contain air-entrained cement (ASTM C260). The addition of air entrainment reduces porosity.[13]

## Surface Treatment

Much controversy exists over the application of surface treatments to increase concrete durability. In freeze-thaw conditions, normal concrete has a tendency to deteriorate quickly. Before specifying a surface treatment to improve concrete durability, the designer should check with the manufacturer for testing results.

Most surface treatments are a temporary coating and need to be replenished periodically. The following chart summarizes research conducted by L.C. Porter for the A.C.I. on the increased durability of concrete through surface coating (See Table 2.5).

**Figure 2.2** *Surface-treated concrete. Aquarium, Baltimore, Maryland.*

**Table 2.4 Suggested Concrete Mix***

| Material | Standard | Weight or volume |
|---|---|---|
| Portland cement Type I, II, or V | ASTM C150 | 112 lbs. |
| Fine aggregate (A natural sand) | ASTM C33 | 210 lbs. |
| Coarse aggregate (Crushed stone, ¾ in. maximum size) | ASTM C133 | 340 lbs. |
| Maximum water-cement ratio (by weight) 0.50 | | 5.5 gal. (49.90 lbs.) |

*\* Procedures and processes for ready mix concrete are covered in ASTM C94.*

**Table 2.5 Surface Treated Concrete Subjected to Freezing and Thawing in Water**

| | | Effect on concrete subjected to freezing and thawing in water | |
|---|---|---|---|
| Mix identity | Coating material | Single coating | Repeated coatings |
| SD | Linseed oil, turpentine and paint | harmful | slight benefit* |
| SE | Zinc fluosilicate | harmful | indeterminate |
| SF | Mg fluosilicate | slight benefit | beneficial |
| SG | Wall seal epoxy | beneficial | beneficial |
| SH | Wall seal epoxy | beneficial | beneficial |
| SO | Pigmented epoxy | beneficial | beneficial |
| SI | Ext. latex paint | beneficial | beneficial |
| SM | Ext. emulsion latex | harmful | indeterminate |
| SJ | Synthetic rubber | questionable | beneficial |
| SP | Chlorinated rubber | harmful | questionable |
| SN | Neoprene (liquid) | beneficial | beneficial |
| SL | Waterproofing sealer | harmful | beneficial* |
| SU | Penetrating sealer (epoxy) | questionable | — |
| SW | Penetrating sealer (epoxy) | beneficial | — |
| TK | Penetrating sealer | questionable | — |

*\* Specimens having 60 days drying following initial application of coating show the opposite. Above reported coatings were dried 7 days.*[14]

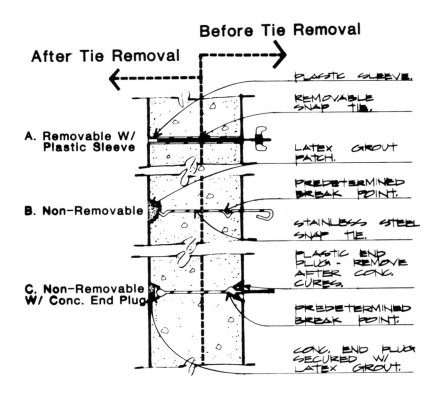

**Before Tie Removal**

**After Tie Removal**

PLASTIC SLEEVE.

REMOVABLE SNAP TIE.

**A. Removable W/ Plastic Sleeve**

LATEX GROUT PATCH.

PREDETERMINED BREAK POINT.

**B. Non-Removable**

STAINLESS STEEL SNAP TIE.

PLASTIC END PLUG - REMOVE AFTER CONC. CURES.

**C. Non-Removable W/ Conc. End Plug**

PREDETERMINED BREAK POINT.

CONC. END PLUG SECURED W/ LATEX GROUT.

**Figure 2.3**          **Snap Tie Patching**

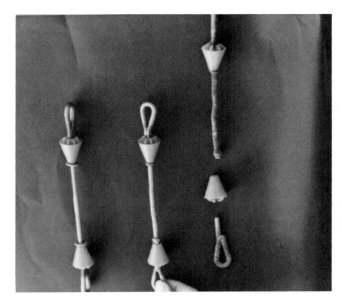

**Figure 2.4** *Snap ties with plastic end caps. Bottom tie with broken end.*

### Snap Ties

Re-usable concrete wall-forming systems usually are held together by thin strips of metal. As concrete is poured into the form, the weight of the concrete creates an outward force. Snap ties ensure that the wall has a uniform thickness and does not bulge under the weight of pouring. Snap ties are normally located every 2 to 4 feet horizontally and at least every 8 feet vertically. Once the forms are removed, the embedded snap tie is either removed or broken off.

Removable types of snap ties are installed in the unpoured wall with a plastic sleeve around the outside of the steel snap tie. This allows the steel to be completely removed. In submerged situations, this type of snap tie generates no rust, but presents a sealing problem. The plastic-lined hole is extremely hard to plug.

Breakable snap ties are manufactured with prestressed joints which are normally located one inch into the concrete wall. This prestressed area creates a predetermined breakage point for the snap tie.

This breakage process leaves part of the snap tie imbedded in the concrete wall. For this reason, noncorrosive stainless steel snap ties should be used.

Because the break is one inch into the face of the wall, the concrete wall has to be repaired after partial removal of the tie. When the ends are broken off, the process normally scars the face of the wall. This necessitates patching of the blemish with a latex-based mortar.

Some manufacturers provide removable plastic end plugs with snap ties. These plugs are conical and create a neatly formed void where the tie can be broken. After the tie end is broken off, a conical-shaped concrete plug is mortared in the void formed by the end plugs.

### Construction Joints

Construction joints are designed for non-movement and are by far the predominantly used joint in fountain construction. Construction joints are utilized in fountain construction to allow for smaller, more manageable pours, or as a means of stopping construction at the end of the day. Monolithic concrete pours are theoretically the most watertight situation but are difficult to pour and finish in large fountains.

Because adjacent concrete pieces are poured at separate times, it is necessary to create good bonding between adjacent concrete and prevent water from seeping through the joint which is created.

Good concrete bonding is achieved by utilizing depressed linear keys in the pour. Keys are usually 2 inches x 4 inches and of a trapezoidal shape to enhance removal after the concrete has cured. Keys are employed between wall panels and floors and sometimes between adjacent floor panels (See Figure 2.5).

In most construction joints the steel reinforcing is extended through to the adjacent pour. This prevents shear at the joint. Water which enters this joint can attack the corrosive steel reinforcing and cause joint failure. The steel reinforcing is protected and watertightness is increased by installing a waterstop at the construction joint. This material should be appropriately located to prevent water from attacking the re-bar (See Figure 2.7).

Properly located construction joints can act as stress relief joints. Stress relief joints are utilized in pool construction to create a predetermined cracking point. The stress relief joint shown in Figures 2.7 and 2.8 will permit a natural concrete contraction during the first 24 to 48 hours after casting. Minimum concrete cover over the reinforcing and the use of a stainless steel dowel allow for the waterstop to be positioned on the top side of the reinforcing.

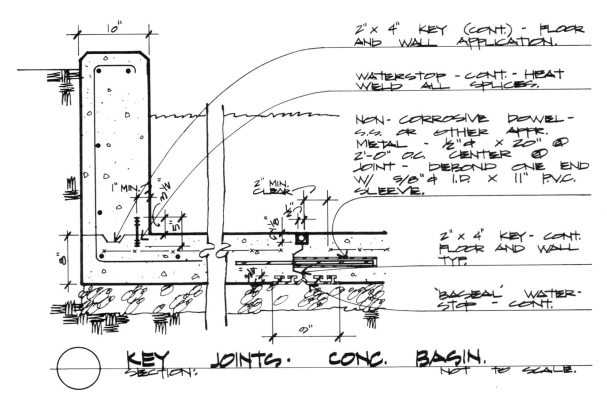

**Figure 2.5**

**Figure 2.6** *Key joint and waterstop. Virginia Beach, Virginia.*

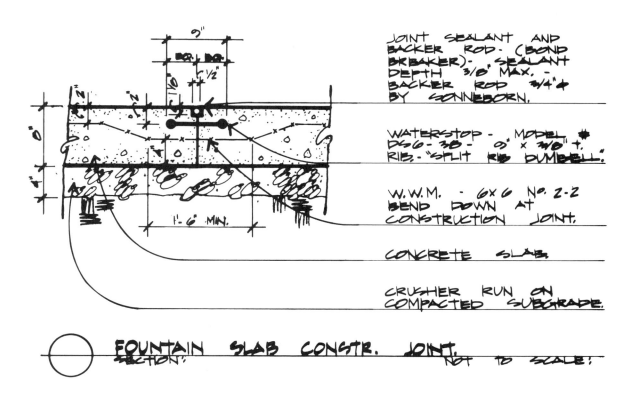

**Figure 2.7**

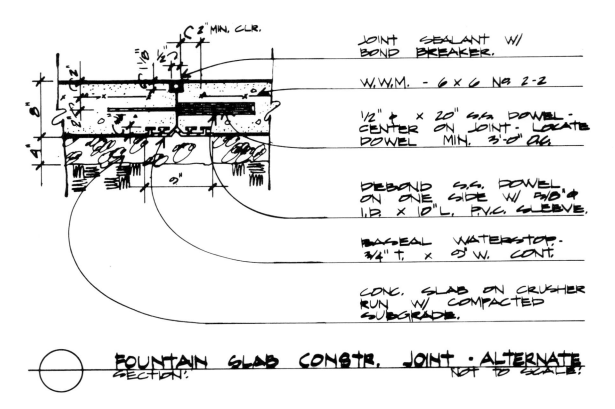

Figure 2.8

## Expansion Joints

Expansion joints may be necessary in walls and floors of large fountains because:

1. Water contained in the fountain basin will expand 9 percent when it freezes.[15]
2. Concrete will expand when the water temperature increases and contract as it cools. In hot weather, water retained in a fountain acts as a coolant and reduces the typical expansion of the concrete. In some cases, the fountain may be drained for cleaning or repair in the summer. For this reason, provisions should be made for the maximum expansion of concrete.
   A. The coefficient of thermal expansion for steel reinforcing is .0000065 or a length increase of approximately 5/64 of an inch per 10 feet of material when there is a temperature change of 100 degrees Fahrenheit.
   B. The coefficient of thermal expansion for concrete with a limestone aggregate is .0000046 or a length increase of approximately 4/64 of an inch per 10 feet of material when there is a temperature change of 100 degrees Fahrenheit.
   C. The coefficient of thermal expansion for concrete with a feldspar aggregate is .0000042 or a length increase of approximately 4/64 of an inch per 10 feet of material when there is a temperature change of 100 degrees Fahrenheit.[16]

3. Large concrete pours can crack due to thermal contraction. Smaller pours will require expansion or construction joints at slab splices.
4. Large pours can be labor intensive. Larger crews are necessary to ensure quality when pouring large sections of concrete. Installing expansion or construction joints will allow for smaller and better quality concrete panels.

Expansion joints can be classified into two types: full movement and partial movement joints. Full movement joints allow displacement in all directions. These joints should not be located in areas subjected to shearing. Shearing of the joint will lead to rupture of the waterstop (See Figure 2.9).

Partial movement joints will allow for movement in one direction only. By inserting a smooth dowel that is bonded to the concrete on one side and debounded on the other, a moveable and shear resistant joint can be created (See Figure 2.10).

## Expansion Joint Treatment

Once the expansion joint has been located, it is important to caulk the joint to prevent water seepage. Caulking selected for sealing joints should be ultraviolet resistant, high in adhesion, resilient, and long lasting. Resiliency of joint caulking is vital. Joint caulking must expand and contract as the concrete moves. Of equal importance is the ability of the material to return to its original shape. If the caulking

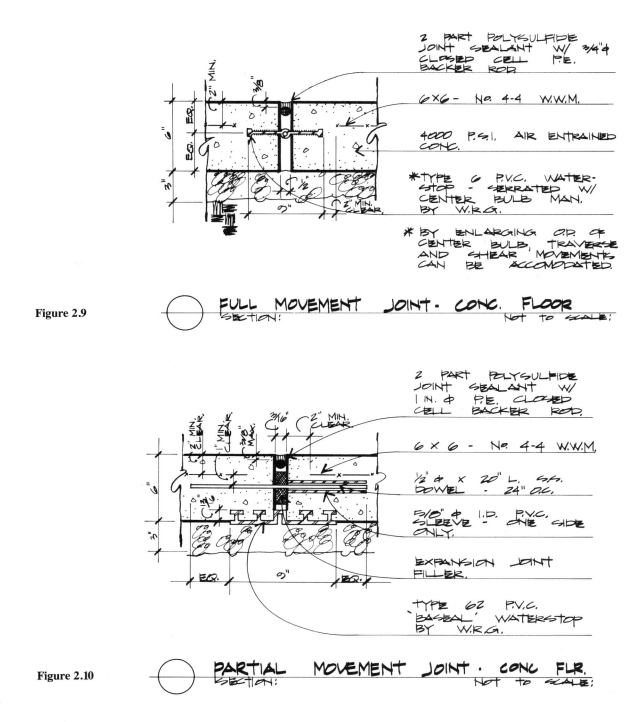

**Figure 2.9**

2 PART POLYSULFIDE JOINT SEALANT W/ 3/4"⌀ CLOSED CELL P.E. BACKER ROD

6X6 - No. 4-4 W.W.M.

4000 P.S.I. AIR ENTRAINED CONC.

*TYPE 6 P.V.C. WATER-STOP - SERRATED W/ CENTER BULB MAN. BY W.R.G.

* BY ENLARGING O.D. OF CENTER BULB, TRAVERSE AND SHEAR MOVEMENTS CAN BE ACCOMODATED.

FULL MOVEMENT JOINT· CONC. FLOOR
SECTION:                    NOT TO SCALE:

**Figure 2.10**

2 PART POLYSULFIDE JOINT SEALANT W/ 1 IN. ⌀ P.E. CLOSED CELL BACKER ROD.

6 X 6 - No. 4-4 W.W.M.

1/2"⌀ X 20" L. S.S. DOWEL - 24" O.C.

5/8"⌀ I.D. P.V.C. SLEEVE - ONE SIDE ONLY.

EXPANSION JOINT FILLER.

TYPE 62 P.V.C. 'BASEAL' WATERSTOP BY W.R.G.

PARTIAL MOVEMENT JOINT· CONC FLR.
SECTION:                    NOT TO SCALE:

material does not rebound to its original form after compression, the width reduction will place stresses on the bonded surface and cause joint failure. When installing the caulking, it is imperative to take precautions to prevent rupture of the caulking when the material is stretched. Bonding of the caulking should only occur on two sides of the joint. (The joint faces [2] perpendicular to the exposed concrete surface.) Caulking will bond a third side of the joint (the joint face), if permitted.

As the joint moves apart, the caulking stretches in the direction parallel to the caulked face of the concrete. If caulking is allowed to adhere to the bottom of the joint, it will prevent free expansion of the caulking and lead to rupture of the sealant (See Figure 2.11). Isolation of the caulking from the joint floor is achieved with a bond breaker. Bond breakers are polyethylene materials inserted into the joint to prevent bonding of the caulking (See Figures 2.11 and 2.12).

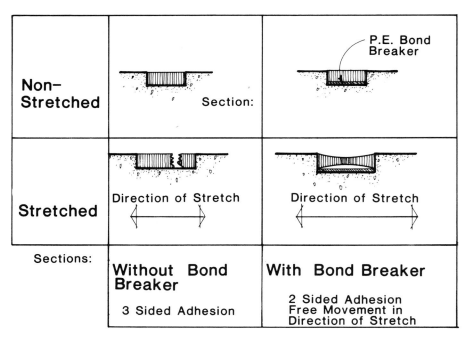

**Figure 2.11**                    **Sealant Failure**

Backer rods are often employed as bond breakers for expansion joints. Backer rods are solid round polyethylene tubes available in rolls of convenient lengths. When installing the backer rod into the joint, the rod diameter should be ⅛ of an inch larger than the expansion joint width. This allows the rod to be wedged between the concrete face. By positioning the backer rod properly, the depth of the caulking can be controlled.

Before specifying the thickness of the caulking, the designer should consult with the caulking manufacturers. Some manufacturers recommend the application of a thin bed (⅛ to ⅜ inch) over a thick bed (over ⅜ inch).[17] The use of a thin bed application tends to reduce the surface stretch and prevents tearing of the caulking (See Figure 2.12).

Width of the caulked joint depends on the specified movement capacity of the caulking (See Table 2.6).

*Example:* It is determined that the maximum movement between an expansion joint in a wall will be ¼ of an inch. Two part polysulfide caulking has a movement capacity of 25 percent of total width. How wide should the caulked joint be?

[Actual joint width in inches] x [Capacity of caulking movement] =
[Maximum movement of concrete at expansion joints, in inches]

By rearranging the equation, we find that:

Actual joint width = $\dfrac{\text{Max. Expansion of Concrete}}{\text{Capacity of caulking movement}}$

$= \dfrac{¼ \text{ inch}}{25\%}$

$= \dfrac{.25 \text{ inch}}{.25}$

Actual joint width = 1 inch

Most caulkings listed in Table 2.6 are suitable for submersed applications. Check with the manufacturer before specifying. In most submersed situations, it is recommended that a primer be applied to surfaces which are to be caulked. Some silicon caulkings have excellent qualities for creating watertight joints but are not recommended for underwater use.[18]

Caulking comes in gun grades for ease of application. This means that the material can be extruded from a caulking gun. Care should be taken to only apply self-leveling compounds on horizontal surfaces (See Figure 2.13). When applied to vertical joints, self-leveling mixes tend to slump and create a weak or bad bond.

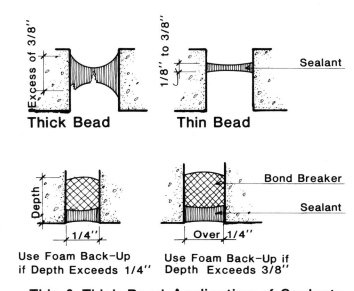

**Figure 2.12**  **Thin & Thick Bead Application of Sealants**

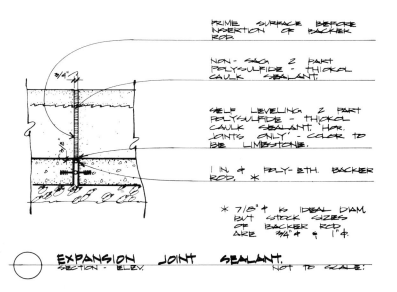

**Figure 2.13**

**Table 2.6 Comparative Evaluation of Joint Sealants**

| | Resistant silicone sealant | Silicone building sealant | Silicone building & glazing sealant | Silicone highway joint sealant |
|---|---|---|---|---|
| Joint Movement Capability, % | ±25 | +100/−50 | ±25 | +100/−50 |
| Recovery, % | 100 | ≥95 | 100 | ≥95 |
| U.V. Resistance | Excellent | Excellent | Excellent | Excellent |
| Weathering Resistance | Excellent | Excellent | Excellent | Excellent |
| Life Expectancy | 20+ Years | 30+ Years | 30+ Years | 30+ Years |
| Service Temperature Range, °F (°C) | −60 to 350 (−51 to 157) | −65 to 300 (−55 to 149) | −80 to 400 (−62 to 205) | −65 to 300 (−55 to 149) |
| Tack-Free Time @ 77°F (25°C) | 15 minutes | 1–3 hours | 15 minutes | 30 minutes to 1 hour |
| Cure Time | 7–14 Days | 7–14 Days | 7–14 Days | 7–14 Days |
| Adhesion | Good to Excellent | Excellent | Excellent | Good |
| Primer | None on Porcelain, Glass Painted Surfaces | None on Concrete Glass | None on Nonreflective Glass | None |
| Color | White, Excellent Stability | Good Range, Excellent Stability | Good Range, Excellent Stability | Gray |
| Submersible | | Yes & No Check with individual manufacturer for application of silicone | | |

**Table 2.6 Comparative Evaluation of Joint Sealants (continued)**

| | Solvent acrylic | Two-part polysulfide | One-part polysulfide | Two-part polyurethane | One-part polyurethane |
|---|---|---|---|---|---|
| Joint Movement Capability, % | ±10 | ±25 | ±25 | ±25 | ±25 |
| Recovery, % | Less than 25 | 60–80 | 60–80 | 90 | 80–90 |
| U.V. Resistance | Good to Excellent | Poor to Fair | Poor to Fair | Fair to Good | Fair to Good |
| Weathering Resistance | Fair | Good | Fair to Good | Good | Good |
| Life Expectancy | 10 Years | 20 Years | 20 Years | 15 Years | 15 Years |
| Service Temperature Range, °F (°C) | −20 to 180 (−29 to 82) | −60 to 180 (−51 to 82) | −40 to 180 (−40 to 104) | −40 to 220 (−40 to 104) | −22 to 220 (−31 to 104) |
| Tack-Free Time @ 77°F (25°C) | 36–72 Hours | 36 Hours to 2 Days | 12 Hours to 1 Month | 3 Hours to 5 Days | 12 Hours to 3 Days |
| Cure Time | Noncuring | 2–4 Months | 6–12 Months | 3–8 Months | 2–6 Months |
| Adhesion | Good | Fair to Good | Fair to Good | Fair to Good | Good |
| Primer | None | Required on Most Surfaces | Required on Most Surfaces | Required on Some Surfaces | Required on Some Surfaces |
| Color | Good Range, Good Stability | Good Range, Poor to Good Stability | Fair Range, Good Stability | Fair Range, Fair Stability | Fair Range, Fair Stability |
| Submersible | No | Yes Primer Neded | Yes Primer Needed | Yes Primer Needed | Yes Primer Needed |

**Figure 2.14** *Flat-ribbed waterstop.*

**Figure 2.15** *Flat-ribbed with center bulb waterstop.*

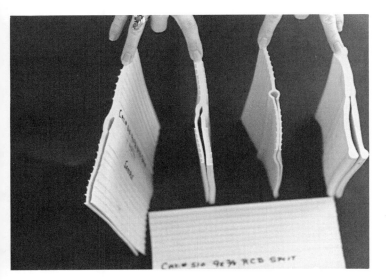

**Figure 2.16** *Split-ribbed waterstop styles. From left: 1) ribbed, 2) ribbed, 3) ribbed with center bulb, 4) dumbbell.*

## Waterstops

Waterstops are flexible strips of plastic used to create a watertight seal at expansion joints or construction joints of *in situ* concrete.

Waterstops are generally manufactured from PVC or vinyl and are available in various styles, thicknesses, and widths. When choosing a style, the designer should consider the exact application of the waterstop. Flat-ribbed styles are best suited for the use in construction joints of walls or slabs, or at the junction of a wall and footing. Joints which employ this style of waterstop should not have any anticipated movement between the members.

Dumbbell styles are preferable for nonmovement construction joints employed in horizontal placement.

Ribbed with center bulb styles are best suited for expansion joint applications where movement between members is anticipated. When installing this type of waterstop, the outside diameter of the center bulb should equal the expansion joint thickness. Care should be taken to locate the center bulb so that it is not embedded into the concrete (See Figure 2.15).

Split ribbed style waterstops eliminate the need for a split form to position the waterstop (See Figure 2.18). This reduces construction cost.

When selecting a waterstop for use in fountains, the designer should consider that concrete does not bond to smooth PVC or vinyl. Ribbed type waterstops create a more favorable condition for adherence of the concrete to the waterstop.

Waterstops are rated to withstand various amounts of pressure created by the height of the water above the waterstop. Most waterstops will withstand pressures produced by water which is 50 feet above the waterstop. This is more than ample for fountain applications.

When installing waterstops, it is important to splice strip ends together with a heat sealing method instead of overlapping the pieces. This ensures that water will not seep out at the splice. Specially molded unions are available for heat-sealing vertical waterstops to horizontal waterstops. Manufacturers should be consulted for their availability.

Nails or wires, used in position waterstops, should be located between the last rib and the end of the waterstop. Positioning holes in an isolated location will prevent water from seeping through the waterstop.

## Wall and Floor Thickness

Wall and floor thickness are dependent on soil type, water depth, freeze-thaw conditions, visual aspects and interacting forces. As a rule of thumb, wall thicknesses range from 8 to 16 inches and will contain vertical and horizontal reinforcing.

Floor thickness ranges from 6 to 10 inches and requires temperature reinforcing or welded wire fabric (WWF). WWF (also known as woven wire mesh or WWM) is used to control expansion and contraction due to temperature change.

| | Application | Non-Movement Joint | Movement Joint |
|---|---|---|---|
| **Flat Ribbed** | | | |
| | Footings, Walls & Slabs | Yes | No |
| **Dumbbell** | | | |
| | Horizontial Applications Only | Yes | No |
| | [1] Max. Joint Width 1/2" | Yes | Yes [1] |
| **Serrated W/ Center Bulb** | | | |
| | Expansion Joint | No [2] | Yes |
| **Split Bulb Types** | | | |
| | Eliminates Split Forms | Yes | Yes [1] |
| | [2]Can be Used in Non-Movement | No [2] | Yes |
| **Special Types** | | | |
| | Expansion Joint | No | Yes |

**Figure 2.17**        Waterstop  Types

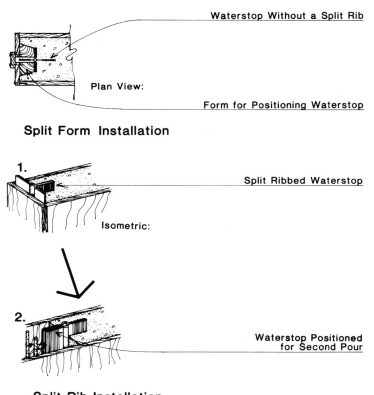

Waterstop Without a Split Rib

Plan View:

Form for Positioning Waterstop

**Split Form  Installation**

1.

Split Ribbed Waterstop

Isometric:

2.

Waterstop Positioned for Second Pour

**Split Rib  Installation**

**Figure 2.18**        Waterstop  Installation  Techniques

**Figure 2.19** *Waterstop for floor and wall application.*

Where soft soil pockets exist, it may be necessary to include reinforcing steel with the WWF to span the unsupportive soil. This steel has tensile strength and will prevent failure of the slab. The following table is for determining WWF size for swimming pool floors and is applicable for fountain design (See Table 2.7). Where slab rebars are spliced together, it is important to overlap the bars to ensure tensile strength. The length of overlap should equal a minimum of 12 bar diameters and should be tied at both ends. All reinforcing should be protected from the corrosive effects of water by providing a minimum of 2 inches of concrete cover.

When concrete is subjected to alternating periods of saturation and drying out, concrete cover over the rebar should be increased to 3 inches to prevent corrosion. This is normal cover for marine applications and will extend the life of the concrete. A recent product, which is anticipated to further extend the life of saturated concrete, is expoxy-coated rebar. This rebar is presently being used in bridge construction and normally comes with a green-colored coating.

## PRECAST CONCRETE

Precast concrete should be specified over *in situ* concrete because it has less tendency to crack and lends itself very well to intricate surface detailing and precise accuracy.[20] Intricate detailing possibilities can be seen in the many statuaries which adorn residential gardens and yards. Sand molds, fiberglass liners and wood forms give flexibility to the shape. Concrete forms are attached to vibratory pouring tables which create excellent pouring conditions.

Because of laboratory-like conditions in some precast factories, comparatively higher strengths can be achieved with precast concrete. Concrete can be poured to achieve compressive strengths of 7,000 to 12,000 psi.

In addition, higher dimensional tolerances are possible with precast concrete. Normal cast-in-place concrete is poured to a tolerance of 1/5 inch derivation from level in a distance of 10 feet for wall tops, and 1/5 inch per 10 foot on floors. In situations where thin layers of water are intended to cascade over the edge of long weirs or elevated basins, a more consistent water thickness is possible by using precast members.

**Table 2.7 Correct Proportion of Steel per Slab Thickness[19]**

| Concrete slab thickness | Area | Temperature reinforcement (WWF) | Temperature reinforcement (new designation) |
|---|---|---|---|
| 4 inch | .029 in² | 6x6 #10/10 welded wire fabric | 6x6 — w1.4 x w1.4 |
| 5 inch | .041 in² | 6x6 #8/8 welded wire fabric | 6x6 — w2.0 x w2.0 |
| 6 inch | .080 in² | 6x6 #4/4 welded wire fabric | 6x6 — w4.0 x w4.0 |
| 8 inch | .108 in² | 6x6 #2/2 welded wire fabric | 6x6 — w5.5 x w5.5 |

In the event that wire fabric is not available, straight deformed billet bars may be used.
Substitution of material is based on area indicated below.

| Size | Area |
|---|---|
| #3 Bar | .11 in² |
| #4 Bar | .20 in² |
| #5 Bar | .31 in² |

In this example, a ¼-inch depth of water is desired to flow over the 10 foot *in situ* weir (See Figure 2.20). If 1/5 of an inch tolerance is allowed, there may be a place on the weir where 1/20 of an inch of water goes over the weir.

By utilizing precast concrete, stricter dimensional standards can be achieved. The size of precast pieces is somewhat limited because of the problems associated with the positioning, shoring, leveling, and transporting of large pieces. Fabricated pieces are transported to the site, where they are lifted into place by cranes. Large pieces should be installed with lifting loops which attach to the crane hook. Loops should be located in an inconspicuous place and to minimize stresses on concrete during lifting. Normally, lifting loops are attached to the steel reinforcing network imbedded inside the piece. In cases of elevated basins, it may be necessary to delete the lifting loops, because there is no inconspicuous area in which to locate them. Shop drawings provided by the manufacturer will locate the loops. Loop placement should be approved by the designer so that patching is not necessary when they are removed.

Precast pieces are normally set into a grout bed which allows for leveling and positioning of the cast piece. Grout is suitable for attachment of smaller pieces which are subjected to minor forces. Weirs, wall panels, elevated basins and sculptural elements subjected to forces which could shear the precast piece from its cast-in-place base, must be fastened or keyed to the concrete base with more than grout. Fasteners should be fabricated out of stainless steel or other corrosion-resistant material. Clips, anchors, tapped plugs, and pins are some of the standard fasteners used by the precast industry. Normally, shop drawings provided by the manufacturer specify the desired method of attachment. Grouting beds should be ½ to 1½ inches thick. In submersed situations, the joint can be raked back and filled with an appropriate caulking and bond breaker. Figure 2.21 illustrates a detail that would be appropriate for installing a precast weir. In this application, the stainless steel pins improve the bond strength between the concrete and mortar, and prevent shearing at the mortar joint.

## PRECAST TERRAZO

Terrazo is a process in which integral color and aggregates are added to concrete. The concrete is allowed to harden; then the surface is ground and water polished. Colors and textures are varied and only limited by the designer's imagination. Terrazo panels can be manufactured to closely resemble marble and granite.

Polished panels are extremely smooth, glassy, and of similar beauty to granite. Because of the smooth nature of terrazo, it becomes very slick when wet. Fountains floors where people may walk should not contain terrazo concrete.

## GUNITE

Gunite is a process in which a dry mixture of cement, sand, and small size aggregate of less than ¾ inch in diameter, is blown through a hose and, at the nozzle, is mixed with water to form a pneumatically-sprayed concrete. This

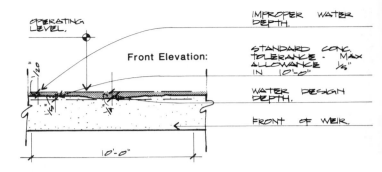

**Dimensional Tolerances of In Situ Concrete Weirs**

**Figure 2.20**

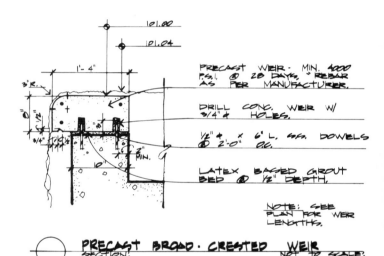

**Figure 2.21**

**Figure 2.22** *Steel rebar for gunite pond.*

**Figure 2.23** *Gunite installation.*

**Figure 2.24** *Gunite fountain. Denver, Colorado.*

process is a widely used construction technique in the swimming pool industry, and is an applicable construction method for free form fountains.

Due to the stiffness of the concrete being sprayed, gunite can normally be formed into almost any shape with limited or no forming. After excavation, steel reinforcing bars are placed to replicate the desired form of the pool or fountain. For a depressed pool, the earth is used as a form to blow the gunite against. When elevated basins or objects are to be formed, wire mesh, stiff fabric supported by stakes, plywood, or inflated bags can be positioned behind reinforcing bars to create a temporary form onto which the gunite can be sprayed.

When using the inflatable air bag technique, the gunite is allowed to harden to the point where the bag can be deflated and the reinforcing and gunite will hold up structurally. Gunite sprayed onto an inflatable bag is being used as a technique to construct concrete shells for earth-sheltered homes. The air bag is reusable and reduces the cost of forming associated with typical concrete construction.

Butt joints are commonly used in gunite construction. These are needed when the operator stops or where he ties a floor panel into a wall panel. These joints are created by installing a smooth board at the start or finish of a sprayed panel. Before work proceeds, the board is removed and the gunite is sprayed against the flush edge.

Most gunite construction does not contain expansion or contraction joints. This is due to the following properties:

1. Gunite has thinner wall dimensions than normal *in situ* concrete. This, along with the absence of forms on at least one side, reduces the amount of generated heat built up in the concrete and alleviates the thermal stresses.
2. Gunite is generally reinforced with heavy high-tensile fabric. Tensile steel content of gunite exceeds that of normal *in situ* concrete.
3. Gunite has a water-cement ratio of 0.33 to 0.35 by weight. Normal concrete has a water-cement ratio of 0.45 to 0.50.
4. Gunite has a compressive strength of 8000 to 9000 psi with equivalent tensile strength.

All of these factors reduce the tendency toward thermal contraction cracking.[21]

Overall gunite quality is dependent on the nozzle operator. Good quality gunite will have uniform density, no voids, consistent thickness and rounded inside corners. Material thickness and reinforcing is determined by the gunite contractor.

Once the base coat of gunite is applied, a finish coat of portland cement plaster is hand troweled on top of the air-placed base coat. The plaster coat is normally ½ to 1 inch in thickness and can be colored or textured to represent a wide variety of materials. (Refer to the discussion on plastering of gunite for further information.)

The process of guniting can require considerable space at the job site. In most cases, bagged cement and dry sand are delivered and stored at the site. Proper quality control of gunite requires keeping the sand and cement dry. Excess moisture in the raw materials and at the nozzle creates lower p.s.i. and weaker concrete. This problem can be prevented by covering materials or by providing covered truck storage.

## SHOTCRETE

Shotcrete is often used instead of gunite to form swimming pools or fountains. Shotcrete, like gunite, is a pneumatically sprayed concrete. Finished shotcrete is virtually undetectable from gunite. Instead of mixing the concrete in the spray nozzle, low slump, ready mixed concrete is poured into a hopper which in turn injects the mixed concrete into a placement pipe.

## SIMULATING NATURE WITH CONCRETE

In recent years, gunite and shotcrete have been used to simulate rocks or soil. Their primary use has been delegated to walls and ponds associated with zoos and animal exhibits. In these applications, attractive, low cost, low weight and water tight native ponds and rocks can be constructed.

When gunite is used to simulate rock, color, sand and/or hand-applied stains and paints are applied to the finish coat to color the concrete. Textures, dimples and cracks are applied with trowels, brushes, sticks or sponges.

In geographic areas where stone is not native, simulated soil along pond edges is more authentic than simulated stone (See Figure 2.25). This effect can be achieved using gunite through several techniques. The simplest and least expensive method requires sand or dirt to be troweled or dusted into the wet finish coat. Dimples and textures are applied with sponges and trowels.

More expensive and realistic methods involve painting and dying the wet gunite with spray bottles. Textures and dimples are applied in the same manner as simulated stone.

Care should be taken when specifying simulated stone and dirt. This type of construction requires skilled artisans to provide quality products.

Most local gunite contractors lack the artistic skills required to simulate rock or soil. Construction specifications should pre-qualify bidders and require a sample panel prior to construction. Several nationally-known gunite and exhibit contractors exist who specialize in this type of construction.

## BRICK

Brick is often used as a primary building material and as a facing material on concrete basins for fountains. Brick used for fountains should have the following qualities:

1. Low water absorption
2. Semi-vitreous nature
3. Low saturation coefficient
4. Ability to withstand freeze-thaw cycles

Due to the shale and clay composition of bricks, capillary pores are created which absorb moisture when the brick comes in contact with free water. In the case of a brick foun-

**Figure 2.25** *Gunite seal exhibit. National Zoo, Washington, District of Columbia.*

tain, much free water is available because of water retention by the brick basin.

The ratio of absorption by simple immersion (24 hour period) to absorption by boiling (5 hour period) is called the C/B ratio or saturation coefficient. Because boiling causes units to absorb more water than they will absorb in normal masonry structures, this ratio is an indication of available pore space into which water can expand upon freezing. Thus, the saturation coefficient along with compressive strength is an indication of the durability of the masonry unit.[22]

Face bricks grade "SW" have good qualities for fountain use. ASTM standard C216 for "SW" brick requires an average of 5 brick units to have less than 17 percent absorption when boiled in water for 5 hours, a maximum saturation coefficient of .78, and a compressive strength of 3000 psi.[23]

In the case of a fountain, where bricks are continually saturated from retained water, it is important to drain the fountain in regions susceptible to freezing. Draining the pool in winter reduces the available free moisture to the pore space and the damaging effects of freezing water. The floors of brick pools should be appropriately sloped at 2 percent or greater towards a floor drain. When the pool is drained for winter, the moisture from rain or snow will be drained off rather than absorbed by the brick.

**Figure 2.26** *Terrazo ground brick basin. Charlottesville, Virginia.*

Paving brick intended for use in areas where the brick may be frozen while saturated with water, are given the classification of SX. This paving brick has slightly better standards than "SW" grade face brick, and falls under ASTM standard C-902-79A. The average of 5 bricks is to have a minimum absorption of 8 percent after being saturated in room temperature water for 24 hours, an average saturation coefficient of .78, and a compressive strength of 8000 psi.

When comparing bricks for use in fountains, the compressive strength and the saturation coefficient should be considered. A compressive strength of over 3000 is appropriate, while, a saturation coefficient of .78 or less is needed. This ensures free unsaturated pore space into which water can move when subjected to freezing, thus reducing the destructive effect of freeze-thaw cycles.

A vitreous clay product is either a brick or tile unit which has been exposed to sufficient temperatures to fuse the grains of the clay or shale and close the water-absorbing pores, making the brick or tile product impervious to water. In this situation, the brick or tile is not absorbing water, so there is no need for free pore space. The lower the saturation coefficient and the percentage absorption after boiling, the more vitreous the product will be.

For high durability, brick units should be chosen to withstand 50 to 100 freeze-thaw cycles.

### Brick Mortar

The mortar type which is best suited to bond brick together in fountains is type "S." Tests indicate that the tensile bond strength between brick and type "M" mortar approaches the maximum obtainable with cement-lime mortars. Type "S" mortar also has a reasonably high compressive strength (See Table 2.8). In the case of a fountain, bond strength is critical to prevent capillary action from

**Table 2.8 Evaluation of Mortar Types**[24]

| | Mortar type | | | Compressive strength of brick units in psi |
|---|---|---|---|---|
| | Type N | Type S | Type M | |
| Allowable tensile stress in psi | 28 | 36 | 36 | — |
| Allowable compressive stresses in solid brick masonry in psi (gross cross-sectional area) | 300 | 350 | 400 | 14,000 plus |
| | 300 | 350 | 400 | 12,000 |
| | 300 | 350 | 400 | 10,000 |
| | 300 | 350 | 400 | 8,000 |
| | 200 | 225 | 250 | 6,000 |
| | 140 | 160 | 175 | 4,000 |
| Assumed compressive strength of brick masonry with inspection, in psi | 3,200 | 3,900 | 4,600 | 14,000 plus |
| | 2,800 | 3,400 | 4,000 | 12,000 |
| | 2,400 | 2,900 | 3,400 | 10,000 |
| | 2,000 | 2,400 | 2,800 | 8,000 |
| | 1,600 | 1,900 | 2,200 | 6,000 |
| | 1,200 | 1,400 | 1,600 | 4,000 |

*Adapted from Building Code Requirements for Engineered Brick Masonry and ANSI Standard A41.1*

sucking water in between mortar joint and brick and weakening the bond during freeze-thaw cycles.

To increase the bonding capacity of type "M" mortar:[25]

1. Mix mortar to the maximum flow compatible with workmanship. Use maximum mixing water and permit retempering.
2. Use brick whose suctions are less than 20 grams of water when laid. Control high suction by wetting brick 4 to 24 hours before installation. If porous brick is not wetted, the brick will pull the available free water out of the mortar and reduce the bond.
3. Use mortars having high water retentivity.
4. Bond mortar to wire cut or roughened surfaces rather than to a die skin.

A latex admixture for mortar will give better bonding strength between brick units. It will also reduce the potential for staining of the mortar due to algae and dirty water. The stronger bond between mortar and bricks should reduce capillary action and create a longer lasting bond and a more watertight joint.[26]

Brick splits can be utilized in fountains with the advent of latex mortars. These bricks have a thickness of ¾ to 1⅛ inch and allow the designer to reduce fountain weight, purchase and handling costs. The latex admixture will be substituted for water in the mortar mix. This product should be used as per manufacturer's recommendations. (See discussion of tile installation using latex mortar.) Some thin set mortars are extremely sticky and make normal brick construction awkward. Check with manufacturer before specifying admixtures.

## Joint Type

Mortar joints should be chosen which will hold minimum water on horizontal surfaces and are also easy to clean if the joint becomes stained with algae or dirt. A rough cut or flush joint would fulfill these requirements. A concave joint would also be acceptable if joints are kept small and the horizontal surface is sloped properly to drain. (For proper mortar setting bed depths, refer to the discussion on the tile mortar.) In most applications, a thin set latex mortar bed is an appropriate installation method for brick.

## Terrazo Grinding of Brick

Terrazo grinding is a process in which horizontal brick surfaces are ground with a terrazo grinder to produce an extremely smooth, plane surface. Terrazo grinding of fountain floors may be appropriate for fountains in which people will walk. However, some bricks may produce a smooth, slick surface when ground which may cause one to slip if the brick is wet. When in doubt, it is best to produce a test panel.

The best results are achieved with hard burned, low porosity brick. Mortar or grout should be similar to the binder in terrazo floors. The mortar which is chosen should have small sand particles. Both of these qualities will reduce crumbling of mortar and brick during grinding. Mortar

**Figure 2.27** *Brick fish pond. See Figure 1.47.*

joints and cushion beds should be allowed to cure one week before grinding is begun.

## Brick Installation

The following details are examples of usage of brick facing as a building material in a fountain basin. Figure 2.28 is an appropriate detail for brick and mortar use on a concrete base. The expansion joint treatment for concrete fountains is also suitable for use with brick facing. Expansion joints should be located as needed, to allow for differential expansion of materials. Care should be taken to ensure that these joints extend from the concrete base straight through the brick facing (See Figure 2.29).

Figure 2.30 is an appropriate detail for building fountain walls completely out of brick. Care should be taken to install a header course every eighth vertical course to create a structural bond in the wall. A header course may be deleted if the brick wall is tied together with galvanized metal ties or reinforcing steel. Metal ties are normally located every 18 to 36 inches on center vertically and horizontally. Local codes will dictate appropriate spacing.

The floor detailing of this fountain should be treated the same as in Figure 2.28. Floor expansion joints should be treated as per Figure 2.29 and in conjunction with the explanation on concrete basins. Due to the necessary tensile strength in the floor, it is recommended that bricks are not used for more than a floor facing material. The information shown in Table 2.9 and Figure 2.30 for constructing a solid structural brick-walled fountain has been adapted from the Structural Clay Products Institute technical notes on reinforced brick masonry swimming pools. These guidelines should be adapted accordingly for the specific fountain, local codes, and local conditions.[27]

Figure 2.31 is appropriate for detailing brick without mortar joints. Instead of mortar, a bituminous setting bed is used to adhere the brick to the concrete base. The bituminous setting bed should consist of 7 percent cement asphalt

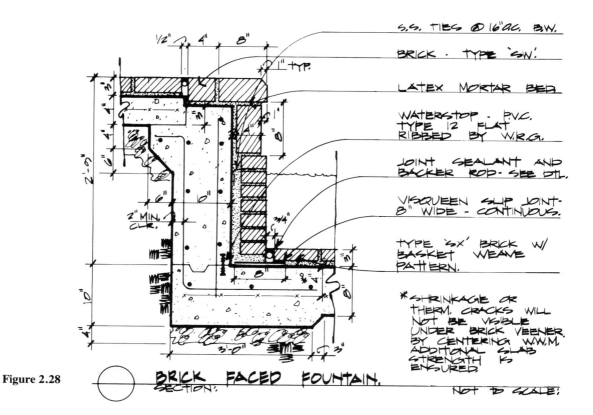

**Figure 2.28**

S.S. TIES @ 16"O.C. B.W.

BRICK - TYPE 'SW'

LATEX MORTAR BED

WATERSTOP - P.V.C. TYPE 12 FLAT RIBBED BY W.R.G.

JOINT SEALANT AND BACKER ROD - SEE DTL.

VISQUEEN SLIP JOINT - 8" WIDE - CONTINUOUS.

TYPE 'SX' BRICK W/ BASKET WEAVE PATTERN.

* SHRINKAGE OR THERM. CRACKS WILL NOT BE VISIBLE UNDER BRICK VENEER. BY CENTERING W.W.M. ADDITIONAL SLAB STRENGTH IS ENSURED.

BRICK FACED FOUNTAIN.
SECTION. NOT TO SCALE.

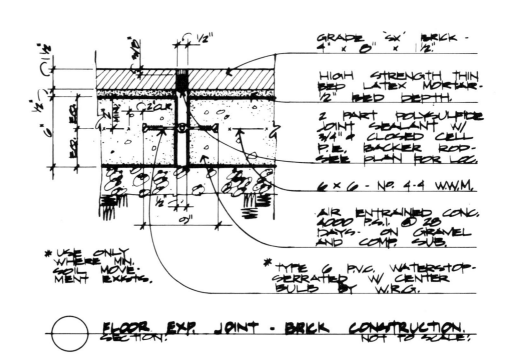

**Figure 2.29**

GRADE 'SX' BRICK - 4" × 8" × 1/2"

HIGH STRENGTH THIN BED LATEX MORTAR - 1/2" BED DEPTH.

2 PART POLYSULFIDE JOINT SEALANT W/ 3/4" Ø CLOSED CELL P.E. BACKER ROD - SEE PLAN FOR LOC.

6 × 6 - No. 4-4 W.W.M.

AIR ENTRAINED CONC. 4000 P.S.I. @ 28 DAYS - ON GRAVEL AND COMP. SUB.

* TYPE 6 P.V.C. WATERSTOP - SERRATED W/ CENTER BULB BY W.R.G.

* USE ONLY WHERE MIN. SOIL MOVE- MENT EXISTS.

FLOOR EXP. JOINT - BRICK CONSTRUCTION.
SECTION. NOT TO SCALE.

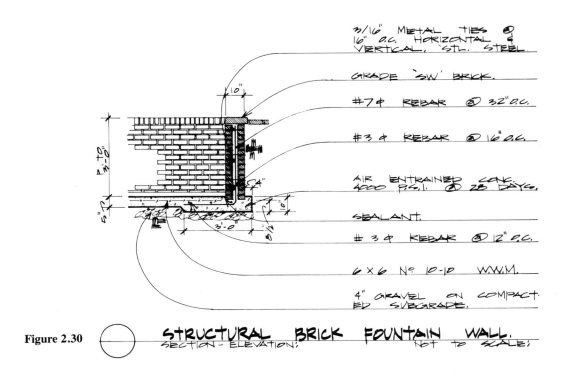

3/16" METAL TIES @ 16" O.C. HORIZONTAL & VERTICAL, STL. STEEL.

GRADE 'SW' BRICK.

#7 Φ REBAR @ 32" O.C.

#3 Φ REBAR @ 16" O.C.

AIR ENTRAINED CONC. 4000 P.S.I. @ 28 DAYS.

SEALANT.

#3 Φ REBAR @ 12" O.C.

6 X 6 No. 10-10 W.W.M.

4" GRAVEL ON COMPACTED SUBGRADE.

**Figure 2.30** ◯ STRUCTURAL BRICK FOUNTAIN WALL.
SECTION-ELEVATION: NOT TO SCALE:

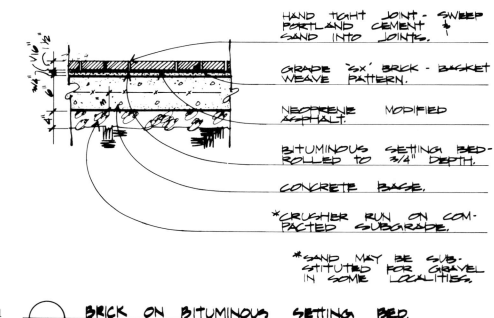

HAND TIGHT JOINT- SWEEP PORTLAND CEMENT & SAND INTO JOINTS.

GRADE 'SX' BRICK - BASKET WEAVE PATTERN.

NEOPRENE MODIFIED ASPHALT.

BITUMINOUS SETTING BED- ROLLED TO 3/4" DEPTH.

CONCRETE BASE.

*CRUSHER RUN ON COMPACTED SUBGRADE.

*SAND MAY BE SUBSTITUTED FOR GRAVEL IN SOME LOCALITIES.

**Figure 2.31** ◯ BRICK ON BITUMINOUS SETTING BED
SECTION: NOT TO SCALE:

**Figure 2.32** *Construction of CMU walls and floor fittings.*

**Figure 2.33** *Construction of CMU walls and floor fittings.*

**Figure 2.34** *CMU walls covered with waterproof membrane and tile.*

**Table 2.9  Fountain Construction Utilizing Solid Brick Walls**

| Wall height in feet* | Footing thickness in inches (vertical) | Footing length in feet (horizontal) | Reinforcing steel** | |
|---|---|---|---|---|
| | | | Bar size | Spacing |
| 3.0 | 10 | 3.0 | #4 | 48″ O.C. |
| 3.5 | 10 | 3.5 | #5 | 48″ O.C. |
| 4.0 | 10 | 4.0 | #5 | 32″ O.C. |
| 4.5 | 10 | 4.5 | #6 | 32″ O.C. |
| 5.0 | 10 | 5.0 | #7 | 32″ O.C. |

\* Measured from top of footing to proposed water level.
\*\* Main reinforcing steel; vertical steel in wall bent into footing.

(ASTM D-3381) and 93 percent fine aggregate (ASTM designation C-136-67) for passing a No. 4 sieve. The dried fine aggregate should be combined with hot asphalt cement and should be heated to 300°F at the asphalt plant. This setting bed should be rolled with a power roller to the depth of ¾ inch.

A coating of 2 percent neoprene modified asphalt adhesive should be mopped, squeezed, or troweled over the setting bed to provide a bond between the brick and setting bed. Once the asphalt adhesive is applied, the pavers can be set in place. A mixture of one part colored portland cement to three parts sand should be swept into hand-tight joints and fogged with water.[28] This detail is best suited for horizontal surfaces. On vertical surfaces, brick should be detailed as per Figure 2.28 or Figure 2.30.

## EFFERVESCENCE AND BRICK

When brick is used in fountain construction, care should be taken with detailing to prevent mineral deposits at the water line. Any salts or chemicals present in the water will be deposited on the brick fountain wall due to water evaporation. In applications where portions of brick are used, these chemicals will be absorbed into the brick and resistant to removal. The inclusion of a tile border will allow the maintenance staff to clean off any deposited chemicals.

## REINFORCED C.M.U. CONSTRUCTION

In geographic areas where freezing is not severe, alternatives to concrete or gunite fountain basins can be considered. When concrete masonry units are used for fountain walls, the blocks are laid on a reinforced footing and supported by vertical rebar located between the block. Additional wall strength is created by including horizontal "ladder type" masonry joint reinforcement and cell grout. Proper wall strength is ensured by grouting all vertical block cells with pea gravel grout. Grout should be compacted by rodding to ensure deletion of air voids in the cells.

Once the walls are fabricated, a concrete floor is constructed between the fountain walls. Suction and discharge devices are best located in the fountain floor to alleviate waterproofing of pipe penetrations in the block walls. Block wall construction should be considered only if the wall exterior material is to be covered with brick, stucco, stone or other masonry material.

41

Because of the porous nature of the concrete block, water-proofing is required in the interior of the fountain. Where tile coverings are used, liquid-applied waterproof membranes create an applicable watertight coating under the tile. When cheaper applications are required, "U.V. safe" waterproof membranes are suitable. In addition, other options such as liquid membrane in conjunction with painted pool plaster can be used.

C.M.U. fountain walls tend to be most cost effective for small fountains which will be covered with finished materials. Block construction is typically cheaper than *in-situ* concrete or gunite. In addition, most gunite contractors are not willing to deal with small garden-scaled projects, which require erection of plywood to spray the gunite against.

## TILE

Tile is a fired clay facing material which can be applied over concrete, brick tile, or fiberglass to achieve rich color and texture. Tiles are available in a rainbow of colors and diverse finishes. Finishes vary between manufacturers. Tiles are manufactured with either a glazed, un-glazing or matte non-slip surface. It tiles are installed on a fountain floor where people may walk, it is advisable to use a non-slip surface such as un-glazed or matte finish.

Mosaics are generally classified as varied colored panels of small tiles usually 1⅜ inch x 1⅜ inch or smaller. Mosaics are often available in large, preassembled sheets. One inch square tiles are attached to a flexible backing which allows many individual tiles to be set at once. This reduces the installation cost considerably.

Smaller tile sizes are more appropriate for covering irregular and curving fountain shapes. They allow the installer to reduce the number of cuts necessary for a desired radius.

Quarry tiles are typically larger squares (6 inch x 6 inch and larger) in a natural color range. These sizes are more appropriate for rectilinear-shaped fountains.

Tile thickness is normally 5/16 to 3/8 of an inch. Because tile is so thin, it is important to specify tiles which do not absorb water. If they are allowed to absorb water in areas subjected to freeze-thaw cycles, they may crack or split due to internal water movement. When selecting tile for use in outdoor fountains, it is important to choose "vitreous" or "frostproof tile." These tile grades ensure that the absorption rate is nil or extremely low.

Tiles are extremely stain resistant and easy to clean. The water lines of gunite and concrete pools are predominantly faced with tile. Due to water evaporation, many dissolved minerals are deposited at the water line, but by using a non-porous material such as tile, the stain is not drawn into the material and can be easily removed.

## TILE COLOR

Ceramic tiles used at the skim line have traditionally been the following colors: black, white, light blue, dark blue and aqua. Black and dark blue tile tend to recede and create a perception of additional depth under the coping. However, darker colors tend to show any chemical deposits. White tile looks incongruous when used under a coping. Clean standing water takes on a natural blue or aqua color. When white tile is used, it interrupts the continuity of the pool color. Therefore, it should not be employed when the water level is closer than 3 inches to the underside of a coping.

Blue-hued tile blends better with the water color and continues the actual color of the white basin vertically. In some applications, 'baby' blue tile can look outdated. In such cases aqua-colored tile tends to create a more modern look.

In any application, tile color should be selected to contrast or complement the overall color scheme of the design and surrounding development. If the entire pool is to be tiled, white or black tiles are preferable. White reflects the natural color of the water, while black creates a reflection and false sense of depth. As a rule of thumb, darker grays and blues act like black pools and create a good contrast against aerating water effects. In most applications, light browns and greens on fountain floors create a muddy appearance. These colors are best suited for walls or as accent colors. A fountain should not be totally lined with light blue tile in an effort to enhance the natural color of water. This particular color creates an articial water color.

### Tile Mortar Beds

Mortar is used as a leveling bed and as a material for adhering or cementing tile to the substrate. Mortar consists of sand, portland cement and water. Bonding strength of the mortar is improved by adding soluble additives, expoxies, or substituting a latex emulsion for water. Mortar takes on a somewhat plastic state and, in contrast to grout, it can not be poured.

When adhering tile to substrate, it is important to have a good shock resistance and bonding qualities in the mortar. Tile tends to be hard and brittle. When using a mortar bed which is somewhat shock absorbent, any impact which occurs on the tile face is transferred to the mortar bed which prevents breakage. As illustrated in Figure 2.37 more leverage occurs on large tiles, thus increasing their chances of breakage. In areas subjected to vandalism, smaller surface dimensioned tiles should be used.

### Epoxy Mortar

Good bond strength is needed to ensure bonding of the tile to the substrate. Epoxy-type adhesives or epoxy-based mortars give best bonding strengths between tile and substrate. Epoxy mortars are substantially more expensive than latex-based mortars or soluble additive mortars. Certain manufacturers do not recommend the use of epoxy as a setting mortar in swimming pools.[29] Fountains are similar in nature to swimming pools and should follow the same recommendations.

**Figure 2.35** *Tile-faced fountain. Oklahoma City, Oklahoma.*

**Figure 2.36** *Tile-faced fountain. St. Louis, Missouri.*

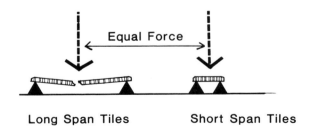

## Leverage on Tile Surfaces

**Figure 2.37**

### Soluble Additive Mortar

Soluble additive mortars are available which are specifically formulated for submersed applications such as swimming pools and fountains. These mortars have low absorption, good bonding strengths, and good impact absorption. Normally these specially bonded mortars have superior qualities to type "M" mortar. Although type "M" mortar is appropriate for some types of brick fountain construction, mortars with higher bonding strengths should be used in tile basin construction.

### Latex Based Mortar

Latex-based mortars are by far the best mortars for adhering tile to a substrate in a submerged situation. Latex-based mortars have good adhesion, shock resistance, flexibility, frost resistance, chemical resistance, and color stability.

When comparing latex-based mortars with other mortars, they are comparatively higher in shear strength but lower in cost. Cost reduction can be attributed to a thin set installation method. (See discussion of thin set mortar.)

Because of the latex additive, the mortar is somewhat flexible, which allows it to absorb physical shock and thermal movement, and withstand expansion and contraction of frost and ice.

Chemical imbalances in the water are caused by acidic conditions. Imbalances can be attributed to purification chemicals, urine, or pollution. These conditions may erode the portland cement mortar and loosen the bond between tile and substrate. Some latex-based mortars are 10 times more resistant to chemicals than portland cement mortars.[31]

Mortars can be colored to match the tile color. Conventional mortars tend to lose their color when exposed to the elements. By using a latex emulsion in the mortar, the pigments are locked onto the mix and protected from bleaching, fading, and washing out.[32]

The following is a manufacturer's specification on latex-based mortar. Mortar selected for adhering tile to fountains should have similar qualities to these mortars.

**Table 2.10 Comparison of Latex Mortar**[30]

| Installation materials | Relative cost | Shear bond strength lbs./sq. in. |
|---|---|---|
| Conventional mortar bed | 37 | 50 |
| Dry set mortar | 10 | 100 |
| Latex mortar systems* | 12 | 580 |

*\* Laticrete.*

**Table 2.11 Qualities of High Strength Latex Thin Set Mortar[33]**

| | |
|---|---|
| Density | 102 lb/cu.ft. (1634 Kg/M³) |
| Water absorption | < 4.0% |
| Compressive strength | > 5,000 psi (352 Kg/cm²) |
| Bond strength | |
| 72 hours | > 500 psi* (35 Kg/cm²) |
| 28 days | > 600 psi (42 Kg/cm²) |
| Tensile strength | > 500 psi (35 Kg/cm²) |
| Coefficient of thermal expansion | Same as concrete |
| Hardness | 72 hours 55–60 (Shore D) |
| | 28 day 70–80 (Shore D) |
| Flame contribution factor | 0 |
| Smoke contribution factor | 0 |

*\* This is more than 400 percent greater than 28 day ANSI 118.1 requirements for shear bond strength of dry set mortars to quarry tile. Conforms to: ANSI A118.4 — 1976 Latex Portland Cement, CTI064-1 Thin Set Portland Cement Mortars. Meets and exceeds water resistance and bond strength requirements of: ANSI A136.1 — 1972 Organic Adhesives, ANSI A118.1 — 1976 Dry Set Portland Cement Mortar.*

**Table 2.12 Qualities of Latex Grout and Mortar[34]**

| | |
|---|---|
| Density | 115 lb/cu.ft. (1842 Kg/M³) |
| Water absorption | < 4.0% |
| Compressive strength | > 3,000 psi (211 Kg/cm²) |
| Bond strength | > 500 psi (35 Kg/cm²) |
| Coefficient of thermal expansion | Same as concrete |
| Flame contribution factor | 0 |
| Smoke contribution factor | 0 |

**Table 2.13 ASTM Designation C 144 for Sand[36]**

| Sieve size | Percent passing |
|---|---|
| No. 4 (4.76-mm) | 100 |
| No. 8 (2.38-mm) | 95 to 100 |
| No. 16 (1.19-mm) | 60 to 100 |
| No. 30 (595-um) | 35 to 70 |
| No. 50 (297-um) | 15 to 35 |
| No. 100 (149-um) | 2 to 15 |
| No. 200 (74-um) | 0 to 2 |

## Grout

Grout is normally a pourable mixture of sand, portland cement, water, and/or admixtures. The grout is poured into the joints between the tiles (⅛ inch) and is squeezed or troweled to fill in the joint and bond the tiles together. This procedure prevents water from penetrating the joint and loosening the tile during freeze-thaw conditions.

Latex-based grouts or acid "R" grouts are best suited for fountain application. Acid "R" grout is general classification given to grouts which withstand acidic water conditions.

Before specifying any mortar or grout product, it is best to check with the tile manufacturer for their recommendations. The following details are appropriate for installing tile in a fountain.

## Colored Grout

Colored grout is best suited for more modern design applications where grout complements or contrasts the tile color. In this situation, the tile will read as one material and will deemphasize the grout joints and irregularities in craftsmanship. In some grouts, chlorine based chemicals associated with water maintenance will bleach color pigments from the dye and create white grout. Check with manufacturers for specific applications.

## Grout Leaching

Epoxy or latex-based grouts should be used on dark fountain tiles which will be continually saturated with fountain water. In this application, traditional grouts will run, bleed, or bleach out milky stains onto the tile. When dark tiles are employed, this staining is very visible and unsightly. The inclusion of latex additives or epoxy grout into the specifications will reduce any potential tile staining due to grout leaching.

## Grout Staining

Like tiled showers, tiled fountains will suffer from grout problems unless properly addressed. Grout staining can be prevented by use of latex additives or of epoxy grouts. The addition of these additives makes the grout impervious to staining.

## Tile Installation With Portland Cement Mortar

*Method No. 1* is the technique recommended by the Tile Council of America for installing tile in pools. Because the number of coats which must be applied and the amount of mortar that is necessary, this installation method is somewhat costly. This detail is appropriate for pools or fountains with uneven walls. The thickness will allow for leveling of the rough surface. The following recommendation refers to the adherence of tile to the wall or floor of a concrete pool or fountain for interior and exterior locations. All materials should conform to the following specifications:[35]

1. Tile should be standard grade conforming with ANSI A137.1 and certified by the manufacturer for use in pools and fountains. Normal average absorption should be one half of one percent.
2. Portland cement is to be ASTM C-150 Type 1.
3. Sand is to conform to ASTM C-144 (See Table 2.13).
4. Lime should conform to ASTM designation C-206 type.

To create a tight bond between the concrete substrate and the mortar, the surface of the concrete should be rough. This can be accomplished by bush hammering, use of high velocity water sprays, or surface retardants to expose aggregate. A scratch coat consisting of 1 part portland cement, ½ part lime, and 4 parts dry sand or .5 parts damp sand should be troweled onto the roughened pool wall. Scraping during the troweling process mechanically keys the mortar to the concrete base, thus creaing a stronger bond between the materials.

Next, a mortar bed should be applied. The mortar bed is normally used as a leveling course and is applied over the scratch coat. When employed on a pool or fountain floor, it should consist of 1 part portland cement and 4 parts damp sand by volume. When applied to a wall, it should consist of 1 part portland cement, ½ part lime, and 5 parts damp sand.[37]

While the mortar bed is still plastic, a bond coat is applied and tile is set in place. The bond coat consists of a portland cement paste and enhances bonding qualities. This method is covered in ANSI A108.1 (TCA method P431).

Once the tile has set, the joints between the tile should be filled with grout. Grout should be of a pourage consistency and should contain 1 part portland cement and 1 part 30 mesh sand by volume. It should be squeezed into the joints. Clean up should take place before grout is allowed to harden on the tile. Damp-curing of the surface is required for proper results.[38]

## Tile Installation With
## Dry-set Portland Cement

*Method No. 2* is similar to Method No. 1 except for the application of a bond coat. In dry-set applications, the mortar bed is allowed to cure. Instead of using a bond coat to adhere the tile to the mortar bed, a dry-set mortar is employed.

Dry-set mortar is a plastic-like mixture of sand, cement, and water retentive additives used to bond tiles to a hardened mortar bed. Dry set mortar is applied to the complete back of the tile and can be as thin as 3/32 of an inch. These mortars are for bonding purposes only and should not be used as a leveling course.[39]

Dry set mortars are not affected by prolonged contact with water. They have excellent water and impact resistance. Complete installation specifications are contained in ANSI A108.5 and ANSI A118.1. (See Figure 2.38).

## Tile Installation With
## High Strength Latex Thin Set Mortars

*Method No. 3* employs a high-strength latex-based portland cement mortar. This method can be adapted to install tile, pavers, brick, marble, and natural stone over concrete, brick, block, and plaster.

Thin bed mortars are usually mortar setting beds which are ¼ to ½ of an inch thick and are possible, due to the increased bond strength of latex mortar.

When using thin bed latex-based mortars, manufacturers' recommendations should be strictly followed. A typical thin bed mixture would consist of 1 part portland cement (one 42-50 kg bag), one hundred pounds 30-60 mesh sand, and 5 gallons of latex mortar additive.[40]

The thin set mortar should be applied to a dust and oil free surface with a notched trowel. Application should be in a scraping fashion to bond the mortar to the substrate.

Tiles should have uniform joints and should be pressed into place with a beating block. This ensures proper bonding.

After the mortar has set, visible joints should be packed with a latex grout. A typical grout would consist of 50 pounds colored grout mix and 1 gallon latex admix. Additional admix should be used to obtain desired consistency.[41] (See Figure 2.39).

## Tile Installation With
## Thick Bed Latex Based Portland Cement

*Method No. 4* — A thick bed method is considered to be any installation technique which uses a mortar bed which is 1 inch to 2 inches thick and is employed where the substrate or facing material is rough, uneven, or varying in thickness. This installation method has similar qualities and installation procedures to the dry-set mortar technique but instead of employing portland cement mortars, higher bond strength latex mortars are used. This tile setting method is appropriate for installing tile, brick, marble, or natural stone. Variations in brick or stone thickness pose no problem in creating a plumb surface when set in thick bed applications (See Figure 2.41).

A typical installation of a thick bed latex-based portland cement mortar bed is as follows: A latex bond coat is applied to the concrete surface. The bond coat consists of a slurry coat of latex-based mortar and is to be applied to the wall with a notched trowel at a thickness of 1/16 of an inch. A typical bond coat consists of one (42-50 Kg) bag portland cement, 100 pounds (45 Kg) of 30-60 mesh sand, and 5 gallons of latex admix.[42]

If walls are rough, uneven, and out of plumb, a leveling bed should be used. A typical leveling bed consists of one (42-50 Kg) bag of portland cement, 3 cubic feet of ASTM

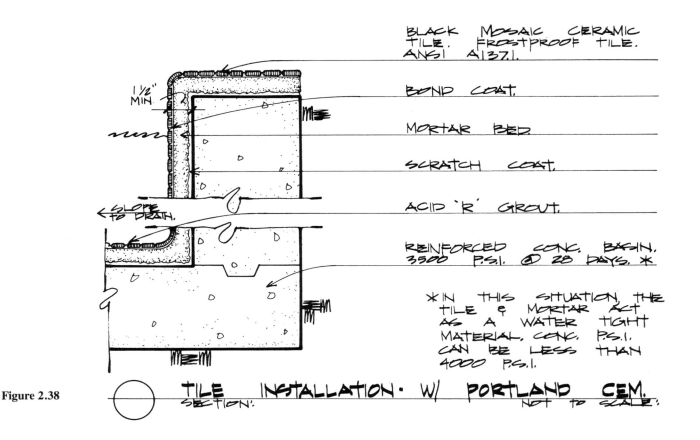

BLACK MOSAIC CERAMIC TILE. FROSTPROOF TILE. ANSI A137.1.

BOND COAT.

MORTAR BED

SCRATCH COAT.

ACID "R" GROUT.

REINFORCED CONC. BASIN. 3500 P.S.I. @ 28 DAYS. *

* IN THIS SITUATION, THE TILE & MORTAR ACT AS A WATER TIGHT MATERIAL. CONC. P.S.I. CAN BE LESS THAN 4000 P.S.I.

1 1/2" MIN

SLOPE TO DRAIN.

**Figure 2.38**

TILE INSTALLATION · W/ PORTLAND CEM.
SECTION: NOT TO SCALE:

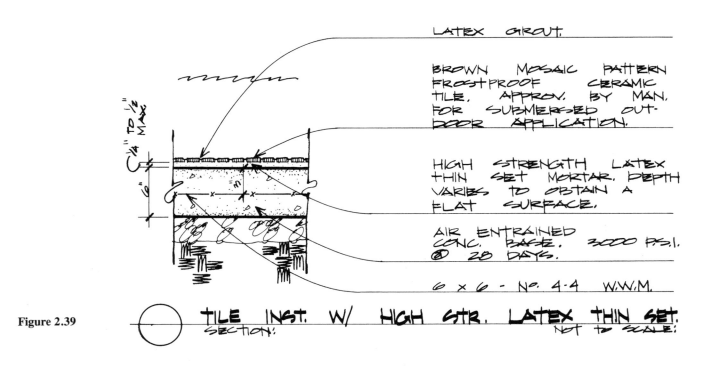

LATEX GROUT.

BROWN MOSAIC PATTERN FROSTPROOF CERAMIC TILE. APPROV. BY MAN. FOR SUBMERSED OUT- DOOR APPLICATION.

HIGH STRENGTH LATEX THIN SET MORTAR. DEPTH VARIES TO OBTAIN A FLAT SURFACE.

AIR ENTRAINED CONC. BASE. 3000 P.S.I. @ 28 DAYS.

6 x 6 - No. 4·4 W.W.M.

1/4" TO 1/2" MAX

6"

**Figure 2.39**

TILE INST. W/ HIGH STR. LATEX THIN SET.
SECTION: NOT TO SCALE:

**Figure 2.40** *Granite and cast iron sculptural element. Charlottesville, Virginia.*

C-144 sand (150 Kg), and 5 gallons of latex admix.[43] Thick bed mortar should be applied over the bond coat or leveling bed. These mortars should not exceed 1 inch in thickness. A typical thick bed mortar consists of one (42-50 Kg) bag portland cement, 3 cubic feet of ASTM C-33 course sand (150 Kg) and 5 gallons of latex admix.[44]

In situations where thick bed mortar is installed over a waterproof membrane, the thickness should be increased to 2 inches. A 2 inch x 2 inch 16 gauge, welded galvanized reinforcing mesh should be layered in the middle of the mortar bed.

When the thick bed mortar is still plastic, a bond coat slurry of 1/16 of an inch should be applied. Application should be with a smooth trowel. Just prior to placing the tile on the bed, a skim coat of mortar should be administered to the back of the tile. After setting has occurred, a latex grout should be packed into the joints.

When specifying the thickness of latex-based mortars, the designer should take into account that thicker is not necessarily better. Thick bed mortars should not be chosen over thin bed mortars because of their increased bonding strength. This is a common misconception. Thin bed mortars often have superior bonding strength and a lower installation cost.[45] Lower installation cost can be attributed to the reduction in material volume.

## STONE

Stone is classified geologically as igneous, sedimentary, and metamorphic. Inherent qualities of stone relate to the geological processes that create it. Suitability for use in fountains is depended on these qualities.

### Igneous Rock

Igneous rocks are products of heat. Granite is the most commonly used igneous building stone. It is available in a wide variety of colors and surface textures. Colors include red, gray, and charcoal. Surface treatments include polishing, split edge, sawed face, and thermal finish. Granite would be chosen as a fountain material because of its resistance to freeze-thaw, compressive strength, tolerance to abrasion, low rate of absorption, and its stately beauty. These qualities make it an excellent choice for use in basins, elevated basins, sculptural elements, or weirs (See Table 2.14).

Water tightness of a granite basin depends on the joint between the stones. Latex mortar can be used instead of

**Table 2.14 Physical Properties of Granite[46]**

| Physical property | Test requirements | ASTM test method |
|---|---|---|
| Absorption by weight max. | 0.40 | C 97 |
| Density min. lb./ft. (kg/m) | 160 (2560) | C 97 |
| Compressive strength min. psi (MPa) | 19,000 (131) | C 170 |
| Modulus of rupture min. psi (MPa) | 1500 (10.34) | C 99 |
| Abrasion resistance min. Ha* | 4 | C 241 |

*\* The minimum Ha value has not been established at this time and is presently a topic of study by Committee C-18.*

47

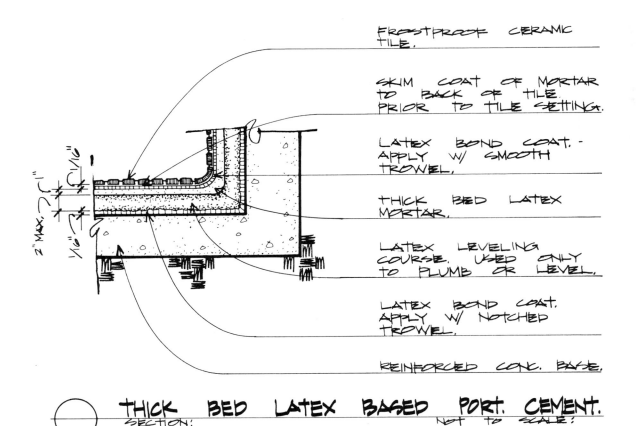

FROSTPROOF CERAMIC TILE.

SKIM COAT OF MORTAR TO BACK OF TILE PRIOR TO TILE SETTING.

LATEX BOND COAT. - APPLY W/ SMOOTH TROWEL.

THICK BED LATEX MORTAR.

LATEX LEVELING COURSE. USED ONLY TO PLUMB OR LEVEL.

LATEX BOND COAT. APPLY W/ NOTCHED TROWEL.

REINFORCED CONC. BASE.

**Figure 2.41**

THICK BED LATEX BASED PORT. CEMENT.
SECTION.                                    NOT TO SCALE.

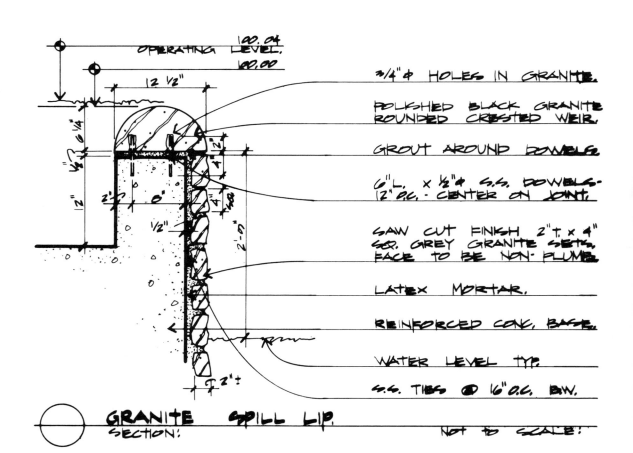

OPERATING LEVEL.    100.04
                    100.00

12 1/2"

3/4" ⌀ HOLES IN GRANITE.

POLISHED BLACK GRANITE ROUNDED CRESTED WEIR.

GROUT AROUND DOWELS.

6" L. x 1/2" ⌀ S.S. DOWELS - 12" O.C. - CENTER ON JOINT.

SAW CUT FINISH 2" t. x 4" SQ. GREY GRANITE SETS. FACE TO BE NON-PLUMB.

LATEX MORTAR.

REINFORCED CONC. BASE.

WATER LEVEL TYP.

S.S. TIES @ 16" O.C. BW.

**Figure 2.42**

GRANITE SPILL LIP.
SECTION.                                    NOT TO SCALE.

48

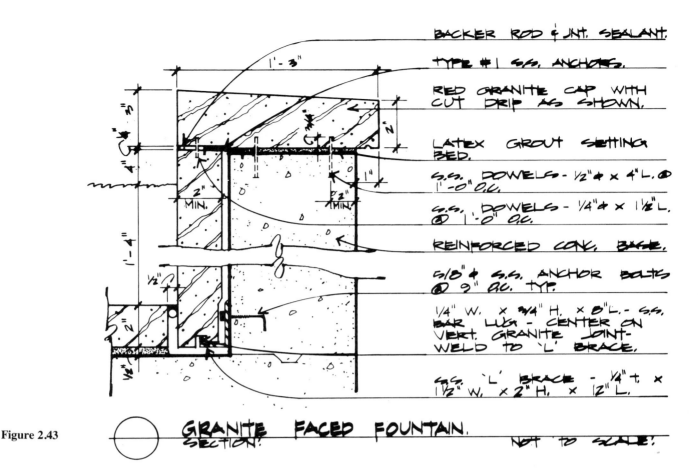

BACKER ROD & JNT. SEALANT.

TYPE #1 S.S. ANCHORS.

RED GRANITE CAP WITH CUT DRIP AS SHOWN.

LATEX GROUT SETTING BED.

S.S. DOWELS - 1/2"∅ × 4"L. @ 1'-0" O.C.

S.S. DOWELS - 1/4"∅ × 1 1/2"L. @ 1'-0" O.C.

REINFORCED CONC. BASE.

5/8"∅ S.S. ANCHOR BOLTS @ 9" O.C. TYP.

1/4" W. × 3/4" H. × 8"L. - S.S. BAR LUG - CENTER ON VERT. GRANITE JOINT-WELD TO 'L' BRACE.

S.S. 'L' BRACE - 1/4" t. × 1 1/2" W. × 2" H. × 12" L.

**GRANITE FACED FOUNTAIN.**
SECTION!

NOT TO SCALE!

**Figure 2.43**

**Figure 2.44** *Thermal finished granite basin with bronze lily pads. Washington, District of Columbia.*

epoxy with the same results, as long as proper stainless steel fasteners are specified. Joints between large panels should be uniform in width and should be raked back and caulked with an appropriate caulking compound. (See expansion joint treatment in concrete section.)

Wall copings and weirs should be set on stainless steel pins to prevent displacement (See Figure 2.42).

Stones exceeding 100 pounds should have Lewis holes for lifting them into place. All Lewis holes and anchorage holes should not come closer than 2 inches to the exposed face of the stone. This prevents shearing of the edges when the stone is lifted. Exceptions to the location of holes should be given to granite veneers.

All construction fasteners should be stainless steel to prevent corrosion. Substrate and fasteners should be fabricated from concrete and stainless steel and follow the prescribed recommendations elsewhere in this book and the granite supplier (See Figure 2.43).

### Sedimentary Rocks

Sedimentary rock consists of silt and skeletal remains of marine life deposited and cemented by ancient seas. Sandstone, limestone, and slate are sedimentary rocks quarried for use in the building industry.

*Sandstone* is comprised of sand particles which are glued together by cementous materials. Deposition of varied materials has created distinct types of sandstone. ASTM Standard C616-80 groups sandstone into three basic

49

categoies. These categories are determined by the free silica content. Free silica consists of detrital quartz grains and authigenic silica.[47] The classifications of sandstone are: Type I, Sandstone, with 60 percent minimum free silica content; Type II, Quartzitic Sandstone, with 90 percent minimum free silica content; and Type III, Quartzite, with 95 percent minimum free silica content.

The amount of free silica influences the suitability of sandstone for use in fountains. Type I sandstone (low in free silica) is soft, very easy to work with and high in water absorption. This type of sandstone has limited application and is best suited for naturalistic waterfalls and pool linings. Because of its high rate of absorption, some additional method of waterproofing is necessary. Various construction methods are available for improving the water retention capabilities of porous materials.

Some designers recommend coating the stone with two applications of clear epoxy.[48] The degree of watertightness of epoxy coats depends upon the amount of basin movement. Any slight surface crack caused by settlement or improper installation of the basin or mortar joints will create an opportunity for water to penetrate the surface treatment.

By veneering the stone to a concrete basin, a semi-watertight vessel will be created. In this situation, the concrete basin is utilized as a water-holding medium. The sandstone acts only as a decorative or a facing material.

In veneer construction, highly absorptive sandstones should be prewetted before installation to prevent sucking of water from the mortar. Latex-based mortars should be specified for stone installation to improve the bonding of stone and mortar.

In regions subjected to freeze-thaw conditions, it is important to prevent highly absorptive sandstones from becoming saturated during winter. The expanded water can crack the stone, spall the surface, or loosen the mortar and eventually dislodge a stone.

Types II and III sandstone have better qualities for use in fountains because of their increased strengths and lower

**Figure 2.45** *Rock-edged basin and waterfall. El Cajon, California.*

**Figure 2.46** *Limestone fountain. Washington, District of Columbia.*

**Table 2.15 ASTM C616 Physical Properties of Sandstone[49]**

| Property | Test requirements | Classifications | ASTM method |
|---|---|---|---|
| Absorption by weight, maximum % | 20 | I Sandstone | C 97 |
|  | 3 | II Quartzitic sandstone |  |
|  | 1 | III Quartzite |  |
| Density, min. lb./ft.³ (Kg.m³) | 140 (2240) | I Sandstone | C 97 |
|  | 150 (2400) | II Quartzitic sandstone |  |
|  | 160 (2560) | III Quartzite |  |
| Compressive strength, min. psi (MPa) | 2000 (13.8) | I Sandstone | C 170 |
|  | 10000 (68.9) | II Quartzitic sandstone |  |
|  | 20000 (137.9) | III Quartzite |  |
| Modulus of rupture, min. psi (MPa) | 300 (2.1) | I Sandstone | C 99 |
|  | 1000 (6.9) | II Quartzitic sandstone |  |
|  | 2000 (13.9) | III Quartzite |  |
| Abrasion resistance | 8 | I Sandstone | C 241 |
|  | 8 | II Quartzitic sandstone |  |
|  | 8 | III Quartzite |  |

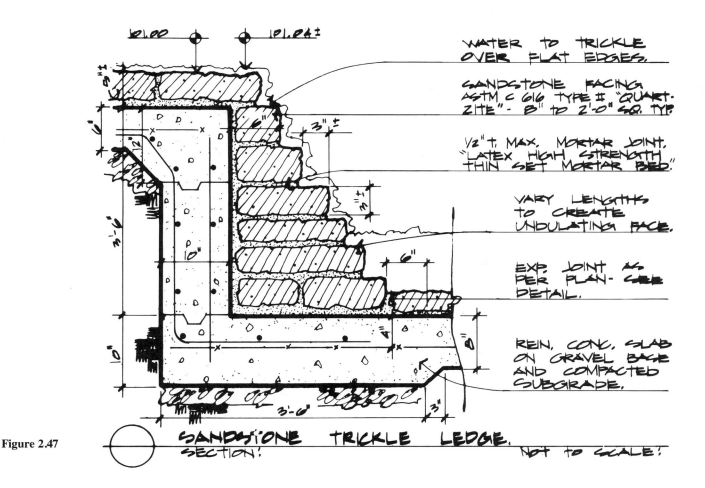

**Figure 2.47**

SANDSTONE TRICKLE LEDGE.
SECTION!

WATER TO TRICKLE OVER FLAT EDGES.

SANDSTONE FACING ASTM C 616 TYPE II "QUARTZITE" - 8" to 2'-0" SQ. TYP.

1/2"± MAX. MORTAR JOINT, "LATEX HIGH STRENGTH THIN SET MORTAR BED."

VARY LENGTHS TO CREATE UNDULATING FACE.

EXP. JOINT AS PER PLAN- SEE DETAIL.

REIN. CONC. SLAB ON GRAVEL BASE AND COMPACTED SUBGRADE.

NOT TO SCALE!

absorption rates. Both types can be used as a building material or as a veneer on a concrete substrate (See Table 2.15).

*Limestone* is a soft sedimentary rock which is easy to carve and shape. However, when exposed to air, limestone develops a hard, long-wearing surface.[50] When specifying limestone for use in fountains, the designer should choose "statuary" or "select" grades. These grades are uniform or fine grained, dense, have no pore spaces larger than 1/25 of an inch, and have only minor grain and texture variations.

Problems often arise with sink holes in regions of the country where limestone is the predominant underlying geology. In these situations, water dissolves the carbonate of lime contained in the stone. For this reason, limestone should be used only in areas not subjected to wetting. Submerged placement may deteriorate the stone (See Figure 2.46).

*Slate* is a sedimentary rock created from layers of high-silica clays and silts. Because of the clays and their deposition into layers, slate splits into thin sheets. Thicknesses of slate range from ¼ of an inch to 2 inches.

Slate is available in at least four colors (blue, green, red, and purple) and in exterior and interior grades. Exterior grade slate has favorable qualities for submersed applications. It has low absorption and high strength (See Table 2.16).

Slate is often used in residential foyers because of its smooth surface and cleaning ease. The smooth surface may become slippery when submerged. For this reason, it is not recommended for use in pool bottoms where people will walk.

In the construction trade, slate is primarily used as a veneer. Veneering is suited for use in fountains as long as mortaring and expansion joints are treated properly. Veneers should be attached to a concrete substrate with a latex-based mortar. Care should be taken to extend the expansion joints of the concrete base straight through the slate surfacing. Expansion joints should be of a uniform thickness and caulked with a resilient caulking. (Refer to the discussion on concrete for proper joint treatment.)

**Metamorphic Rock**

Metamorphic rock is formed by the gradual change in character and structure of igneous or sedimentary rock. Marble is the most commonly used metamorphic stone for building purposes.

*Marble* is a crystalline rock composed of various minerals. Basic mineral composition determines the classification of marble. ASTM standard C503-79 designates marble as follows:

1. Calcite
2. Dolomite
3. Serpentine
4. Travertine

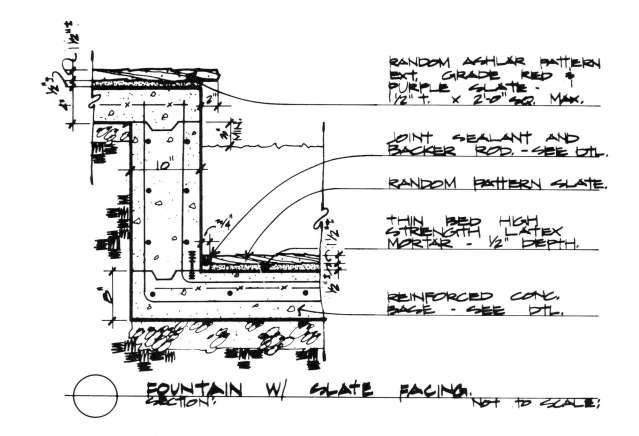

RANDOM ASHLAR PATTERN
EXT. GRADE RED &
PURPLE SLATE.
½" t. × 2'-0" SQ. MAX.

JOINT SEALANT AND
BACKER ROD. - SEE DTL.

RANDOM PATTERN SLATE.

THIN BED HIGH
STRENGTH LATEX
MORTAR - ½" DEPTH.

REINFORCED CONC.
BASE - SEE DTL.

FOUNTAIN W/ SLATE FACING.
SECTION:                    NOT TO SCALE:

**Figure 2.48**

**Figure 2.49** *Sandstone entry fountain. Richmond, Virginia.*

**Table 2.16 ASTM C 629 Physical Properties of Slate[51]**

| Property | Test requirements | Classifications | ASTM test methods |
|---|---|---|---|
| Absorption, max. % | 0.25 | I Exterior | C 121 |
| | 0.45 | II Interior | |
| Modulus or rupture min. psi (MPa): | | | |
| Across grain | 9000 (62.1) | I Exterior | C 120 |
| | 9000 (62.1) | II Interior | |
| Along grain | 7200 (49.6) | I Exterior | C 120 |
| | 7200 (49.6) | II Interior | |
| Abrasion resistance | 8.0 | I Exterior | C 241 |
| | 8.0 | II Interior | |
| Acid resistance, max. inches (mm) | 0.015 (0.38) | I Exterior | C 217 |
| | 0.025 (0.64) | II Interior | |

**Figure 2.50** *Marble sculptural element. Kansas City, Missouri.*

When compared to granite, marble is normally weaker in compressive strength. Rate of absorption, color range, and beauty closely parallel the qualities of granite (See Table 2.17).

Care should be taken in selecting the proper marble for exterior use. Marbles vary greatly in their abilities to withstand the elements. Some crumble under severe weather conditions and pollution. Also certain marbles will deteriorate in the presence of water.

Marble contains more natural faults than granite. These fault planes may cause stones to split apart from weathering. Marble grades "A" and "S" are preferable for fountain use because of their limited natural faults.

Construction procedures for installation of marble are similar to granite. Marble is suited for elevated basins, weirs, and sculptural elements. When installing marble veneers, panels should be inspected for natural faults. Marble suppliers repair these faults and lines of separation by reinforcing, sticking, and waxing. (For detailed information on the installation of marble, refer to the discussion on granite.)

## METAL BASINS

Various metals have been used over the years for basins or fountain liners. The following outlines the utilization of these materials.

### Lead Sheeting

Lead sheeting was one of the first metals used to line water-holding basins. It is relatively soft and consequently easy to shape and work with, but recent literature on lead poisoning recommends that lead in any form not be used in a publicly-accessible area.

**Table 2.17 ASTM C 503 Physical Properties of Marble[52]**

| Physical Property | Test requirements | Classification | ASTM test method |
|---|---|---|---|
| Absorption by weight, max. % | 0.75 | I. II. III. IV. | C 97 |
| Density, min. lb./ft.³ (Kg.m³) | 162 (2595)<br>175 (2800)<br>168 (2690)<br>144 (2305) | I. Calcite*<br>II. Dolomite*<br>III. Serpentine*<br>IV. Travertine* | C 97 |
| Compressive strength, min. psi (MPa) | 7500 (52) | I. II. III. IV. | C 170 |
| Modulus of rupture, min. psi (MPa) | 1000 (7) | I. II. III. IV. | C 99 |
| Abrasion resistance min. hardness** | 10 | I. II. III. IV. | C 241 |

\* See Definitions C 199 for definitions of calcite, dolomite, and travertine marbles.

\*\* Pertains to foot traffic only. Where two or more marbles are combined for color and design effects, there should be no greater difference than 5 points in abrasion resistance. In stairways, floors, and platforms subject to heavy foot traffic, a minimum abrasion hardness of 12.0 is recommended.

## Copper

Copper is an excellent choice for use in fountains due to the following qualities:

1. Resists attack by air and moisture (Non-corrosive)
2. Extremely durable
3. Easy to work and join
4. Attractive.

Copper can be used as a basin liner, sculptural element, or covering for a raised pool or weir. The cost of solid copper is quite prohibitive for most situations but can be reduced substantially by using sheet copper.

Sheeting is available in various thicknesses. In the building industry, thickness or gauge of copper is expressed in terms of "ounces per square foot."[53] For example, this means that a 12 inch by 12 inch sheet having a certain thickness would weigh 20 ounces. Sheeting having a weight of 12 to 20 "ounces per square foot" is best suited for use in fountains. Sheeting having a weight of 12 "ounces per square foot" is the most economical (See Table 2.18).

Sheet copper is available in three types: 1) 110 cold rolled copper; 2) 110 soft copper; and 3) lead-coated copper. Cold rolled copper is used extensively in the building industry to waterproof roofs, and is by far the best choice for fountain basins. Soft copper is extremely malleable and therefore not suited for basins. Lead-coated copper should be avoided in fountains due to the potential harm of lead poisoning.

When using 110 cold rolled copper, it is important to provide a proper backing or structural support for the sheeting material. Relative strength is dependent on the strength of the base. Strength of the material can be increased by introducing shapes into the sheeting (See Table 2.19).

*Installation of Copper Sheeting.* Copper can be applied over wood, brick, stone, stucco, or concrete. Wooden bases for copper sheeting should be smooth, kiln-dried, and free of any corrosive fire-retardant treatment. Surfaces such as stone, brick, and stucco should be smooth and free of bumps. Concrete intended for use as a copper substrate

**Figure 2.51** *Copper and brick fountain. Charlottesville, Virginia.*

**Figure 2.52** *Copper spill lip. Charlottesville, Virginia.*

should be made smooth by applying a wash of smooth cement or heavy coats of asphalt paint.

Before sheet copper is installed on any substrate, apply a layer of roofing felt followed by a layer of building paper. Roofing felt used should be an asphalt or coal tar saturated felt weighing not less than 15 pounds per 100 square feet, while the building paper should be a rosin sized unsaturated paper weighing approximately 6 pounds per 100 square feet.

When using copper sheeting in fountain basins, care should be taken to design a watertight joint between sheets. Submerged joints should be soldered flat, locking seams. Joints should be tinned before connection. Solder should conform to ASTM standard B-32 and consist of 50 percent lead and 50 percent tin. A soldered joint physically bonds the two materials together, creating the most watertight seal for use underwater. By locking the seam and soldering, the joints become rigid.

Loose seams and joints allow for expansion but do not provide a watertight joint when submerged. They are best suited for situations in which wetting may occur (See Figure 2.53). In some instances, it may be necessary to physically attach the sheeting to the substrate. This can be achieved by cleating, nailing, or screwing.[56] Cleating allows for fastening without puncture of the sheeting, reducing the chance of future leaks. All fastening should be of copper or copper alloy. In situations where nails or screws are needed, the heads can be soldered over to form a tight seal. Basins must be designed to accommodate differential expansion. The substrate and copper sheeting may expand or contract at dif-

ferent rates causing failure of the seam. Successful copper fountain construction should consider the following items:

1. What type of joints are needed?
2. Is attachment to substrate needed?
3. What is the best method for attachment of sheeting?
4. Will there be differential expansion of materials?
5. When using rigid joints, will attachment of sheeting to substrate cause failure of seams?
6. How will differential expansion of material be handled?

Due to the interaction of dilute sulfurous and sulfuric acid (acid rain), copper sheeting tends to develop a patina (copper sulfate). Patina is characterized by a blue-green or a gray-green color. It creates a protective coating which inhibits further corrosion.

Some people consider a rich patina to be desirable and attractive. To accelerate the formation of patina, ammonium chloride or ammonium sulfate may be applied to the sheeting.

To discourage this process and preserve the bright natural color and high reflectivity of copper, one can wax, oil, or coat the surface. Oil and waxes tend to dissipate when exposed to the elements and would need reapplication periodically.[57] A more permanent, protective measure would be an air-drying, clear, organic coating.

The following details are ideas for copper use in fountains (See Figures 2.55 and 2.56).

**Table 2.18 Thickness of Gauge of Sheet Copper[54]**

| Weight per sq. ft. | | Thickness (inches) | | Nearest gauge no. (B&S) | Nearest fractions (inches) |
|---|---|---|---|---|---|
| ounces | pounds | nominal | minimum | | |
| 32 | 2 | .0431 | .0405 | 17 | |
| 24 | 1½ | .0323 | .0295 | 20 | 1/32 |
| 20 | 1¼ | .0270 | .0245 | 21 | |
| 16 | 1 | .0216 | .0190 | 23 | |
| 12 | ¾ | .0162 | .0143 | 26 | 1/64 |
| 10 | ⅝ | .0135 | .0115 | 27 | |
| 8 | ½ | .0108 | .0090 | 29 | |

**Table 2.19 Effect of Shape and Weight on Strength of 110 Cold Rolled Copper[55]**

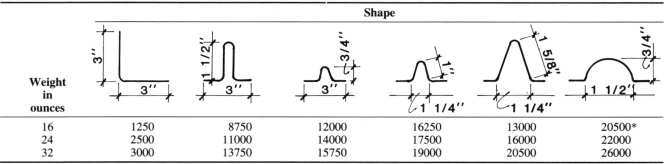

| Weight in ounces | Shape | | | | | |
|---|---|---|---|---|---|---|
| 16 | 1250 | 8750 | 12000 | 16250 | 13000 | 20500* |
| 24 | 2500 | 11000 | 14000 | 17500 | 16000 | 22000 |
| 32 | 3000 | 13750 | 15750 | 19000 | 20500 | 26000 |

*Columnar rigidity-stress in pounds per square inch.*

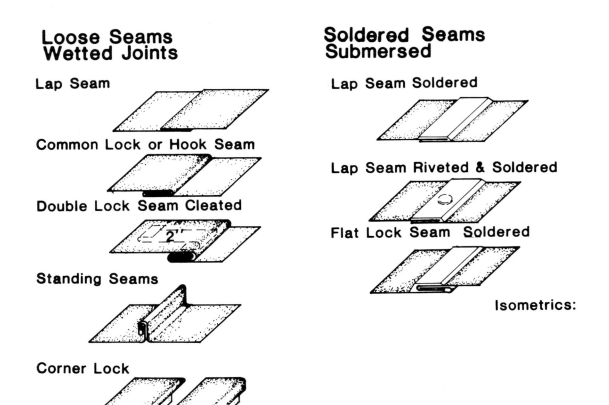

## Loose Seams
## Wetted Joints

### Lap Seam

### Common Lock or Hook Seam

### Double Lock Seam Cleated

2"

### Standing Seams

### Corner Lock

Single
Seam

Double Seam

## Soldered Seams
## Submersed

### Lap Seam Soldered

### Lap Seam Riveted & Soldered

### Flat Lock Seam Soldered

Isometrics:

**Figure 2.53**    **Jointing Methods of Copper Sheet**

### Brass

Brass is defined as a copper alloy containing copper and zinc. Brass can be cast, stamped, rolled into sheets, and drawn into pipes or tubing. Colors range from golden or reddish to yellow.

Because brass is an alloy of copper, it has similarities to and advantages over copper. Joining, workability, and corrosion resistance are similar to copper. Strength and ductility are greater than copper. Brass is more expensive than copper. It would be specified over copper for applications where rich color and increased strength are needed. (Refer to the discussion on copper for further information.)

### Bronze

Bronze is a copper alloy containing copper and zinc, or copper, silicon, and manganese. It is a rich brown metal suitable for castings, or sheeting. Colors range from bronze-red to a light copper.

Because bronze is an alloy of copper, it has similarities and advantages over copper. Corrosion resistance, workability and joining are similar to copper. Bronze has greater strength than copper and is more expensive. It would be specified over copper for applications where increased strength or richness of color is needed. (Refer to the discussion on copper for further information.)

**Figure 2.54** *Sculptural copper mushrooms. Philadelphia, Pennsylvania.*

56

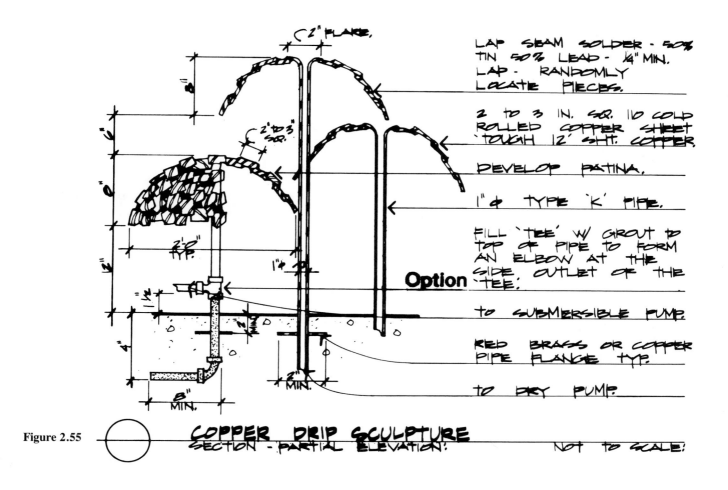

LAP SEAM SOLDER - 50% TIN 50% LEAD - ¼" MIN. LAP - RANDOMLY LOCATE PIECES.

2 to 3 IN. SQ. 16 COLD ROLLED COPPER SHEET 'TOUGH 12' SHT. COPPER.

DEVELOP PATINA.

1" ⌀ TYPE 'K' PIPE.

FILL 'TEE' W/ GROUT TO TOP OF PIPE TO FORM AN ELBOW AT THE SIDE OUTLET OF THE 'TEE.'

**Option**

TO SUBMERSIBLE PUMP.

RED BRASS OR COPPER PIPE FLANGE TYP.

TO DRY PUMP.

**Figure 2.55**  COPPER DRIP SCULPTURE
SECTION - PARTIAL ELEVATION.          NOT TO SCALE!

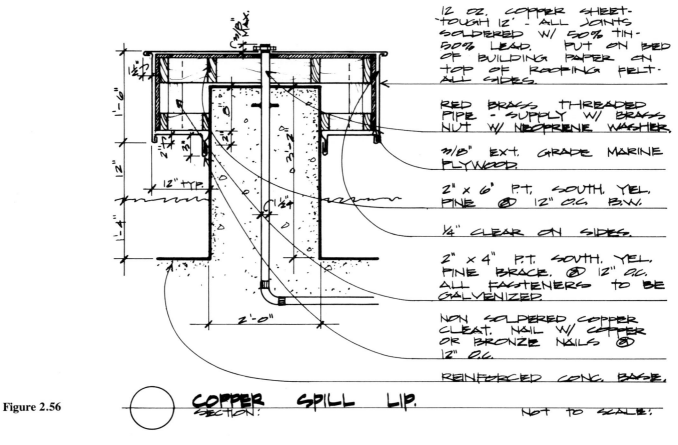

12 OZ. COPPER SHEET-TOUGH 12' - ALL JOINTS SOLDERED W/ 50% TIN-50% LEAD. PUT ON BED OF BUILDING PAPER ON TOP OF ROOFING FELT- ALL SIDES.

RED BRASS THREADED PIPE - SUPPLY W/ BRASS NUT W/ NEOPRENE WASHER.

⅜" EXT. GRADE MARINE PLYWOOD.

2" × 6' P.T. SOUTH. YEL. PINE @ 12" O.C. B.W.

¼" CLEAR ON SIDES.

2" × 4" P.T. SOUTH. YEL. PINE BRACE @ 12" O.C. ALL FASTENERS TO BE GALVENIZED.

NON SOLDERED COPPER CLEAT. NAIL W/ COPPER OR BRONZE NAILS @ 12" O.C.

REINFORCED CONC. BASE.

**Figure 2.56**   COPPER SPILL LIP.
SECTION.                    NOT TO SCALE!

**Figure 2.57** *Bronze sculptural element. Santa Fe, New Mexico.*

**Figure 2.59** *Bronze sculpture and fountain. Richmond, Virginia.*

**Figure 2.58** *Bronze sculpture and fountain. Richmond, Virginia.*

**Figure 2.60** *Bronze sculpture and fountain. Richmond, Virginia.*

**Figure 2.61** *Cast iron fountain and basin. Kansas City, Missouri.*

**Figure 2.63** *Cast iron fountain.*

**Figure 2.64** *Cast iron fountain. Charleston, South Carolina.*

**Figure 2.62** *Intricate surface detailing of cast iron. Courtesy of Robinson Iron Works.*

### Cast Iron

Any iron containing 1.7 percent carbon and poured into molds is classified as cast iron. Cast iron is brittle, high in compressive strength, hard, and relatively crystalline in nature. Cast iron used for fountains is sand cast Class 30 gray iron.[58] This iron has a tensile strength of 30,000 psi and falls under classification ASTM A48. Cast iron fountain walls should not be less than ⅜ of an inch thick. This will ensure long life and proper tensile strength.

Cast iron fountains and basin are of special interest to the preservationist. The use of cast iron fountains in the United States predates the Civil War. The relative strength and casting capabilities of the iron allow for the construction of thin basins, light visual forms, and delicate tiered effects. These qualities are very distinctive of iron casting and are hard to achieve in other materials except molded plastics.

Packed sand molds are constructed in the reverse of the desired design. The sand molds permit excellent surface detailing. The use of surface detailing is seen in many of our older fountains and is typified in form by fluted edges, slender cranes, friendly dolphins, griffins, cattails, and lilies. The size of fountains is somewhat limited by molding and the capability of the foundry.

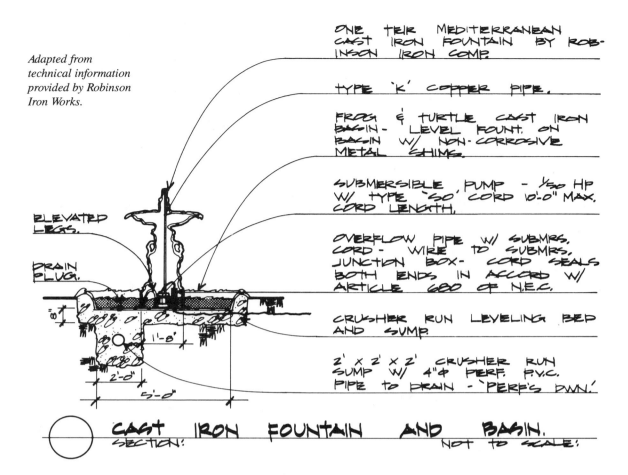

*Adapted from technical information provided by Robinson Iron Works.*

ONE TIER MEDITERRANEAN CAST IRON FOUNTAIN BY ROBINSON IRON COMP.

TYPE 'K' COPPER PIPE.

FROG & TURTLE CAST IRON BASIN - LEVEL FOUNT. ON BASIN W/ NON-CORROSIVE METAL SHIMS.

SUBMERSIBLE PUMP - 1/50 HP W/ TYPE 'SO' CORD 10'-0" MAX. CORD LENGTH.

OVERFLOW PIPE W/ SUBMRS. CORD - WIRE TO SUBMRS. JUNCTION BOX- CORD SEALS BOTH ENDS IN ACCORD W/ ARTICLE 680 OF N.E.C.

CRUSHER RUN LEVELING BED AND SUMP.

2' X 2' X 2' CRUSHER RUN SUMP W/ 4"∅ PERF. P.V.C. PIPE TO DRAIN - 'PERF'S DWN.'

ELEVATED LEGS.

DRAIN PLUG.

8"

1'-8"

2'-0"

5'-0"

**Figure 2.65**

CAST IRON FOUNTAIN AND BASIN.
SECTION:                                    NOT TO SCALE:

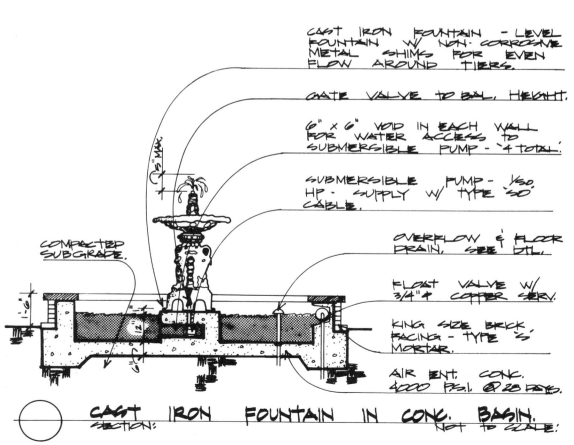

CAST IRON FOUNTAIN - LEVEL FOUNTAIN W/ NON-CORROSIVE METAL SHIMS FOR EVEN FLOW AROUND TIERS.

GATE VALVE TO BAL. HEIGHT.

6" X 6" VOID IN EACH WALL FOR WATER ACCESS TO SUBMERSIBLE PUMP - '4 TOTAL.'

SUBMERSIBLE PUMP - 1/50. HP - SUPPLY W/ TYPE 'SO' CABLE.

OVERFLOW & FLOOR DRAIN, SEE DTL.

FLOAT VALVE W/ 3/4"∅ COPPER SERV.

KING SIZE BRICK FACING - TYPE 'S' MORTAR.

AIR ENT. CONC. 4000 PSI. @ 28 DAYS.

COMPACTED SUBGRADE.

**Figure 2.66**

CAST IRON FOUNTAIN IN CONC. BASIN.
SECTION:                                    NOT TO SCALE:

**Figure 2.67** *Stainless steel sculptural elements. Denver, Colorado.*

**Figure 2.68** *Aluminum sculptural element. Philadelphia, Pennsylvania.*

Larger fountains are often comprised of many individually cast pieces. These pieces are welded with a nickel welding rod according to AWS standards. Larger fountains require stainless steel bolts and welding to hold pieces together.

Cast iron exposed to air and moisture will oxidize if not protected. Once oxidation occurs on the surface, it produces a protective layer which prevents further oxidation. This rust will stain adjacent surfaces and care should be taken to prevent this. Most manufacturers paint cast iron fountains as a rust prevention measure.

Paint coatings include primer, finish coat and an optional antique finish coat. The primer consists of a two-part epoxy. This is then covered with an urethane enamel finish coat. Non-corrosive atmosphere areas are given a finish coat of an alkali industrial enamel. As an option, green alkali enamel is hand rubbed over the top of a gloss black finish coat.[59]

Cast iron is an extremely watertight material. However, problems with waterproofing may occur when pipes or nozzles penetrate the basin. A watertight joint can be achieved by using gaskets, threaded unions, or compressive fittings.

Some fountains are available pre-plumbed. In this case, the manufacturer has installed the pipe and unions at the factory. Pipes will be stubbed-out at the base of the fountain and will require simple hookup at the job site. If unions are to be installed on the job site, workmen should follow the procedures specified by the shop drawing.

The following are typical cast iron fountain installation details (See Figures 2.65 and 2.66).

### Steel

Steel is not ideally suited for use in fountains because of surface corrosion. However, with proper coatings, steel could be employed in a fountain but maintenance is necessary to prevent corrosion. Certain steel alloys can be used.

*High strength low-alloy steels* are a group of patented alloy steels called weathering steel. These steels are better known to the construction industry by their trade names — Cor-ten, Mayari-R, and Dynalloy.[60] These steels are normally specified because of their increased strength and corrosion resistance.

Weathering steels are not suited for direct burial or submerged applications.[61] For this reason, weathering steels are preferable for sculptural elements in pools. When used in fountains, they should be located in areas subjected to limited wetting.

Weathering steel forms an oxide film on its surface. This oxide creates a protective film which seals the surface of the member and protects against further corrosion. During the formation of the oxide film, the steel will lose about 0.002 inches (0.051 mm) in thickness.[62] This film assumes a pleasing texture and color ranging from brown to warm purple, depending on exposure. Oxide film has a tendency to stain adjacent materials and the designer should anticipate this problem and design accordingly.

Flexible design form and ease of fabrication are inherent qualities of steel. Design form can be achieved by using the available stock members — plate, bars, sheeting, tubing, channels, angle, and beams. Fabrication is also versatile and would include a combination of the following: cutting, shearing, forming, milling, punching, riveting, and welding.

*Stainless steel* is a steel alloy containing 11.5 percent or more chromium. As more chromium is added to steel, it becomes more resistant to corrosion.[63] Enough chromium is present in stainless steel to permit the formation of a film of chromium oxide on the surface. If this oxide is scratched, a proper oxidizing agent should be applied to reform the protective film. Presently, there are 40 types of stainless steel on the market. Type 302 is best suited for use in fountains. It is a basic chromium-nickel stainless steel, employed in a wide range of applications in all kinds of architectural work. It is easy to form and fabricate and has excellent resistance to corrosion and weather exposure.

Stainless steel is available in a variety of finishes. They range from a non-reflective matte finish to a highly polished, reflective mirror-like finish. Finish types are assigned a number one through eight. Type one is a matte finish while type eight is a mirror finish.

Stainless steel is an excellent choice for fountains due to the following qualities:

1. Corrosion resistant
2. Non-stainable
3. Easy workability
4. Beauty
5. Strength.

Stainless steel is available in standard metal shapes such as angle, channels, bars, sheeting, and tubes. Sheeting can be used as a substrate liner for smaller pools or as a cover for elevated weirs or pools. When using stainless steel, the degree of watertightness in a basin is dependent on the joint.

Stainless steel has a high rate of expansion when exposed to heat. Detailing should account for this property.

The relative high cost of the material has limited its use in fountains to sculptural elements and smaller scale fountains. Sculptural elements can be built out of a combination of standard metal shapes. The diversity of available shapes affords great design freedom, which is one good reason for selection of stainless steel.

## Aluminum

Aluminum could be specified for fountain use when reduced weight, and corrosion resistance is needed. Pure aluminum develops a spontaneous oxide film when exposed to air. This oxide gives aluminum its corrosion resistance.

Various alloys of aluminum are presently on the market. Pure aluminum is moderately strong and by adding alloys, it can achieve strengths of 20,000 to 68,000 psi.[64] As alloy content increases, aluminum tends to lose its corrosion resistance. When choosing an alloy, gains and losses in strength and corrosion resistance should be considered, respectively. Alloys 5005, 5050, and 5052 are appropriate for fountain application. These alloys have good workability, superior strength, and corrosion resistance and are of suitable quality for use in basins, elevated weirs, or sculptural elements.

Anodizing, an electrolytic process which encourages the formation of oxide on the surface, is often used to increase the corrosion and abrasion resistance of aluminum.

Aluminum has several similarities to steel. It can be fabricated by shearing, cutting, milling, forming, punching, riveting and welding. Like most watertight skins, aluminum's retention capabilities depend on the use of proper joints. Aluminum has been employed for many years as a building material in swimming pools.

Welding of joints creates the best insurance against leakage, and is predominantly performed by the inert-gas shielded arc method. In this process, an electric arc is used to heat and fuse the metal, and the melted metal is shielded from contact with the air by an inert gas (usually helium).

Design form is flexible because of the available stock components. Stock shapes include bars, rods, angles, channels, beams, plate and sheet.

## Combined Use of Metals — Galvanic Action

When two dissimilar metals are in contact in the presence of an electrolyte, a liquid capable of conducting electricity, an electric current is generated (as in a battery). An electric current will flow from one metal to the other metal (the cathode). In this process the anode will be eaten away while the cathode will remain intact. This process is called galvanic action.[65] Care should be taken when using dissimilar metals in fountains. Pool or fountain water may contain salts or chemicals which would increase the conductivity of water. This would cause destructive corrosion of submerged metals. The effects of two metals in the presence of an electrolyte can be determined by knowing the metals location on the galvanic scale[66] (See Table 2.20).

**Table 2.20 Galvanic Series of Metals Used in Construction***

| | |
|---|---|
| Anodic | Magnesium |
| | Magnesium alloys |
| | Beryllium |
| | Aluminum (commercially pure) |
| | Manganese |
| | Zinc |
| | Cadmium |
| | Aluminum 2024 (active) |
| | Iron or steel |
| | Cast iron |
| | Stainless steel 301, 302 (active) |
| | Lead |
| | Tin |
| | Nickel (active) |
| | Brass |
| | Copper |
| | Bronze |
| | Chromium stainless steel |
| | Silver |
| | Titanium |
| | Platinum |

*\* Each metal, as listed, will be corroded by the metals listed below it. The further apart metals are located on the galvanic scale, the greater will be the corrosion. Corrosion caused by galvanic action can be inhibited or prevented by treating metals with protective coatings.*

**Figure 2.69** *Pressure-treated wood waterfall. Philadelphia, Pennsylvania.*

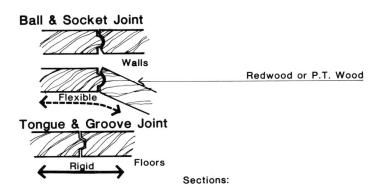

**Watertight Joints – Hot Tubs**

**Figure 2.70**

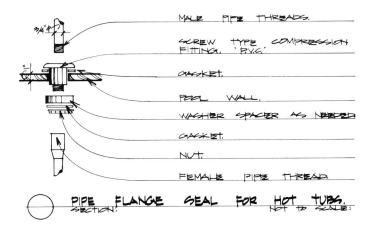

**Figure 2.71**

## WOOD

Wood has been used to retain liquids for several centuries. Water, vinegar, and spirits are often stored in wooden kegs or barrels, staves of which are held in compression by steel or wooden bands. The staves are beveled on the edge perpendicular to the banding so that the joint angle radiated out from the barrel center. The barrel staves, made from air or kiln-dried wood, absorb moisture when subjected to free water and expand slightly. Because of the radial joint, the expanded wood fibers thrust the wedge-shape staves outwards towards the banding. This outward force against the inward compression of the banding causes the joint to tighten further.

Our modern day hot tubs work on the same principle. A hot tub shell can be used as a basin for a residential fountain or as a water feature in conjunction with the hot tub. Tubs are available in various types of wood, including redwood, mahogany, and white oak. Redwood will normally last longer in an outdoor setting without painting or treating.

To create a tighter joint between the staves, most manufacturers use tongue and groove, ball and socket joints, or a combination of both joints. Tongue and groove joints are best suited for floors and walls while ball and socket are best suited for wall construction. Ball and socket joints will allow for curvature while still providing a watertight joint (See Figure 2.70)

The penetration of any piping or fixture through the wood wall or floor can cause a waterproofing problem if not handled properly. Most hot tub manufacturers have compressive screw flanges which expand in diameter as they are tightened against the wall. This creates an excellent watertight seal between the pipe and the wall or the flange and the wall (See Figure 2.71).

Wooden climbers and play structures are ideal for use in spray pools and fountains. These manufactured play pieces are sculptural, easily altered and assembled, and somewhat durable.

When ordering a climber for use in fountains, the specifier should make sure that the wood is (chromated copper arsenate or equal) pressure-treated pine, which has good resistance to rotting, or redwood. Many manufacturers will pre-drill vertical members to permit the insertion of a pipe. This allows a spray nozzle to be positioned at the top of the sculptural wood element. Troughs can be routed through the top face of horizontal members to produce channels for water spillage (See Figure 2.72). This creates additional water interest.

If drilled vertical members are allowed to split, it may create a route for water to seep from in a submerged situation. By installing a corrosion-resistant collar or flashing, this problem can be prevented.

When a metal collar enlarges due to thermal expansion, both the inside and outside diameters enlarge. The expanding collar will press outward against the concrete when temperatures rise. This expansion should be absorbed in an expansion joint to prevent damage to the concrete.

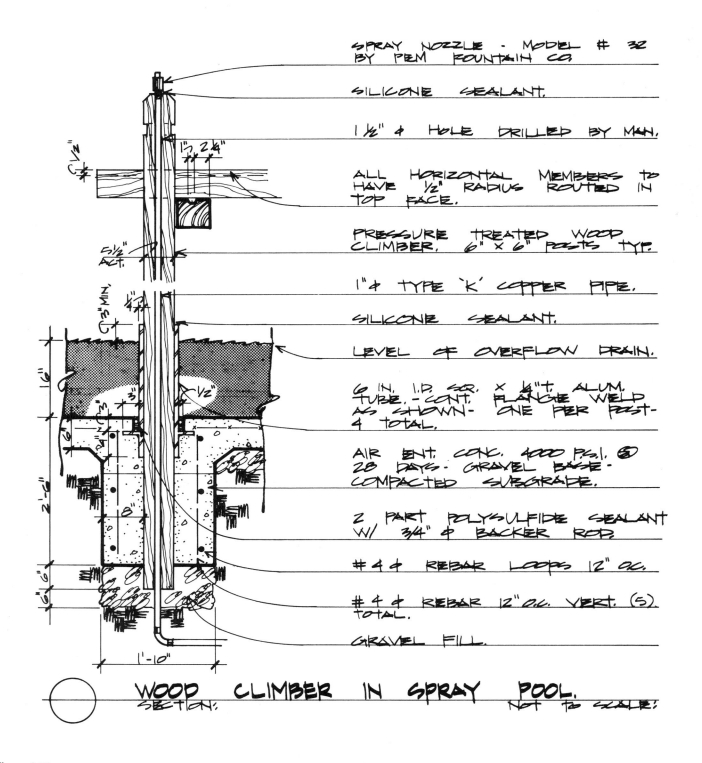

SPRAY NOZZLE - MODEL # 32
BY PEM FOUNTAIN CO

SILICONE SEALANT.

1 ½" Ø HOLE DRILLED BY MAN.

ALL HORIZONTAL MEMBERS to
HAVE ½" RADIUS ROUTED IN
TOP FACE.

PRESSURE TREATED WOOD
CLIMBER, 6" × 6" POSTS TYP.

1" Ø TYPE 'K' COPPER PIPE.

SILICONE SEALANT.

LEVEL OF OVERFLOW DRAIN.

6 IN. I.D. SQ. × ⅛"t. ALUM.
TUBE. - CONT. FLANGE WELD
AS SHOWN - ONE PER POST -
4 TOTAL.

AIR ENT. CONC. 4000 P.S.I. @
28 DAYS - GRAVEL BASE -
COMPACTED SUBGRADE.

2 PART POLYSULFIDE SEALANT
W/ ¾" Ø BACKER ROD.

#4 Ø REBAR LOOPS 12" O.C.

#4 Ø REBAR 12" O.C. VERT. (5)
TOTAL.

GRAVEL FILL.

## WOOD CLIMBER IN SPRAY POOL.
SECTION:                              NOT TO SCALE:

**Figure 2.72**

**Figure 2.73** *Water running over split log. Colorado.*

**Figure 2.74** *Fiberglas sculptural element with water cascading over umbrella. Dutch Wonderland, Pennsylvania.*

When the collar cools, the inside diameter will constrict. Wood is somewhat flexible and should withstand the inward pressures created by the collar. Caulking should also be provided on the inside of the collar to prevent water from entering the collar interior.

## FIBERGLASS

Fiberglass is a name given to materials composed of layers of polyester or epoxy resin and glass fibers. A glass mat is combined with wet resins in successive layers to achieve the desired thickness. A finish coat or gel coat, consisting of colored plastics, is applied to the exposed faces of the material to form a smooth colored surface. The gel coat is then sanded and buffed.

Fiberglass is a good choice of material for use in fountains. One-piece fiberglass pool shells are being employed quite successfully by the swimming pool industry because it is light in weight, easily molded and shaped, strong in tensile strength, and extremely waterproof. The cloth-like nature of the un-resined glass mat allows fiberglass to be shaped easily. The glass mat is placed over a smooth polished mold and hardened by applying the resin.

Fiberglass is high in tensile strength due to the layering of the combined materials, with strengths reaching 50,000 psi. Care should be taken when using fiberglass in areas of high vandalism. Most fiberglass is fairly rigid. The surface may crack or chip when hit by bricks, rocks, or hammers.

Fiberglass basins are extremely waterproof when molded in one piece. Compression fittings, and gasket fittings are best suited for creating a watertight joint where pipes or nozzles penetrate the skin.

## ACRYLIC

Acrylics are plastics better known in the industry as plexi-glass, lucite, or korad. Acrylics are normally rigid transparent plastics which are available in sheets or molded forms.

Acrylic is desirable as a fountain material because of its durability and transparency. Acrylic sheeting is often specified instead of glass in architectural construction because of its resistance to breakage. The transparency of acrylic will be lost when subjected to surface abrasion; care should be taken to prevent this.

Because of its transparency, many so-called "tricks" can be achieved through acrylic use in fountains. Water can be made to float or originate in mid air or it can be formed into striking volumes such as oozing cubes.

The watertightness of basins or sculptural elements employing clear sheet acrylic is dependent on the joints. Solvents can be applied to sheeting which chemically bond the sheets together. Added joint strength can be achieved by fastening the acrylic together with screws.

Recent advances in the spa industry have developed colored acrylics. These acrylic shells are very similar to fiberglass, except that they resist crazing and blistering when exposed to chemicals or extreme heat. Colored acrylic is best suited

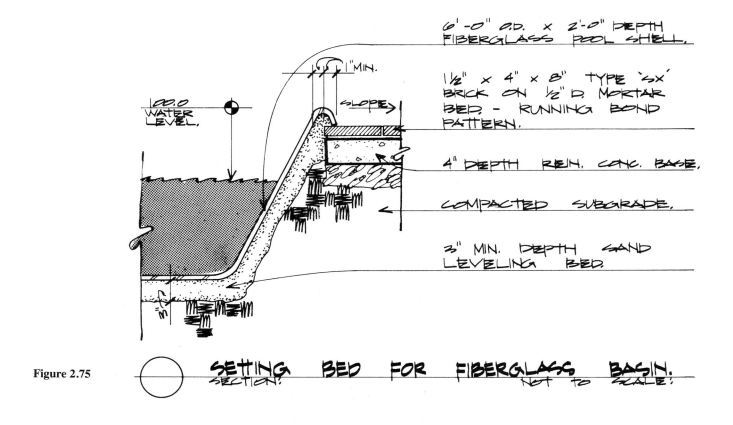

**Figure 2.75**

SECTION: SETTING BED FOR FIBERGLASS BASIN.
NOT TO SCALE.

6'-0" O.D. x 2'-0" DEPTH FIBERGLASS POOL SHELL.

1½" x 4" x 8" TYPE 'SX' BRICK ON ½" D. MORTAR BED - RUNNING BOND PATTERN.

4" DEPTH REIN. CONC. BASE.

COMPACTED SUBGRADE.

3" MIN. DEPTH SAND LEVELING BED.

100.0 WATER LEVEL.

1" MIN.

SLOPE

for use in fountain basins but basin size is somewhat restricted because of molding limitations.

## WATERPROOFING MEMBRANES

Waterproofing membranes have been used for several years as an impermeable material for flat roofs, reservoirs, or man-made lakes. Waterproof membranes are elastic sheets of PVC, Butyl and/or EPDM, fiberglass-reinforced latex rubber, and liquid membranes. Membranes vary in thickness. They are available in thicknesses of 1/32, 1/16, 3/32, or 1/8 of an inch and are used in two types of construction:

1. As a membrane sandwiched between two materials
2. As a membrane applied to the surface.

### Sandwiched Membranes

Various waterproofing membranes are available for use as a sandwiched material. They are typically enclosed between:

1. Concrete substrate and tile facing
2. Concrete substrate and brick facing
3. Concrete substrate and stone facing
4. Concrete substrate and concrete surface coat.

Due to the cost of this material and installation, its use should be restricted to fountains which are on roof tops or

**Figure 2.76** *Water cascading over an acrylic tube. New York City.*

66

**Figure 2.77** *Oozing acrylic cubes. Oklahoma City, Oklahoma.*

**Figure 2.78** *Oozing acrylic cubes, Oklahoma City, Oklahoma.*

over livable spaces. Normal tile, brick, porous stone, gunite, and concrete construction are porous enough to allow small amounts of water to pass through them. When built in an in-ground situation, which is not over any inhabited space, there is no problem with this minor leakage. In cases where leakage could penetrate a living space, waterproof membranes create a watertight seal and prevent destruction of the interior building materials. Typically, waterproof membranes of 1/8 inch thickness will pass less than a pint of water over 10 years. By comparison, a square yard of porous concrete an inch thick will pass some 70 gallons in the same period.[67] When selecting a product for use, care should be taken to choose one with high tensile strength and good concrete bonding strength (See Table 2.21 and Figure 2.80).

**Table 2.21 Physical Properties of Sandwiched Membranes**[68]

| | |
|---|---|
| Water Permeability | (30 ft. Hydro/1 Atmos.) Nil. |
| Tensile Strength | > 2000 lb./linear inch (357.2 Kg./cm.) |
| Service Temperature | −70° to 350°F (−57° to 175°C) |
| Cleavage | < 400 psi (72.6 Kg./cm²) |
| Thickness of Membrane | 0.125 inch (3mm) nominal |
| Compressive Strength | 2,000 psi (140 Kg./cm²) |
| Bonding Strength to Concrete | 200 psi min. (14 Kg./cm²) |
| Fire Rating | Non Combustible |

### Surface Membranes

Surface membranes are normally of the EPDM and Butyl or PVC composition. Manufacturers should be consulted for appropriate application of the product. Some materials are extremely sensitive to ozone and ultra-violet radiation and these products are best suited for sandwich application. Surface membranes are preferable for use in fountains over inhabited space, as a repair material for leaking fountains, or as a lining for lake fountains.

Membranes come in varying sizes; some manufacturers provide 20 foot x 100 foot sheets and they can be easily spliced to form larger sheets. Membrane sheeting is often lapped up into 6 inches at the union and is heat-sealed or sealed by adhesives. Joint width is determined by hydrostatic pressure. Splicing should be performed as recommended by the manufacturer. Attachment of the liner to the subbase and proper flashing of edges are to be completed as recommended by the manufacturer (See Figure 2.82).

Several techniques exist for membrane application in lake fountains. One technique is 100 percent coverage of the lake bottom. Complete coverage of the dirt base increases water clarity and reduces water losses, but may lead to membrane bubbling and rupture. Lining failure is caused by ground

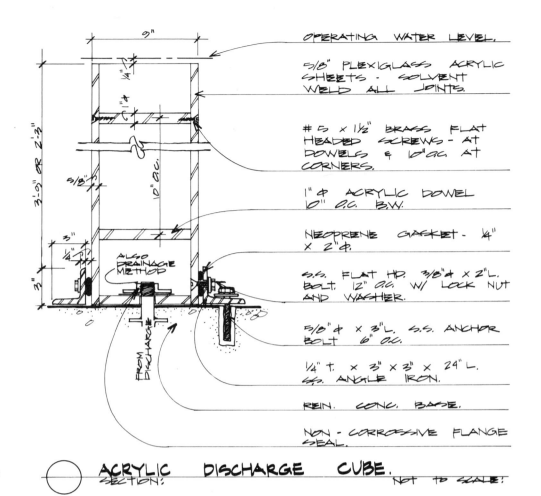

OPERATING WATER LEVEL.

5/8" PLEXIGLASS ACRYLIC SHEETS - SOLVENT WELD ALL JOINTS.

#5 x 1½" BRASS FLAT HEADED SCREWS - AT DOWELS & 10" O.C. AT CORNERS.

1" ⌀ ACRYLIC DOWEL 10" O.C. B.W.

NEOPRENE GASKET - ¼" X 2" ⌀.

S.S. FLAT HD. 3/8" ⌀ X 2" L. BOLT. 12" O.C. W/ LOCK NUT AND WASHER.

5/8" ⌀ X 3" L. S.S. ANCHOR BOLT 6" O.C.

¼" t. X 3" X 3" X 24" L. S.S. ANGLE IRON.

REIN. CONC. BASE.

NON - CORROSSIVE FLANGE SEAL.

ALSO DRAINAGE METHOD

FROM DISCHARGE

9"
¼"
1" ¼
5/8"
3"
¼"
3"
10" O.C.
3'-0" OR 2'-3"

**Figure 2.79**    ACRYLIC DISCHARGE CUBE.
SECTION:                                    NOT TO SCALE!

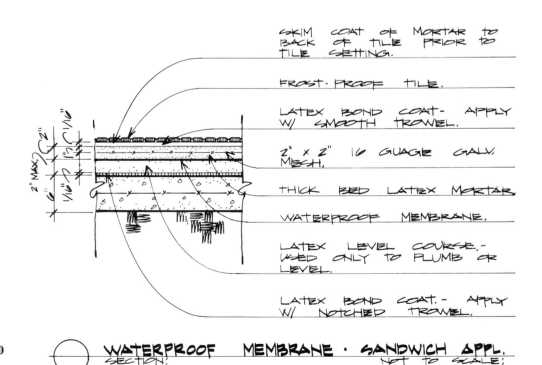

SKIM COAT OF MORTAR TO BACK OF TILE PRIOR TO TILE SETTING.

FROST-PROOF TILE.

LATEX BOND COAT - APPLY W/ SMOOTH TROWEL.

2" X 2" 16 GUAGE GALV. MESH.

THICK BED LATEX MORTAR.

WATERPROOF MEMBRANE.

LATEX LEVEL COURSE - USED ONLY TO PLUMB OR LEVEL.

LATEX BOND COAT - APPLY W/ NOTCHED TROWEL.

2" MAX.

**Figure 2.80**    WATERPROOF MEMBRANE · SANDWICH APPL.
SECTION:                                    NOT TO SCALE!

68

**Figure 2.81** *Flashing of a surface-applied waterproof membrance.*

water seepage and high water tables creating an upward pressure on the membrane.

Another method employs a 10 to 15 foot strip, starting at the water's edge and extending this width into the water. This method allows ground water pressure to equalize in the soil not covered by the membrane, preventing the possibility of membrane failure. By lining the edge, shallow depth water will have clarity while the deeper areas will be semi-murky due to the dirt bottom. When using this method, the deeper unlined soil should be down a minimum of 3 feet. This will create a water depth in which water and dirt can stratify to increase clarity. Before specifying lake depth check with local authorities for allowed depths. The soil conservation service can be very helpful in providing information about water tables and soil characteristics for a particular site.

In both installation techniques, proper edge treatment is required for improved aesthetics. Care should be taken to maintain a level edge so that the black membrane is not exposed or is exposed at a consistent dimension along the entire edge. When water level is anticipated to fluctuate, it is best to provide a 3 foot wide stone band to prevent a somewhat unnatural looking lining from being visible.

## PLASTERING *IN SITU* CONCRETE

Plaster is a sand and cement mixture used as a surface treatment for gunite and concrete pools and fountains. Some designers recommend plastering of poured-in-place *(in situ)* concrete basins as a method of waterproofing.[69] Generally

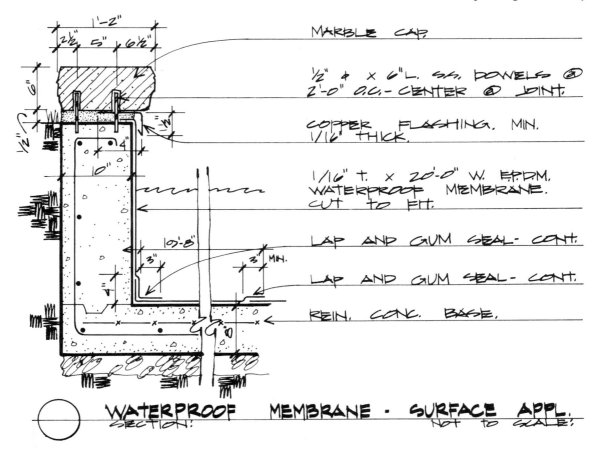

**Figure 2.82**

speaking, if the concrete is specified properly, there is no need to plaster the surface. Proper construction would include air-entrained and high strength concrete. Installation of waterstops at construction joints is also necessary.

Plastering of concrete basins is a somewhat successful method for water-tightening pools which do not contain waterstops. In this situation, the plaster coats prevent water from attacking the unprotected steel reinforcing which is exposed at the construction joint.

Watertightness of the plaster coat depends upon the concrete substrate. If the substrate cracks, breaks will appear in the plaster coat. When applying plaster to *in situ* concrete, it is important to have proper bonding between the plaster and the smooth concrete. By exposing the coarse aggregate of the concrete by grit blasting, bush hammering, or high-velocity water jets, a better bond can be created. This surface preparation can be deleted by using a latex-based mortar or by applying a scratch coat to the concrete before plastering begins. A scratch coat is a firm rough surface which improves plaster bonding and consists of 1 part portland cement and 1½ to 2 parts clean, sharp, dry sand. It normally has the consistency of a slurry and is scratched or combed to key the material to the wall. Because the material is less than 2 mm, it is important to spray it with water one hour after application to ensure proper curing.[70]

## Plastering of Gunite

The plastering of gunite swimming pools is a common practice. Plaster is normally applied in two coats to form the finished surface. Plaster should not be considered as a cure-all waterproofing material. Properly applied gunite makes an excellent waterproof shell.[71]

Plaster is primarily used as a leveling course in gunite construction because of the method of application. Air-placed base courses are rough and uneven. By troweling the plaster on the base course, the surface can be made smooth, even, and suitable for swimming or wading. The rough surface of the gunite base makes an excellent bonding surface for the base coat of plaster. The first coat applied to the walls is normally ⅜ to ½ inch thick. Thickness is dependent on the unevenness of the surface. If the thickness exceeds one inch it is advisable to use light-weight stainless steel mesh for reinforcing.

Portland cement should be of a high-alumna or sulphate-resistant type. These cements will prevent acid from attacking the plaster coats. Acidic conditions often exist in the water due to an imbalance in water chemistry.

The plaster mix should consist of one part portland cement and 3 parts clean dry sand, dampened prior to application. The surface of the first coat should be combed or scratched to form a key for application of the final coat. The second wall coat should consist of 1 part portland cement to 3½ parts sand. The surface of the final coat should be floated with a wood float to form a dense level surface.

Proper curing practices are important to produce a sound plaster coat. The plaster coat should be protected from drying air and hot sun. Before the second coat is applied, allow the plaster to cure for 24 hours.

The floor application of plaster should be applied in one coat. The thickness should be from 1¼ to 2½ inches.

Most swimming pools are plastered with a concrete base plaster system containing marble dust. The addition of white marble dust adds increased durability and increased resistance to slippage. This coating is commonly referred to as "white-coat" or "Marlite."

Once the final finish coat is applied to the pool shell, moisture must be applied to the plaster finish to prevent checking or cracking of the plaster. In extreme heat applications, water is added to the lower pool depth while the walls are plastered. In addition to this, moisture protection must be provided to the plaster finish during draining of the pool in summer. Maintenance of the bright plaster color is achieved through acid etching of the plaster. This process reduces the thickness of the white-coat or plaster and makes it necessary at sometime to replace the coating. In replacement of the white-coat, the original plaster is roughened to increase bonding of the new plaster. Roughening is accomplished through sandblasting or hatchet chipping of the finish. In addition to this precaution, a "latex" based bonding agent will increase bonding capabilities.

Roughening of the existing plaster partially removes the plaster finish of the pool. All existing tile, floor fittings and wall fittings are sawn around so that the added thickness of the new plaster can be tapered back to the original wall or floor fitting.

## LEAK REPAIR

Pool and fountain leaks can be classified as *structural cracks* which are leaks caused by error in design, and leaks due to expansion and contraction of the ground; or *non-structural cracks* which are cracks created by thermal stresses and drying shrinkage, and leaks caused by porous areas and honeycombing. Pools and fountains containing *structural cracks* should be repaired in the following manner:[72]

1. External piers or buttresses of reinforced concrete bonding into the walls.
2. An internal lining of reinforced gunite; or new walls and floor of *in situ* concrete constructed inside the existing pool shell. The new *in situ* concrete may or may not be bonded into the old concrete according to the structural design of the new work.
3. A combination of external piers or buttresses and internal gunite lining.
4. Providing a new independent inner pool shell of aluminum.
5. A combination of external piers and internal lining of a suitable waterproof membrane.

*Non-structural cracks* are best repaired by:[73]

1. Cutting out the crack in the pool shell to form a V and filling with a high-quality mortar.
2. Crack injection using polymer resins.
3. Repair with a flexible channel section.
4. The application of a polymer resin (epoxide or polyurethane) by brush or spray, with or without glass-fibre mesh reinforcement; or the application of a proprietary "bandage."
5. Line the inside of the basin with a flexible waterproof membrane.
6. Cut out the crack and fill with a resilient caulking.

When using method "1," the crack should be widened to ½ inch and deepened to 1 to 1¼ inches. The widened joint should be in the form of a "V" and free of dirt and dust. The joint should be packed with a latex-based mortar for best bonding results. This treatment is not satisfactory for cracks when future movement is anticipated. Flexible channel section epoxied in place or resilient caulkings are more suitable where movement is anticipated (See Figure 2.83).

Plaster coating should be considered as a method of repairing concrete basins which have numerous surface cracks. The plastic-like material will fill in the cracks and create a more watertight surface. In this case, the plaster seals the cracks while creating a more attractive surface coat. Basins with surface cracks should be expeditiously repaired. These cracks will allow water to enter. Expansion of water in surface cracks can cause deterioration of the basin during freeze-thaw cycles.

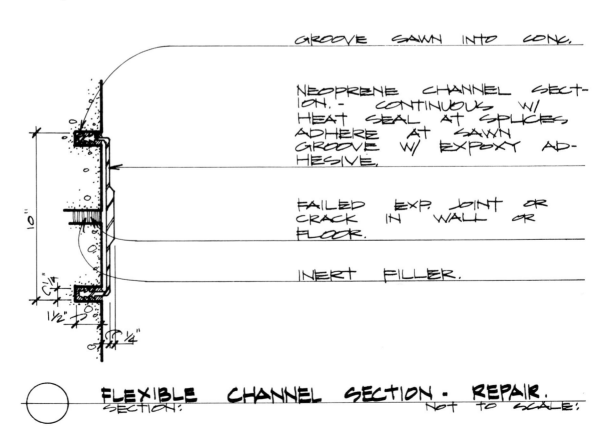

GROOVE SAWN INTO CONC.

NEOPRENE CHANNEL SECT-ION. - CONTINUOUS W/ HEAT SEAL AT SPLICES ADHERE AT SAWN GROOVE W/ EXPOXY AD-HESIVE.

FAILED EXP. JOINT OR CRACK IN WALL OR FLOOR.

INERT FILLER.

**Figure 2.83** FLEXIBLE CHANNEL SECTION - REPAIR. SECTION: Not to Scale:

**Table 2.22 Evaluation of Fountain Construction Materials**

| Material | Waterproof nature | Crack resistance | Durability | Weather resistance | Stain resistance | Achievable surface texture | Relative strength | Weight | Achievable surface detailing | Degree of craftsmanship needed for fabrication | Used as a surface treatment | Primary building material | Fountain basin | Sculptural element within pool | Affects water clarity |
|---|---|---|---|---|---|---|---|---|---|---|---|---|---|---|---|
| In-Situ Concrete | M-H[1] | M | M | M[15] | M | H-M | M | M | M | M | No | Yes | Yes | Yes | No |
| Pre-Cast Concrete | H-M | M-H | M-H | M-H[15] | M | H | H | M | H | H | No | Yes | Yes | Yes | No |
| Terrazo | H-M | M-H | M-H | M-H[15] | H | M | H-M | M | L | H | Yes | Yes | Yes | Yes[26] | No |
| Gunite | H-M | M | M-H | M-H[15] | M | H | M | M | H-M | H | Yes | Yes | Yes | Yes | No |
| Brick | H-M[2] | H-M[7] | H-M | M[15] | M | H-M | H-M | M-H[22] | H-M | H-M | Yes | Yes | Yes | Yes | No[28] |
| Tile | H[2] | H-M[7] | H-M[7] | H | H | H | M | M[22] | H-M | H-M | Yes | No | Yes | Yes | No[28] |
| Granite | H[2] | H | H | H | H | H[20] | H | H | H | H | Yes | Yes[24] | Yes | Yes | No |
| Sandstone | M[2]H[3] | M[8] | M[8] | L-M[15] | H-M | M-H | M | H[22] | M | M | Yes | Yes[25] | No[27] | Yes | Yes |
| Limestone | H-M[2] | H | M-H[10] | L-H[10] | H | H-M[20] | M-H | M-H[22] | H | H | Yes | Yes | No[27] | Yes | Yes |
| Slate | H[2] | M[8] | M[8] | M | H | M | M | H | L | M | Yes | No | Yes | No | No |
| Marble | H[2] | H-M[8] | M[10] | L-H[10] | H | H[20] | M-H | H | H | H | Yes | Yes[24] | No[27] | Yes | No |
| Lead | H[4] | H | M-H | H | H | N.A. | L-M | H | N.A. | M | Yes | No | Yes | No | Yes |
| Copper | H[5] | H | H | H[16] | H-M | H-M[21] | M | M | H-M | M-H | Yes | Yes[24] | Yes | Yes | Yes |
| Brass | H[5] | H | H | H[16] | H-M | H[21] | M-H | M | H | M-H | Yes | Yes[24] | Yes | Yes | Yes |
| Bronze | H[5] | H | H | H[16] | H-M | H[21] | M-H | M | H | M-H | Yes | Yes[24] | Yes | Yes | Yes |
| Cast Iron | H[6] | H-M | H[9] | M-H | H-M | H[21] | M-H | M-H | H | H | No | Yes | Yes | Yes | No |
| Steel | H[5] | H | M | M[17] | M | H-M | H | M-H | H-M | M | No | Yes | No[27] | Yes | Yes |
| High Strength — Low Alloy Steel | H[5] | H | H | H[16] | M | H-M | H | M-H[23] | H-M | M | No | Yes | No[27] | Yes | Yes |
| Stainless Steel | H[5] | H | H | H[16] | H[11] | M-H | H | M-H[23] | H-M | H | Yes | Yes[24] | Yes | Yes | No |
| Aluminum | H[5] | H | H-M[11] | H[16] | H | H-M[21] | M-H | M-L[23] | H-M | H | Yes | Yes | Yes | Yes | No |
| Wood | H-M[5] | M | M[12] | M[18] | M | H | M | M | H | M | No | Yes | Yes[27] | Yes | No |
| Fiberglas | H[6] | H-M[9] | M[9] | M-L[19] | H | H | M-L | L | H | H | No | Yes | Yes | Yes | No |
| Acrylic | H[6] | H | M-H[9] | M | H | H | M-L | L | H | H | No | Yes | Yes | Yes | No |
| Waterproof Membrane Surface | H[5] | H | M[13*14] | M[14] | H | L | M | L-M[23] | L | H | Yes | No | Yes | No | No |
| Sandwiched | H[5] | H-M | H-M[14] | N.A. | N.A. | N.A. | M | L-M[23] | L | M | Yes | No | Yes | No | No |
| Plaster | M | M[7] | M[7] | M[15] | M | H-M | M | M[23] | H | M | Yes | No | Yes | Yes | No |

## NOTES ON TABLE 2.22

L = Low
M = Moderate
H = High
N.A. = Not Applicable

1. Susceptible to surface cracks.
2. Watertightness depends on mortar joints.
3. Depends on specific stone selection.
4. Not recommended for fountain application due to possible lead poisoning.
5. Depends on joint treatment.
6. One piece molded. Problems may occur at pipe penetrations.
7. Depends on mortar type and substrate.
8. Natural planes of weakness may be present.
9. May chip or crack if impacted.
10. May dissolve in a submerged application.
11. Some alloys are soft and less durable.
12. May splinter or crack.
13. May be cut or torn.
14. Some products are affected by ozone and ultra violet rays.
15. Freeze-thaw damage.
16. Protective surface oxidant develops.
17. Material may oxidize if not treated properly.
18. May rot without pressure treatment.
19. May develop surface cracks due to heat and chemicals.
20. Texture due to surface carving.
21. Casting capabilities increase surface texture.
22. Overall weight depends on substrate type and thickness.
23. Weight depends on substrate and/or material thickness. Reduced material thickness is achievable because of strength.
24. Somewhat cost prohibitive.
25. Limited application due to porosity.
26. Difficult due to grinding required.
27. Material effected by submersion.
28. Acid cleaning products may effect water quality.

# MECHANICAL SYSTEM

The mechanical system of a fountain can be broken down into three sub-categories. These sub-categories are the water effects system, the filtration system, and the drainage and water level control devices.

## WATER EFFECTS SYSTEM

The water effects system includes the nozzles, pump, piping, etc. which produce the various water movements of the fountain. These effects consist of water coming from the weirs, channels, nozzles, spray rings, eyeballs, and/or pipes. A water effects system requires a suction line to bring water to the pump, a discharge line to supply water from the pump to the nozzles, and a pump system to generate water pressure.

### Suction Line

When the pump is started, suction is created in one of the lines. This suction pulls water to the pump where it enters, and is pushed through a discharge line to create some type of water effect. The pipe which pulls water from the basin to the pump is called a suction line. For the pump to operate properly, the quantity of water being drawn through the suction line should equal the quantity of water dispersed from the nozzles and eyeballs.

Suction gpm = Discharge gpm

The suction line, which supplies the pump with water, consists of piping, fittings, suction shut-off valve, anti-vortex plate, and sump and strainer (See Figure 3.1).

### Anti-Vortex Plate and Sump

An anti-vortex plate and sump is a depressed box and cover set into a fountain floor. This device is used to collect water for the suction line.

The flat cover or the anti-vortex plate is slightly elevated on legs to allow water to access the sump from the sides. This prevents swirling water from occurring at the suction line (See Figure 3.3).

Downward-pulling vortexes have accounted for the drowning of humans and animals in rivers. In the case of a fountain, the plate prevents entrained air from entering the piping. When specifying anti-vortex plates, the designer must consider the following:

1. Is gpm of the anti-vortex plate and sump rated for the same gpm as the discharge? Manufacturers' literature will rate the gpm of this device. More than one sump can be used to match the discharge gpm.

2. Does the anti-vortex plate come with a sump or must a sump be constructed? In concrete fountains, a void form can be used to construct a sump in the fountain floor.

3. Is there minimum concrete cover and proper reinforcing under the bottom of the sump? (2 inches minimum).

4. Is the sump and anti-vortex plate located appropriately in the pool? In long narrow pools, it is necessary to locate the suction line in the center of the pool to prevent wave motion.[74] Additional suction lines may be located in isolated basin corners to prevent stagnation of the water (See Figure 3.2).

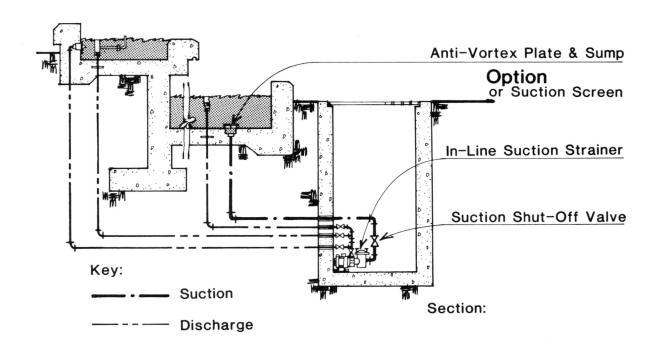

**Anti-Vortex Plate & Sump**

**Option**
or Suction Screen

**In-Line Suction Strainer**

**Suction Shut-Off Valve**

Key:

———·—— Suction

——— – –— Discharge

Section:

**Figure 3.1**      ## Suction Line of Water Effects Pump

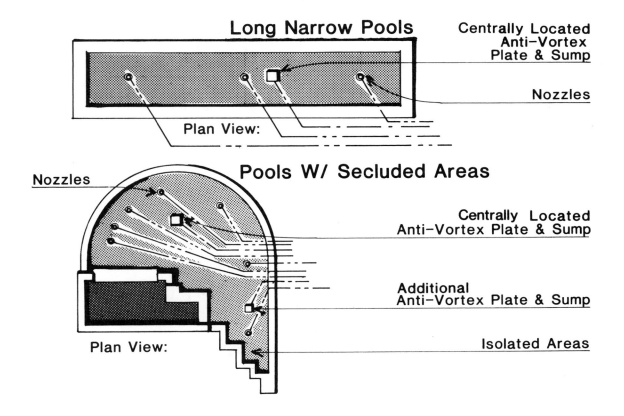

### Long Narrow Pools

Centrally Located
Anti-Vortex
Plate & Sump

Nozzles

Plan View:

### Pools W/ Secluded Areas

Nozzles

Centrally Located
Anti-Vortex Plate & Sump

Additional
Anti-Vortex Plate & Sump

Isolated Areas

Plan View:

**Figure 3.2**      ## Anti-Vortex Plate & Sump Location

## Suction Strainer

A suction strainer is a screen covered metal box or cylinder which is located on an elevated pipe in the fountain basin. This is an alternate device used to collect water for the suction line. The suction strainer can be located at water level or 2 inches above the fountain floor. Consult the manufacturer for installation details.

Some manufacturers recommend the substitution of a suction strainer for an anti-vortex plate and sump. A suction strainer is particularly helpful in fountains where waterproof membranes are used. An anti-vortex plate and sunken sump can be especially difficult to waterproof when used in conjunction with a surface-applied waterproof membrane. The elevated strainer and flange create a tight seal between the membrane and the strainer and reduce chances of leakage (See Figure 3.6).

A suction strainer may allow the designer to delete the line strainer. The small holes in the face of the strainer collect dirt and trash and prevent debris from entering the pipe. When specifying a suction screen the following must be considered:

1. The strainer must be rated for a gpm equal to the discharge. Two or more strainers can be used to obtain the gpm. Undersizing of the suction screen is a common error. This can lead to rapid clogging of the screen and potential pump damage.

2. The openings in the suction screen must be small enough to prevent clogging of the nozzle orifice. The manufacturer will specify the minimum nozzle orifice size suitable for use with the strainer.

3. The opening of the screen must be small enough to prevent suspended debris from damaging the pump impeller.

4. The openings of the screen must not be too small. If holes are too small, increased velocity will pull leaves against the strainer and reduce pump efficiency.

## In-Line Suction Strainer

An in-line suction strainer is a device used to prevent dirt and debris from entering the pump. Any dirt which settles in the water will be pulled through the suction line. It is extremely important to prevent this dirt from damaging the pump impeller and being further transported to the small orifice of a discharge nozzle. Small diameter orifices of jet clusters, finger clusters, or water castles are easy to clog and hard to dislodge. A suction strainer should prevent this.

In-line strainers are located next to the pump in the mechanical room. Most strainers contain a wire basket which collects the transported dirt and prevents it from entering the pump. This basket must be periodically cleaned to prevent a reduction in the gpm being drawn through the suction line. When specifying an in-line suction strainer, the designer should consider the following:

1. Does the specified pump contain an integral strainer? If so, a separate strainer is not needed.

**Figure 3.3** *Anti-vortex plate.*

**Figure 3.4** *Anti-Vortex plate prior to floor construction.*

**Figure 3.5** *Suction Strainer.*

76

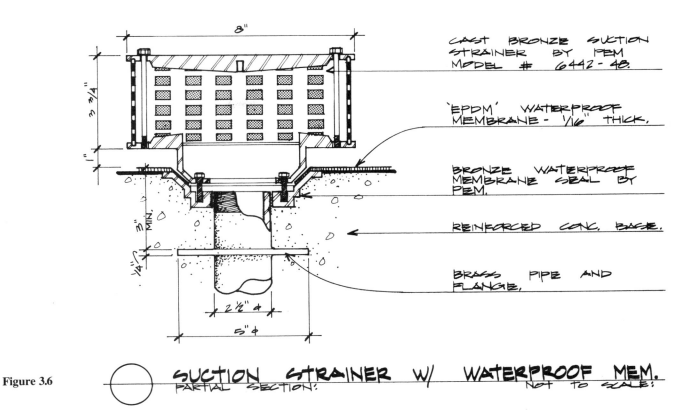

CAST BRONZE SUCTION STRAINER BY PEM MODEL # 6442-48.

'EPDM' WATERPROOF MEMBRANE - 1/16" THICK.

BRONZE WATERPROOF MEMBRANE SEAL BY PEM.

REINFORCED CONC. BASE.

BRASS PIPE AND FLANGE.

**Figure 3.6**

SUCTION STRAINER W/ WATERPROOF MEM.
PARTIAL SECTION.
NOT TO SCALE:

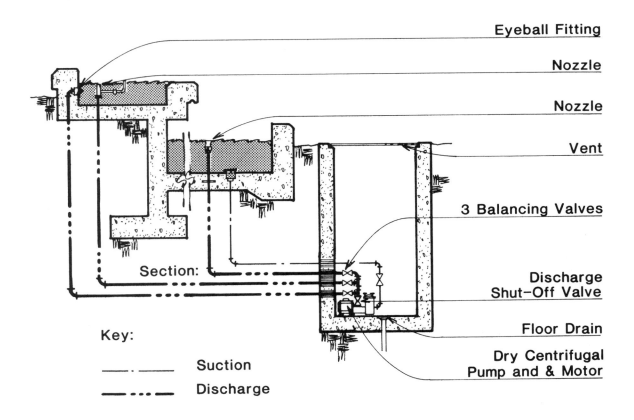

Eyeball Fitting

Nozzle

Nozzle

Vent

3 Balancing Valves

Discharge Shut-Off Valve

Floor Drain

Dry Centrifugal Pump and & Motor

Section:

Key:

— . —  Suction

— .. —  Discharge

**Figure 3.7**        **Discharge Line of Water Effects Pump**

2. Does the suction line diameter match the inlet diameter of the strainer?

3. Is there enough space in the mechanical room to remove the trash basket?

## Suction Shut-Off Valve

A suction shut-off valve is located between the pump and the in-line strainer. Traditionally, a gate, globe or butterfly valve has been used as a shut-off valve.

Because the suction line is normally lower than the bottom water level in the basin, water is siphoned out of the fountain basin when the strainer is opened for cleaning. Closing this valve prevents water from entering the pump room when the strainer basket is removed for cleaning. The height of the discharge should never be regulated by partial closing of a suction shutoff valve.[75] This may damage the pump.

## Discharge Line

The discharge line is responsible for transporting water from the pump to the nozzle(s) to achieve the desired water effect. The various elements included in the discharge line are a shut-off valve, balancing valves, pipe, fittings, nozzles and/or eyeballs (See Figure 3.7)

## Discharge Shut-Off Valve

A discharge shut-off valve is a globe valve, gate valve, butterfly or electronic valve located between the pump and the balancing valve. Normally, this valve is located in the equipment pit. It is used to regulate flow after the nozzles have been balanced in height, or as a valve to prevent water from entering the pump room while cleaning the suction strainer.

A gate valve is not intended for continual regulation and will soon leak if subjected to such wear.[76] In situations where continual use is anticipated, a globe valve is more appropriate.

Often an electronic valve is employed as a discharge shut-off valve. Some electronic valves work in full open, partial open, and fully closed positions. Extensive pump operation while the electric valve is fully closed will create back pressure on the pump seals and shorten its life. When used in conjunction with a wind sensor and wind control panel, the overall height of the water from the nozzles can be reduced to prevent splash out of the side of the basin during moderate winds. Other electronic valves which operate in the opened or closed position, can be closed to bypass the main flow of water through a smaller diameter pipe. The reduction in pipe diameter will reduce the gpm and lower the water effects (See Figure 3.8). When an electronic valve is used in conjunction with a bypass pipe, a manual shut-off valve is also required.

When using aerating nozzles with air snorkel pipes, similar water height reduction can be achieved by attaching an electric valve to the air intake pipe.

## Balancing Valves

Balancing valves are gate, butterfly, globe, motorized or electronic valves which are predominantly located in the pump room of the fountain basin. These valves are installed between the nozzle and the discharge shut-off valve and are used to set the desired height of water coming from the nozzle. Each nozzle contained in the fountain will have its own balancing valve. This is extremely important when there are two or more nozzles designed to have the same water height. These valves allow the designer to field adjust the gpm of the nozzles, thus balancing the nozzle heights.

When locating the balancing valve in the pump room, it is necessary to run a separate discharge line to each nozzle. Often a single discharge line is run from the pump room to the fountain. At the fountain, the pipe branches out to each nozzle. Balancing valves are then located at the base of each nozzle on the fountain floor.

Placing the balancing valves in the bottom of the fountain allows the designer to reduce the amount of pipe run from the pump room to the fountain, but has some drawbacks as well. Balancing valves located in the bottom of the fountain may present a maintenance problem. These valves are hard to clean and easy for vandals to alter. If balancing valves are located in the fountain bottom, it is important to remove the valve handle after water levels are adjusted.

In all cases, the farther away the balance valve is from the nozzle, the better the nozzle will perform. When the balance valve is adjacent to the nozzle, the sharp edges of the valve interior tear the laminar flow in the pipe and distort the water pattern.

Electronic balancing valves are often used in conjunction with a timer to create a changing water effect. The chosen electronic valve operates in an open or closed position. The flow adjustment stem allows the designer to regulate the quantity of water which flows through the valve in an open position. As the timer proceeds through its preprogrammed sequence, the valves are automatically closed or opened. This type of fountain can be extremely attractive due to the intermittent water effects.

Motorized valves are those which gradually close as operated. These valves are of particular interest because of

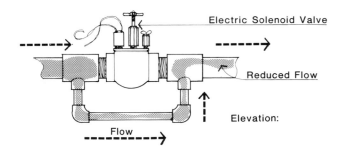

## Flow Pattern When Valve is Closed

**Figure 3.8**

**Figure 3.9** *Nozzles out of balance.*

Photo by Theodore D. Walker

**Figure 3.10** *White froth from aerating nozzles. Salt Lake City, Utah.*

the varying amounts of water which they allow through the nozzles. This function creates an everchanging water effect. The valves require a timer and control panel for operation and should be located in an equipment vault.

### Check Valves

Discharge and suction devices located below the static water level in the upper levels of a multi-level fountain can cause accidental drainage of these basins when the fountain is turned off. Whenever the fountain is turned off, the water in the upper basins creates water pressure in the fountain pipes much like a municipal water tank. This pressure pushes water through the pump and displaces this water into the lower basin of the fountain. In most applications, this displaced water is expelled into the fountain overflow drain.

To prevent this periodic water wastage, a check valve is normally installed on those lines leading to the upper level devices located below the static water level. This valve allows water to flow through the pipe in a one-way direction and prevents drainage of the basin.

Low water pressure, which occurs when the pump shuts off, activates the check valve and closes the line to water flow. Consult valve manufacturers for operating pressures of check valves.

### Fountain Nozzles

As described by Campbell, fountain nozzles can be broken down into four basic types of jets: aerating nozzles, spray heads, smooth-bore nozzles, and formed nozzles.[77] Both Campbell and McCulley give excellent descriptions of the visual effects of each nozzle. In making a design decision about an appropriate nozzle, the designer should consult these texts.[78]

When selecting the appropriate nozzle, the designer will be forced to consider both scale and project budget. Generally speaking, as the height of the water increases, greater pressure and gpm are required to operate the nozzle. This increased water demand may require larger pipe and more powerful pumps. These increases generally translate into additional budget and operating costs of the pump. It may be necessary to down scale the whole fountain to bring the project in under budget. In this situation, both scale and fountain purpose should be studied before making the decision.

### Aerating Nozzles

This group of nozzles are known in the trade as either bubbler jets, foam nozzles, geyser nozzles, aerating nozzles, jet pods, or aeration-jet clusters. These jets are characterized by a white frothy water effect which is visible from considerable distance. The white water effect is achieved with an air-water combination. This mix is accomplished by locating the nozzle under the water level, by drawing air-water through a submerged-perforated cover at the bottom of the nozzle, or by drawing air through an air induction tube. Because water must be pushed out of the way before the water jet reaches the surface, more head pressure is required to operate an aerating-type nozzle. When compared to a smooth-bore nozzle, an aerating-type nozzle requires a larger horsepower pump. (High head pressure low gpm.)[79]

Because air and water are combined, aerating-type nozzles normally require an exact amount of water cover for correct operation, some nozzles must be submerged below the operating water level (bubbler and geyser), while others must be partially above the operating water level (foam, aerating, jet pods, jet clusters). The nozzle manufacturer should be consulted for the proper installation heights.

A common mistake is the location of the nozzle in reference to the static water level instead of the operating water level. In some instances this may lead to improper air induction and a reduction in nozzle performance. Nozzles in the bottom level of multi-level pools are most affected by this problem.

If a nozzle is rated as a "waterlevel independent nozzle," it means that the nozzle can be located at any height the designer desires. Some waterlevel independent aerating nozzles are presently available.[80] Check with the manufacturer for availability.

Aerating nozzles, jet pods, and aerating clusters consist of a double sleeve which creates a venturi effect when the nozzle operates. The air and water which is pulled through the perforated sleeve of the nozzle will draw any surface debris to the nozzle. In fountains subjected to high volumes of litter, this may lead to clogging of the aerating nozzle. Most manufacturers sell trash screens which surround the nozzle and prevent clogging (See Figures 3.22).

## DESIGNING WITH AERATING NOZZLES

Aerating nozzles are extremely visible due to the air content of the nozzle. These nozzles are best suited for background locations or applications where viewing distances are excessive. Locating aerating nozzles in groups or grids is very popular. Because of the extreme visibility of this nozzle, form and shape are easily defined. The general shape of tall aerating foam jets is pyramidal and extremely visible, making it an ideal choice for lake locations or settings where viewing distances are large.

When locating aerating nozzles in groupings, evenly spaced grids of nozzles are best used when ample space is left between each nozzle. This spacing will create negative and positive volume which will make the nozzle more visible. In addition to increasing visibility, overall balance should be considered when specifying nozzle spacing.

Aerating nozzles of random heights located on an asymmetrical spacing are very attractive in fountains. As the viewer moves around the fountain an ever-changing view is created. In this application ample space between nozzles is not as critical as the overall balance of the nozzle composition.

In windy locations, aerating nozzles tend to perform better than other nozzle types. Nozzle distortion is covered up by the aeration at the edge of the water effect.

In regards to noise, aerating nozzles create enormous amounts of high energy sound. The noise typically fluctuates

Photo by Theodore D. Walker

**Figure 3.11** *Aerating nozzles. Indianapolis, Indiana.*

**Figure 3.12** *Air tube of aerating nozzle. Virginia Beach, Virginia.*

**Figure 3.13** *Bubbler and foam jet.*

**Figure 3.14** *Plexiglas surge baffle at the edge of a weir. Oklahoma City, Oklahoma.*

**Figure 3.15** *Spray head.*

as the nozzle moves. In addition, as the nozzle fluctuates, the water in the pool can rock and create additional noise.

### Aerating Nozzles and Surge

When water is propelled from an aerating-type nozzle, the pool water deflects the water ejected from the nozzle and creates an uncontrolled situation. The splash created when uncontrolled water falls, is greater than from most other nozzle types. Extensive water surge in the fountain basins may occur due to an improperly used aerating nozzle. In particular, surge problems arise when aerating nozzles are used in circular, confined, or small pools.[81]

Although surge may be attractive in some instances, excessive surge should be addressed by the designer. Excessive surge creates:

1. Wave-like motions which reach the level of the overflow drain. This will lower the water level and continually activate the water level control device to fill the pool. Unnecessary water waste should be prevented.

2. Wave-like surges which periodically lower the water below the proper operating level of the nozzles. This reduction in water height will reduce the water force which is restraining the ejected water and will cause a higher-than-anticipated burst of water.

### Reducing Surge with Baffles

Baffles are often used in conjunction with aerating nozzles to reduce surge potentials. Baffles are usually constructed of concrete curbs, Plexiglas, or perforated brass collars (See Figure 3.23). In general, these baffles encircle the nozzle and run from the floor to just below the operating level of the water.

Another method employed to reduce surge problems is the horizontal installation of a fine mesh at the operating level of the pool (See Figure 3.23). This dissipates the energy of the falling water and, in turn, creates a less turbulent pool.

### Spray Heads

Spray heads are characterized by delicate combinations of clear thin water jets. A spray head consists of a distribution head in the shape of a circle or fan with exposed tube nozzles or holes drilled into the face of the head. Spray head nozzle types include: water castle fountain heads, jet clusters, finger clusters, finger jets, finger nozzles, crown jets, and columnar jets.

Because of the small orifice within the nozzle, a suction strainer or an in-line strainer is mandatory to prevent nozzle clogging. Spray heads are often used in children's spray pools because of the delicate water patterns created by the nozzle. When specifying a spray head for use in a spray pool, a drilled orifice is preferable to a tube orifice spray head. The tube orifice spray head may be dangerous if fallen against, and is also easy for vandals to destroy (See Figure 3.25).

## DESIGNING WITH SMOOTH BORE NOZZLES

Smooth bore nozzles generate a clear round shaft of water. Due to the transparent nature of this water effect, these nozzles are best used where there is a contrasting background or where the nozzles are used in groupings or spray rings.

Generally speaking, smooth bore nozzles are more visible when closely spaced. The overall water volume creates moderate visibility. In applications where nozzles are required to provide horizontal or near horizontal projections, no other nozzle can provide the same effect. These nozzles can be directed to create an accurately positioned water jet. Generally speaking, these nozzles create a less active and fluctuating effect than an aerating nozzle. In regards to noise, these nozzles create less noise than an aerating nozzle of equal design height. Horizontally-directed smooth bore nozzles create a slight soft trickle. Traditional aerating nozzles require water cover to provide aeration. A horizontal positioning of a water level dependent aerating nozzle provides a less than desirable effect due to the constant depth of water required over all sides of the nozzle.

## MASKS AND SMOOTH BORE NOZZLES

Smooth bore or pipe nozzles are often mounted in a horizontal position above the operating level of the fountain. These nozzles either drip or squirt small volumes of water into the basin. They are normally small in size and produce a small trickling noise in the basin reminiscent of falling rain. In some cases these nozzles are mounted in elevated walls and covered with a decorative cover plate. These cover plates vary in design and are available in material such as stone, lead, iron, or bronze.

Older versions of these plates resembled human or animal faces and were called masks. A current resurgence of classical design influence has created a renewed use of these decorative masks (See Figures 3.18 to 3.21).

## DESIGNING WITH SPRAY HEADS

Spray heads typically create a subtle effect which is best suited to small garden fountains. This effect is best seen when backlighted with sun or light. In regards to sound, these nozzles create a gentle rain-like tinkle which is very soothing.

In bigger installations where space will allow larger effects, cascade-shaped spray heads create an impressive image. In most cases single centrally located spray heads are specified. Single nozzles are usually chosen because of the dominance in shape and quality of sound which a single nozzle creates.

### Smooth Bore Nozzles

A smooth bore nozzle is typified by a clear, pencil-like solid stream jet of water which eventually breaks up into fine droplets as it reaches its maximum height. Most smooth bore nozzles are constructed of cast bronze and contain a single smooth bore channel through which the water

**Figure 3.16** *Smooth bore nozzles. Royal Lemington Spa, England.*

**Figure 3.17** *Smooth bore nozzles. Royal Lemington Spa, England.*

**Figure 3.18** *Lion mask and obelisk. England.*

**Figure 3.19** *Animal mask. Chatsworth, England.*

**Figure 3.20** *Lion mask. Norfolk, Virginia.*

**Figure 3.21** *Human mask. Newport, Rhode Island.*

is emitted. Because of this smooth channel, a very controlled stream of water can be created (See Figure 3.26).

Smooth bore type nozzles comprise the following: smooth bore jets, spray rings, spray bars, swivel jets, and plain jets. These jets are excellent choices for use with smaller horsepower pumps as they require less head pressure but more gpm than aerating nozzles.[82] Because of the accuracy of a smooth bore jet, a slight deflection off of plumb is easily detected. When installing plumb stub-outs for single jets, vertical nozzle placement is difficult to achieve. A swivel jet allows for minor adjustment of the nozzle after installation. The ball fitting allows up to a 15 degree deviation from center adjustment. Soft copper pipe connected to the nozzle will also allow for vertical adjustment, but permits vandals to alter the setting.

Smooth bore nozzles are often installed in other than vertical positions. As the nozzle is moved farther from vertical, the length of the water effect will increase.

When designing with a nozzle off of vertical, the horizontal throw of the water is more important than the vertical height. Controlling the correct horizontal dimension will prevent the jet from shooting outside of the basin. Most manufacturers' nozzle ratings only specify vertical heights

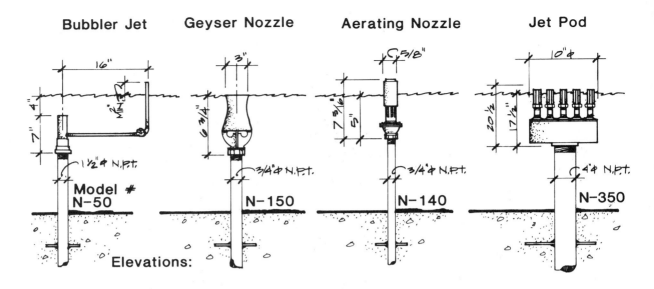

**Figure 3.22**  **Aerating Type Nozzles**

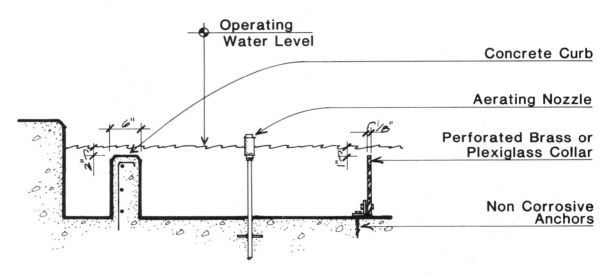

**Figure 3.23**  **Surge Reduction Devices**

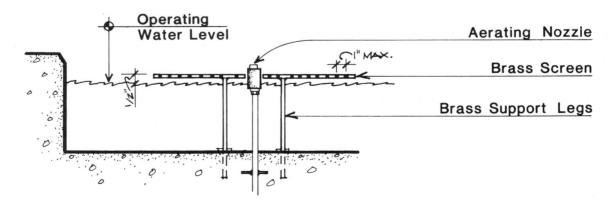

**Figure 3.24**  **Surge Reduction Devices**

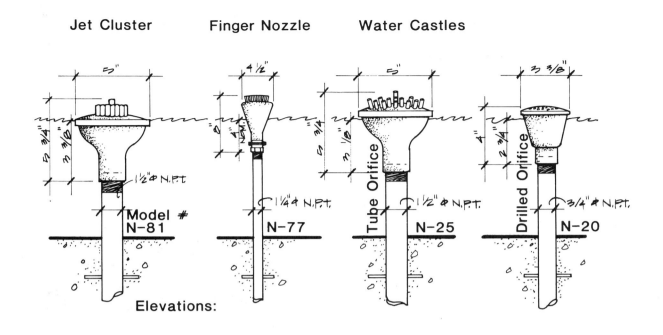

Jet Cluster    Finger Nozzle    Water Castles

Model #
N-81    N-77    N-25    N-20

Elevations:

**Figure 3.25**    **Spray Head Type Nozzles**

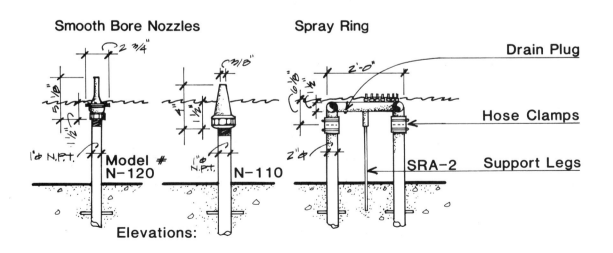

Smooth Bore Nozzles    Spray Ring

Drain Plug

Hose Clamps

Model #
N-120    N-110    SRA-2    Support Legs

Elevations:

**Figure 3.26**    **Smooth Bore Type Nozzles**

of the water effect. Table 3.1 will allow the designer to establish the head and gpm of the nozzle for a prescribed horizontal dimension.

**Example:** A smooth bore nozzle, which will reach a vertical height of 5 feet, requires 3.6 gpm and 7 feet of head pressure to achieve this height. The same nozzle is to be installed at 35 degrees off of vertical and will project to a horizontal distance of 5 feet. By looking at the chart, we find that a nozzle installation that is 35 degrees off of vertical requires 37 percent capacity of the same nozzle in a vertical position. To achieve an equal water length:

| gpm vertical position | × | percent of vert. requirement from chart | = | gpm for nozzle at prescribed angle |
|---|---|---|---|---|

$$3.6 \text{ gpm} \times 37\% =$$
$$3.6 \text{ gpm} \times .37 =$$
$$= 1.33 \text{ gpm}$$

The same jet which is now creating a 5 foot horizontal length of water requires 1.33 gpm and 7.0 feet of head pressure.

## Spray Ring with Smooth Bore Nozzles

Some manufacturers supply the spray ring pre-assembled with nozzles, manifold, and make-up lines. Other manufacturers supply the nozzles and suggest that the contractor build the manifold.

On larger diameter spray rings, it is necessary to install two make-up lines to equalize pressure to each nozzle. If unequal pressure is created, the height of the water emitted from the jets will become progressively lower as it leaves the inlet pipe (See Figure 3.26).

The fountain shown in Figure 3.29 defies these general suggestions. In this situation, each individual jet of the spray ring is fitted with an adjustable screw valve and each jet coming from the spray ring was randomly set at a different height. This fountain is extremely attractive because it deviates from the standard conformation of a spray ring.

## Formed Nozzles

Formed nozzles are typified by a thin sheet of water which originates in the formed jet. Size and shape of the water sheet are varied. Shapes range from mushrooms to morning glories.

Formed-type nozzles include: fan jets, calyx jets, calyx hollow stream jets, dandelion spheres, bell jets, and morning glory nozzles (Figure 3.33).

Because these nozzles utilize thin sheets of water for their effects, tolerances in the jet are very exact. Any dirt which is transported through the discharge line will be deposited in the jet opening and may lead to clogging or deforming of the jet pattern. For proper performance of these nozzles the designer must:

1. Situate the nozzle in a non-windy area. The delicate water sheet is easily affected by wind.

**Table 3.1 Capacity Reduction of Smooth Bore Nozzles in a Nonvertical Position**

| Desired Spray Off the Vertical | Desired Spray Off the Horizontal | Percentage of the Vertical Requirement* |
|---|---|---|
| 85° | 5° | 5% |
| 75° | 15° | 12% |
| 65° | 25° | 18% |
| 55° | 35° | 28% |
| 45° | 45° | 28% |
| 35° | 55° | 37% |
| 25° | 65° | 52% |
| 15° | 75° | 93% |

* Applicable for smooth bore and aerating nozzles.[83]

**Figure 3.27** *Large spray ring. Oklahoma City, Oklahoma.*

**Figure 3.28** *Smooth bore nozzle of a spray ring. Oklahoma City, Oklahoma.*

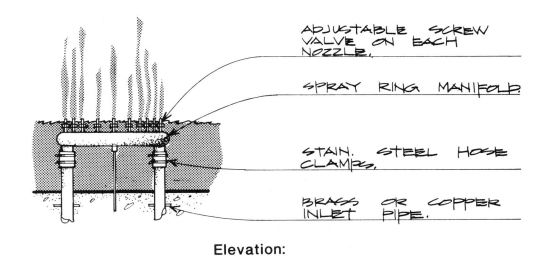

ADJUSTABLE SCREW
VALVE ON EACH
NOZZLE.

SPRAY RING MANIFOLD.

STAIN. STEEL HOSE
CLAMPS.

BRASS OR COPPER
INLET PIPE.

Elevation:

**Figure 3.29**   **Random Height Water Effect from Spray Ring**

**Figure 3.30** *Grid of formed nozzles. Fort Worth, Texas.*

Photo by Theodore D. Walker

**Figure 3.31** *Mushroom nozzle. Virginia Beach, Virginia.*

**Figure 3.32** *Custom formed nozzle. Norfolk, Virginia.*

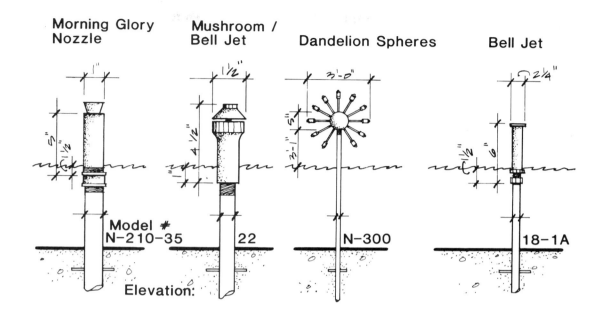

Morning Glory Nozzle

Mushroom / Bell Jet

Dandelion Spheres

Bell Jet

Model #
N-210-35

22

N-300

18-1A

Elevation:

**Figure 3.33**    **Formed Type Nozzles**

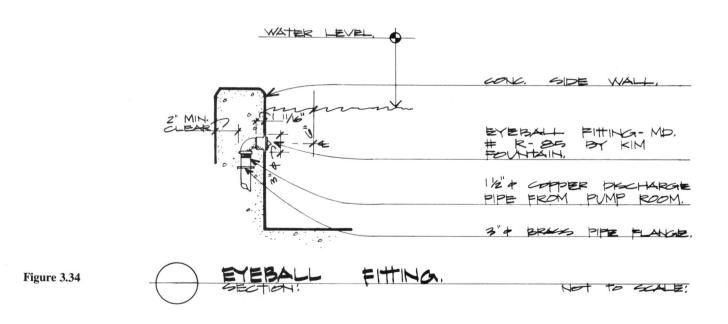

WATER LEVEL.

CONC. SIDE WALL.

2" MIN.
CLEAR?

EYEBALL FITTING- MD.
# R-85 BY KIM
FOUNTAIN.

1½"⌀ COPPER DISCHARGE
PIPE FROM PUMP ROOM.

3"⌀ BRASS PIPE FLANGE.

**Figure 3.34**    EYEBALL FITTING.
SECTION!                                              NOT TO SCALE:

89

2. Provide suction or in-line strainers to prevent dirt from entering the jet. In-line strainers are normally located on the discharge line and are known in the trade as dandelion discharge strainers.

3. Provide non-turbulent (laminar) flow in the pipe. This is achieved by providing non-twisted water at the nozzle.

Formed nozzles are not dependent on the water level of the pool, so they can be located any distance above the water level.

## DESIGNING WITH FORMED NOZZLES

Because of the unusual shapes created by formed nozzles, shape, balance and form of the fountain and effects must be considered to provide proper design. Grids of formed nozzles tend to create a misty and powerful appearance. Spacing between nozzles needs to be adequate so each nozzle can be perceived individually. In addition, formed nozzles too closely spaced will deform the clear "paper-like" shapes of each adjacent nozzle.

In regards to sound, formed nozzles create a soft, gentle noise. This noise is extremely soft because the water effect is continuous from the nozzle to the water. Since the falling distance of the water is short, very little noise is generated.

Drawbacks to this nozzle are related to shape and potential wind distortion. Some formed nozzles produce such a dominant effect that only a single nozzle is appropriate. These nozzles can be static and uninteresting. In addition, wind drastically alters the shape of the nozzle effect. These nozzles are relatively low and must be viewed from short distances.

## COMBINATION OF NOZZLES

Combining several different nozzle types, heights and or shapes can expand the limited varieties of nozzles which are currently available. Combining of nozzles can expand on standard shapes, contrast of textures, form and height to spread ratio of standard nozzles. In addition to this, custom shaped nozzles can be custom fabricated to create custom site specific effects.

## COMBINING WATER EFFECTS

The current trend in design of urban and commercial water effects is to combine several different effects to create additional interest and variety for the observer. In most applications two to three groups of water effects are combined in one fountain. Typically water effects such as water channels, waterfalls, water steps, aerating nozzles and/or smooth bore nozzles are used in conjunction with each other. The use of specialty nozzles such as formed nozzles, in this instance, normally is not successful due to their strong form. Like all design solutions, balance, form, repetition, hierarchy and volume must be considered to achieve good design solutions. When water effects are combined, balance and hierarchy are the most important design motifs to consider. In most applications, a visual balance of water volume

**Figure 3.35** *Combined water effects. Norfolk, Virginia.*

**Figure 3.36** *Design balance with nozzle height and spacing. Washington, District of Columbia.*

**Figure 3.37** *Design hierarchy with nozzle volume and spacing.*

**Figure 3.38** *Formed nozzles altered by wind patterns. Oklahoma City, Oklahoma.*

**Figure 3.39** *Simple pipe nozzles. Oklahoma City, Oklahoma.*

is successful. Vertical water effects can be balanced with horizontal effects of low nozzles or water steps. Vertical nozzles can be balanced with several low aerating nozzles, while waterfalls can be balanced with bubblers or low water steps (See Figure 3.35). In addition to balance, a general hierarchy of water effects should be created so that one element in the fountain is more dominant than the other. Dominance can be achieved by increasing height, aeration, noise, width or volume of one of the effects in the fountain. This will allow one element to be the main focal point, while others create background or enhance it (See Figures 3.36 and 3.37). In applications where there is no hierarchy of water effects the overall outcome is too powerful and usually distracting. Since the two elements are of equal importance they compete with each other and create a visual distraction.

### Pipe Nozzles

A pipe nozzle can be easily constructed from copper pipe. By partially smashing or reducing the end diameter of the pipe, an appropriate residential scale nozzle can be created. The gpm requirements for the nozzle are easy to establish. To find the gpm, the proposed pipe nozzle should be held over a one gallon bucket. With the aid of a stop watch, the minutes needed to fill a one gallon bucket can be determined. This will enable the designer to establish gpm.

To establish pressure requirements for the nozzle, the designer must incorporate a simple pressure gauge at the nozzle base and attach the nozzle to a hose or other water source. Measurements should be taken after the design height is set.

**Example:** By operating the proposed nozzle at the desired height, it takes 30 seconds (0.5 minutes) to fill a one gallon bucket. What is the gpm of the nozzle?

$$\frac{(x) \text{ minutes}}{1 \text{ gallon}} = \frac{1 \text{ minute}}{(y) \text{ gallons}}$$

$$\frac{0.5 \text{ minutes}}{1 \text{ gallon}} = \frac{1 \text{ minute}}{(y) \text{ gallon}}$$

$$(y) = 2 \text{ gallons}$$

2 gallons/minute required

### Eyeball Fittings

Eyeball fittings are a water discharge device often used to supply water for weirs. When installed, the eyeball is generally located 6 inches below the water level of the fountain. By locating the water input below the water level, surface turbulence can be reduced.

Eyeballs contain a flexible ball union which allows the designer to field adjust the direction of the water coming from the orifice of the eyeball. Some manufacturers have eyeballs which adjust to 40 degrees from the centerline of the nozzle.[84] By adjusting the water input direction, surface turbulence can be reduced. When selecting an eyeball for

91

use, the designer should check the maximum gpm rating for the eyeball as it may be necessary to install more than one eyeball when large volumes of water are needed.

Other water discharge devices can be constructed from copper pipe and fittings. Designers often use a vertical pipe with a "tee" or a downward pointed 90° elbow as a substitute for an eyeball (See Figure 3.43).

Large tees and elbows will carry greater volumes of water than an eyeball. In cases where large quantities of water are necessary to operate weirs, a pipe discharge device is more cost effective than several eyeballs.

Field adjustment of pipe fitting input devices, to reduce surface turbulence, becomes very time consuming. Minor adjustment may necessitate draining of the fountain to re-solder the pipe joints. This problem can be easily prevented with threaded fittings. Pipe fittings used as a water discharge element should be carefully located in a participatory fountain where people will walk. For this application, the pipe should be positioned in a wall or floor niche to prevent tripping (See Figures 3.40 and 3.44).

## ENCOURAGING WATER FLOW

In special applications eyeball fittings can be used to push surface debris towards skimmers, to encourage channel flow or stimulate turbulence. When designing water channels, eyeball fittings located at various locations along the channel wall will encourage faster water flow in level channels.

Most eyeball fittings have optional directional insert fittings which reduce water pressure but increase water velocity. When pointed towards the water surface, these inserts simulate turbulence similar to stone washboards in streams.

## DISCHARGE DEVICES

Other water discharge devices can be constructed from pipe and fittings or preformed P.V.C. sumps (See Figures 3.41 and 3.42).

Preformed plastic anti-vortex plates and sumps normally used for suctioning make excellent discharge devices to provide a water source for weirs, waterfalls or watersteps. These devices are easily inserted in concrete floors and require no forming to create the sump.

In fountain designs where the walls are constructed of block or brick, waterproofing around wall-mounted discharge devices such as eyeball fillers is difficult. In some applications, floor-mounted discharge devices such as anti-vortex plates and sumps can be substituted for eyeball fillers. This allows the device to be mounted in poured concrete thus making a good seal around the device.

### Generation of Pressure for Nozzle Operation

Many early fountains relied upon elevated dam structures to create pressure for nozzle operation. The raised height of the dam above the nozzle produced enough water pressure to power the nozzles. Such famous fountains as Ville d'Este at Tivoli operate on this principle.[85]

These systems required extensive reservoirs to create water pressure, and needed a continual water supply to fill the dam

**Figure 3.40** *Discharge elbow and sump. Richmond, Virginia.*

**Figure 3.41** *PVC pipe supply for watersteps. Washington, District of Columbia.*

**Figure 3.42** *Schedule 80 PVC pipe supply and butterfly valves. Washington, District of Columbia.*

92

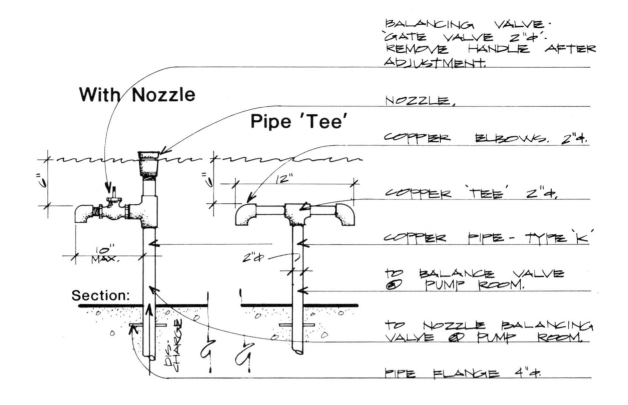

**With Nozzle**

**Pipe 'Tee'**

BALANCING VALVE. 'GATE VALVE 2"∅'. REMOVE HANDLE AFTER ADJUSTMENT.

NOZZLE.

COPPER ELBOWS. 2"∅.

COPPER 'TEE' 2"∅.

COPPER PIPE - TYPE 'K'

TO BALANCE VALVE @ PUMP ROOM.

TO NOZZLE BALANCING VALVE @ PUMP ROOM.

PIPE FLANGE 4"∅.

Section:

**Figure 3.43**     **Types of Pipe Discharge Devices**

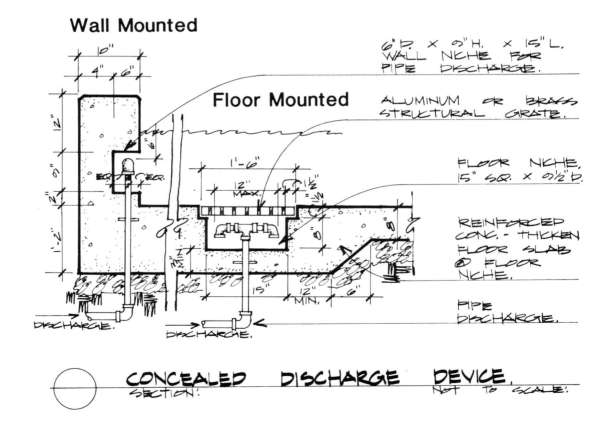

**Wall Mounted**

**Floor Mounted**

6"D. X 0"H. X 15"L. WALL NICHE FOR PIPE DISCHARGE.

ALUMINUM OR BRASS STRUCTURAL GRATE.

FLOOR NICHE, 15" SQ. X 0½"D.

REINFORCED CONC. - THICKEN FLOOR SLAB @ FLOOR NICHE.

PIPE DISCHARGE.

DISCHARGE.

DISCHARGE.

**Figure 3.44**     CONCEALED DISCHARGE DEVICE.
SECTION:     NOT TO SCALE.

as no water was ever recycled. Once the water was emitted from the nozzle, it was drained into a river of a lower elevation. Because of the high cost of diverting rivers and building dams, modern day fountains are predominantly designed as closed systems. Water held in the basin is continually recycled from the basin by the pump, to the nozzle or eyeball, and back to the basin again. Once the fountain is filled, a pump mechanism generates pressure to recycle the water.

Pumps used to operate the water effects of a fountain are predominantly powered by electric motors. As the water effect increases in magnitude, more complicated pumping systems are required.

### Submersible Pumps

One of the simplest pumping systems is a submersible pump. A submersible pump is a watertight electric motor and pump set into the water of the fountain basin. Submersible pumps are usually equipped with a 1/20th to 1 horsepower electric motor and are intended for use in fountains where low volumes of water are needed (3 ft. head at 120 gpm).[86]

These pumps have built-in suction lines and suction strainers, and require only minor installation procedures. When installing a submersible pump, only an electrical line must be run from the basin exterior. This reduces the number of pipes which penetrate the basin wall, thus decreasing the potential of a leak. Discharge lines from the pump to the nozzles will need to be installed. In some cases, the nozzle and discharge line may need to be anchored to the floor of the basin.

Large submersible pumps used for pumping of sewage do not conform to the data described. These pumps can range in size up to 50 horsepower and larger. Due to the size of these pumps, it is necessary to construct a recessed pit in the floor of the fountain. These pits are normally 3 feet x 3 feet x 3 feet and require a perforated brass sheet to prevent accidental falls into the pump pit.[87] The pit also provides proper water cover for the pump. The cost of this type of pump and motor may be higher than that of a dry pump of similar capacity. When selecting a submersible pump, the designer should consider the following advantages and disadvantages:

#### Advantages

1. The pump is easy to install.

2. The system requires no isolated pump room for equipment storage.

3. The system is generally less expensive than other pumping systems. It requires shorter pipe runs because the pump is located in the fountain basin.

4. Submersible pumps require less pipe penetrations through the basin wall. This reduces the possibility of leaks.

5. The pump is located in the fountain basin and will not create water siphoning when strainers are opened for cleaning. In this application, a discharge and suction shut-off valve will not be needed to prevent water siphoning. Any excess water will be deposited into the basin. However, a discharge shut-off valve may be necessary to regulate overall water effects height.

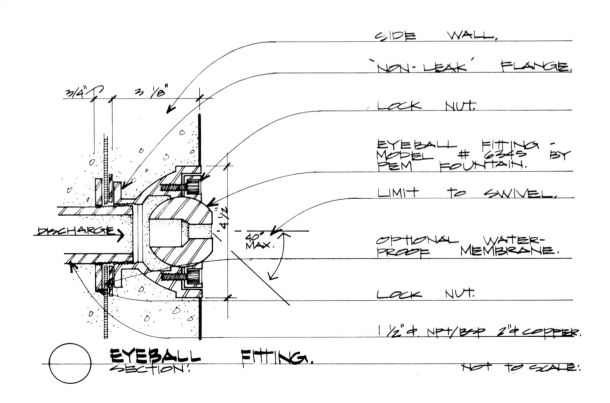

**Figure 3.45**

EYEBALL FITTING.
SECTION.

SIDE WALL.

'NON-LEAK' FLANGE.

LOCK NUT.

EYEBALL FITTING - MODEL # 6345 BY PEM FOUNTAIN.

LIMIT TO SWIVEL.

OPTIONAL WATER-PROOF MEMBRANE.

LOCK NUT.

1 1/2"Ø NPT/BSP 2"Ø COPPER.

NOT TO SCALE.

**Figure 3.46** *Two HP sewage pump for lake fountains.*

### Disadvantages

1. Discharge rate of the pump is normally limited to 100 gpm.

2. The 110 volt electric service and motor is in direct contact with water which could cause electrical shock. All submersible pumps should be fitted with a ground-fault circuit interrupter to prevent electrical shock in the instance of a faulty circuit. This prevents the use of energy efficient motors rated at 208–230 volt 3-phase.

3. Pipe and pump are exposed and fall prey to vandalism.

4. People who enter fountain may trip on piping and pump. Concealed pipe and pump covers should be employed in fountains where people will walk.

5. Pump must be covered with water to operate properly. Pump may be damaged if water level inadvertently drops.

6. Winterization of fountain may require the removal of the pump.

### Dry and Remote Pumps

These pumps are located in an isolated-dry equipment vault which is in proximity to the fountain. Equipment rooms are construction of *in situ* concrete or are available in preassembled fiberglass units available from some fountain parts manufacturers.[88]

Because the pump and other equipment are located in an isolated vault, running pipe from the vault to the fountain is necessary. Water may enter the pump room due to cleaning of the in-line strainer or possible leak. This water must be prevented from entering the pump and damaging the non-submersible motor. In some situations, a floor drain located at a low point in the equipment pit floor will provide adequate protection. In instances where the equipment pit floor

is too low to provide gravity flow to the storm or sanitary sewer, an automatic sump pump may be necessary.

Pumps used in a dry pump installation are normally a dry centrifugal or vertical turbine pump.

### Dry Centrifugal Pump

A dry centrifugal pump system consists of a pump, electric motor, a suction line, and a discharge line and is most commonly used for larger water features.[89] They range in size from ¼ to 100 horsepower and have ample capacity to supply water.

The suction line for the pump is normally located at an elevation lower than the water level of the lowest basin of a multi-level fountain.[90] Sloping the line towards the pump creates free flow of water to the pump and reduces the amount of force the pump has to exert to produce water pressure (See Figure 3.47).

When installing the suction line to the pump, it is important to reduce the head pressure which the suction line must exert to carry the water from the basin to the pump. Vertical rises in the suction line should be held to a minimum. This will reduce head pressure requirements of the pump (See Figure 3.47). Excessive vertical rises will reduce the performance of the pump. Rises should never exceed 33.94 feet. The forces of gravity prevent suction lifts higher than this.

In Figure 3.48 water is allowed to enter the suction line by gravity. This reduces the energy which the pump must exert to lift the water to the nozzle.

Kim Lighting recommends that the center of the suction line, where it attaches to the pump, be at or below the floor elevation of the pool floor. In the case of a multi-level pool, the suction center line should be at or below the floor of the lowest basin. Exceptions to these rules are possible but require larger horsepower pumps (See Figure 3.49).

Often the discharge line and suction line are larger in diameter than the pipe flange of the pump. This necessitates the use of a pipe reducer to match the two diameters. By employing a conical type reducer, the turbulence and friction loss created by a straight-necked pipe reducer will be diminished (See Figure 3.50).

Straight-necked pipe reducers as shown in Figure 3.51 should not be used.

### Vacuum Switch for Centrifugal Pumps

Since a dry-centrifugal pump is located in an isolated vault, it is extremely hard to detect a pump which is running dry due to a clogged pipe or an inadvertently drained fountain. To prevent this occurrence, a vacuum switch can be installed in the suction line of the pipe. These switches allow the pump to run as long as there is water in the suction line. In the event that water ceases to flow in the line, the vacuum is broken and the switch shuts off the pump.

### Vertical Turbine Pump

Vertical turbine pumps are often used in irrigation systems or in municipal water systems. These pumps move

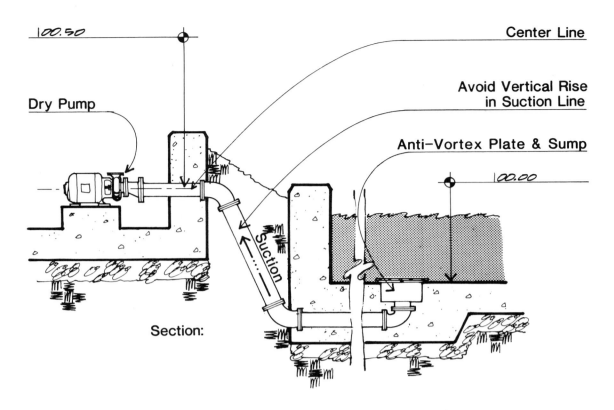

**Figure 3.47**    **Vertical Rise in Suction Line**

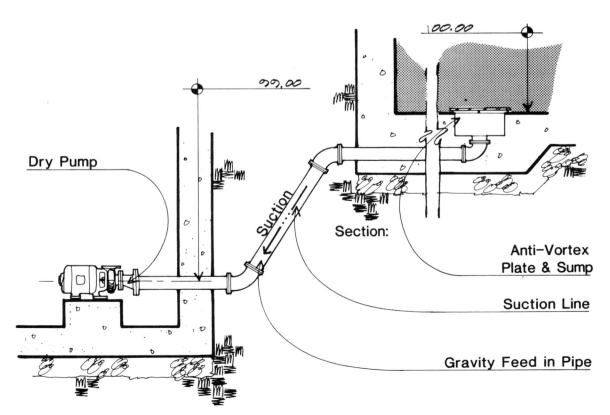

**Figure 3.48**    **Gravity Feed Suction Line**

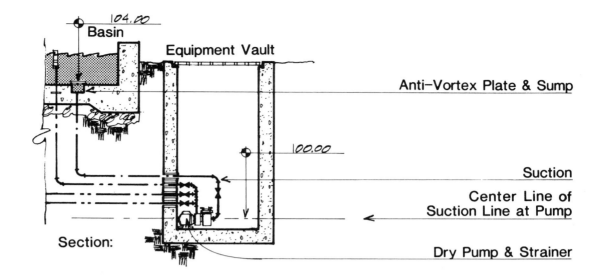

**Figure 3.49**     **Center Line of Pump Suction Below Fountain Floor**

tremendous amounts of water and should be considered for use in large water features. A vertical turbine pump requires the pump and motor, a water sump located in the equipment vault, a gravity feed mechanism to fill the sump, and a discharge line. These pumps are normally more energy efficient than those with suction lines. This is because the energy used to run the pump is only operating a discharge line. This pump exerts no energy to move the water to the pump. Water flows to the pump by gravity and thus reduces the amount of work exerted by the pump.

The water sump is located so that a pipe or inlet will gravity feed the sump with water. When a level feed mechanism is used, the water in the sump will rise to the same elevation as the water in the lowest basin of the fountain. The turbine pump is suspended in the sump so that the suction shaft sits in the water of the sump. Sumps should be designed so they are accessible for cleaning. Strainers must also be designed to prevent trash from entering the sump or clogging the suction shaft of the pump (See Figure 3.52).

Because the sump feeds by gravity, vortexing caused by typical suction lines can be avoided. Sump and inlet size need to be large enough to prevent the pump from running dry during operation. Consult with the pump manufacturers for these sizes.

The designer should consider the following advantages and disadvantages before specifying a dry pump installation:

**Advantages**

1. Pump capacities of up to 5,000 gallons per minute are possible.

2. The electrical motor of the pump is not submersed in water. This reduces the potential for electrical shock and the need for costly watertight seals.

3. The pump is concealed from vandals.

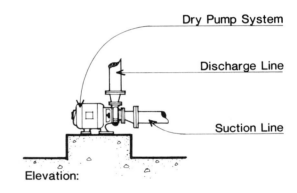

**Figure 3.50**     **Flange Reducer**

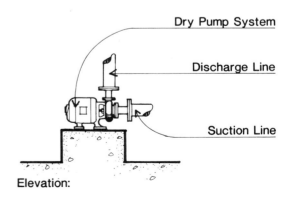

**Figure 3.51**     **Straight Necked Reducer – Improper Method**

97

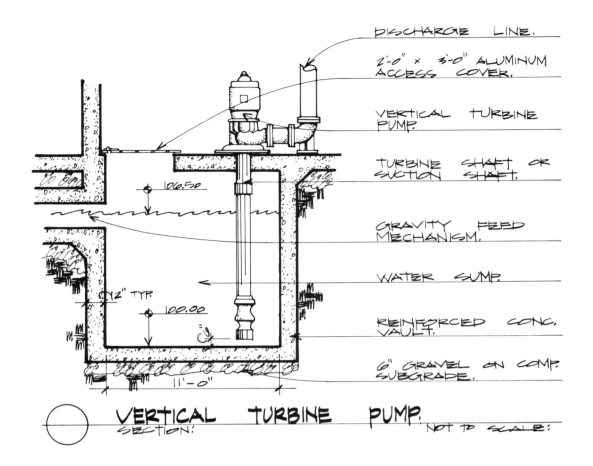

DISCHARGE LINE.

2'-0" x 3'-0" ALUMINUM ACCESS COVER.

VERTICAL TURBINE PUMP.

TURBINE SHAFT OR SUCTION SHAFT.

GRAVITY FEED MECHANISM.

WATER SUMP.

REINFORCED CONC. VAULT.

6" GRAVEL ON COMP. SUBGRADE.

106.50

12" TYP.

100.00

11'-0"

**Figure 3.52**

**VERTICAL TURBINE PUMP.**
SECTION: NOT TO SCALE:

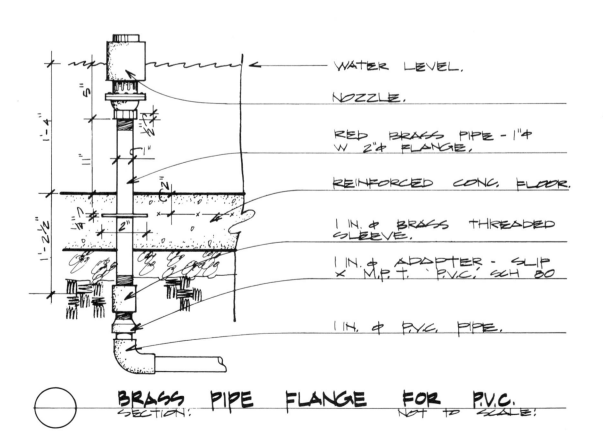

WATER LEVEL.

NOZZLE.

RED BRASS PIPE - 1"∅ W 2"∅ FLANGE.

REINFORCED CONC. FLOOR.

1 IN. ∅ BRASS THREADED SLEEVE.

1 IN. ∅ ADAPTER - SLIP X M.P.T. P.V.C. SCH 80

1 IN. ∅ P.V.C. PIPE.

**Figure 3.53**

**BRASS PIPE FLANGE FOR P.V.C.**
SECTION: NOT TO SCALE:

**Figure 3.54** *Direct burial pump vault and air tubes. Portsmouth, Virginia.*

**Figure 3.55** *Direct burial pump vault. Richmond, Virginia.*

**Figure 3.56** *Partially buried pump vault. Virginia Beach, Virginia.*

## Disadvantages

1. A separate equipment vault must be constructed in close proximity to the pool. The pump vault should be a maximum of 150 to 200 feet from the fountain.[91] Short pipe lengths will reduce friction losses through the piping and permit the use of smaller pumps. Increased pipe lengths and vault construction increase the project budget.

2. The equipment vault must be ventilated to prevent overheating of the pump.

3. Drainage must be provided in the floor of the equipment vault to prevent flooding of the motor. Because leaks occur and the system is normally drained for winter, a drain must be provided.

4. Pipes must be run from the equipment vault to the fountain. Leaks may occur where pipes penetrate the fountain basin or where pipes are disturbed by construction.

## DIRECT BURIAL PUMP VAULTS

In fountain applications where pump rooms are impractical or excessive pipe runs from the fountain to the pump are required, factory-built direct burial pump vaults are the ideal solution. These systems are custom built by various fountain manufacturers to meet each individual design application. Each system is supplied with the appropriate number of balancing valves, pumps, and control panels as specified by the designer.

Typically, each vault is supplied with a fiberglass burial shell, an aluminum access hatch, access ladder, safety light, exhaust fan, ventilation duct, and sump pump. The sump pump is connected to the sanitary sewer to prevent flooding of the vault during maintenance of the pump and filter system.

Although this system is more expensive than its individual components, the cost of site labor to install the equipment is considerably reduced. Each system is totally fabricated and tested at the factory. The responsibility of fabrication and errors in installation rests on the fountain manufacturer. Applications in which local craftsmen have little expertise in wiring and plumbing fountains make these systems ideal. In addition, site-built problems which occur when craftsmen substitute components or combine non-compatible products are alleviated.

Typical installation of this system would require excavation and bedding for the vault, connection to the various fountain pipes and provision of required public utility connections.

Fountain manufacturers should be consulted for the available pump, filter and accessory options. (As a rule of thumb, as the pumping and electrical functions and accessories are increased, the pump vault size will increase.) This size increase will accommodate code-required clearance at electrical control panels (See Figures 3.54 to 3.56).

## Pre-Engineered Fountain Kit

Most manufacturers produce a pre-designed and engineered fountain kit. These systems are package deals which include a submersible pump and motor, lights, piping, nozzles and valves. These units are assembled and tested at the factory. The cost of labor needed to assemble and test the unit makes a pre-engineered fountain more expensive than the individual components. Installation requires the on site construction of a basin and a minor electrical connection.

In some instances, these kits are mounted in a stainless steel float system and anchored in lakes. The incorporation of the float, motor and nozzle in one unit prevents problems associated with lake fountains. The float rises and descends with the lake level, maintaining a constant height of water over aerating nozzles commonly used in lakes. In some applications a floating unit may be more economical than a permanent nozzle riser due to footing costs and extensive pipe lengths.

## FOUNTAIN PIPING

Piping will be needed for the water effects pump, the filter pump, and the drainage and water level control devices. Local plumbing codes should be consulted before specifying various piping materials as these codes may restrict the use of particular pipe materials in certain situations.

Flow rates of water traveling through the piping system should not exceed 6 to 8 feet per second. At higher velocities any dirt suspended in the water will cause water scouring of the pipes.

Water traveling through fountain pipes will normally flow at high gpm and low pressure. Pipe joints which are to be embedded in the fountain wall or floor should be pressure tested before they are encapsulated by the fountain building material to prevent costly repair of undetected leaks.

## PRESSURE TESTING PIPE

Solvent joints of P.V.C. piping often leak and cause extensive problems when encased in concrete. Joint leakage should be checked prior to pouring concrete around pipes. To pressure test piping, a temporary cap should be solvent welded to each pipe end. Each interconnected manifold or pipe run should also be fitted with pipe adaptors to accept a proper pressure gauge and an air insertion device.

Pressure gauges should be chosen so that their calibration reads in excess of 10 to 20 P.S.I. above the test pressure for the pipe manifold. Often gauges are pressurized with the needle touching the higher limit pin of the gauge. This causes an unknown excess pressure to be exerted on the pipe run and gauge. Any pressure loss in the pipe system will not be detected until it drops below the pressure set by the limiting pin of the gauge. Ten to 20 P.S.I. pressure loss in the pipe system could occur before the needle moves away from the limit pin.

In addition to selecting a proper gauge, it is important to pressure test pipe a minimum of 24 hours prior to pouring of concrete and periodically during the entire construction project.

## Flushing

Piping should be thoroughly flushed prior to installing the fountain nozzles. This will prevent dirt, deposited in the line during construction, from clogging a nozzle.

## Pipe Penetrations

Pipes with straight penetrations through the floor or wall of a fountain must be provided with flange collars to prevent capillary action from encouraging water seepage between the pipe wall and the fountain basin. These collars are necessary on pipe and conduit; they must be at least twice the diameter of the pipe itself.[92] When using copper pipe, sheet copper can be soldered to the pipe to form this flange. In some instances, it may be necessary to change the pipe material which penetrates the fountain. This material change is required to increase durability and ease of collar construction.

When pipe materials vary, penetrating pipes are kept to a minimum length. This will reduce the cost and allows for the use of red brass or copper penetrating pipe. Dissimilar metals in contact with water may corrode due to galvanic action. Select the pipe material accordingly.

PVC pipe is very slick and will not allow concrete to bond to the pipe exterior but increased adherence can be achieved by roughening the exterior with a wire brush. When using PVC pipe, better bonding can be achieved by changing the piping material which will penetrate the basin. By changing the pipe material which penetrates the fountain, a more watertight and durable component is created. Installing a slip to thread adaptor at the end of the PVC pipe will permit the use of a metal pipe to penetrate the pool wall (See Figure 3.53). PVC pipe is very economical for fountain construction but should not be used to support nozzles.

When using threaded adaptors to convert from metal to plastic pipe, a plastic male fitting and metal female fitting should be employed. This will reduce internal stresses and rupture of the plastic fitting (See Figure 3.53).

Pipe flanges are hard to install on pipes which penetrate cut stone fountains. By caulking around the pipe and installing a pipe flange as soon as possible, leakage can be prevented. In cases where a cut stone fountain basin is set on an *in situ* concrete base, the base is an appropriate location for the flange (See Figure 3.57).

## Draining Piping

All fountain piping should be drained in regions susceptible to freezing to prevent pipe rupture due to expanded water. Ease of pipe draining can be facilitated by sloping the pipe towards the equipment vault. Here the water can be emptied by means of small in-line valve which empties the water into an appropriate drain. When piping will not allow complete drainage, antifreeze should be poured into them to provide additional protection. Submersible pumps and piping will be hard to drain by means of gravity and should be completely removed to prevent winter damage.

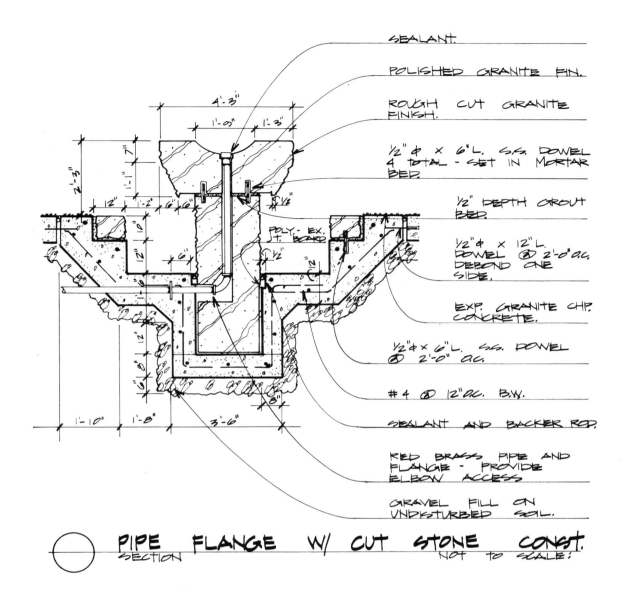

SEALANT.

POLISHED GRANITE FIN.

ROUGH CUT GRANITE FINISH.

½"∅ X 6"L. S.S. DOWEL 4 total - SET IN MORTAR BED

½" DEPTH GROUT BED.

½"∅ X 12"L. DOWEL @ 2'-0" O.C. DEBOND ONE SIDE.

EXP. GRANITE CHP. CONCRETE.

½"∅ X 6"L. S.S. DOWEL @ 2'-0" O.C.

#4 @ 12"O.C. B.W.

SEALANT AND BACKER ROD.

RED BRASS PIPE AND FLANGE - PROVIDE ELBOW ACCESS

GRAVEL FILL ON UNDISTURBED SOIL.

**Figure 3.57**

PIPE FLANGE W/ CUT STONE CONST.
SECTION          NOT TO SCALE.

## Steel Piping

Black iron, steel, or galvanized pipe should never be used in fountains.[93] These materials will rust and eventually restrict the water flow through the pipe. Rust which accumulates on the pipe interior can easily dislodge and become deposited in the fountain nozzle. This can cause clogging of the fine orifice of a nozzle.

## Cast Iron Piping

Cast iron is suitable for use as large piping material. This material is different from steel pipe as rust will not collect on the pipe interior. If a cast iron system is shut down for long periods of time, small traces of rust will be present in the water. This residue has a potential for staining and precautions should be taken to prevent permanent discoloration.

## Copper Piping

Copper has been used for many years as a piping material in fountains. Copper pipe is low in corrosion, easy to join, and durable.

Copper piping and fittings are connected by soldering of the joints. Copper pipe is available in annealed (soft copper) or hard drawn. Annealed copper is soft and can be shaped by hand to bend corners. This type of copper is often used to bring the water service from the water meter to the site. Hard drawn copper is rigid and requires fittings to change directions.

When selecting pipe for fountain use, the designer should consider its wall thickness. Wall thickness is rated as type K, L, and M. Type K has the thickest wall and will withstand higher internal pipe pressures. The designer should choose a pipe whose wall thickness will tolerate the water pressures of the fountain system (See Tables 3.2 and 3.3).

Type K pipe is often specified because of the increased

durability ensured by its wall thickness. A trade-off between durability and cost may require the designer to choose type L or M pipe. When choosing these types of pipe, it is important to check the plumbing code and allowable internal pressures before specifying these less expensive, thinner-walled pipes. Additional corrosion protection must be provided when copper pipe comes in contact with concrete.

## PVC Piping

Polyvinylchloride (PVC) pipe has been used in increasing amounts as a pipe material for residential and commercial plumbing. PVC pipe is lower in price than copper and requires only a hack saw and solvent for attachment of fittings. PVC pipe is generally used in conjunction with metal valves. Plastic valves which are compatible with PVC pipe are generally more expensive and less durable than comparable brass or copper valves.

Slip to thread adaptors must be installed on the PVC pipe to allow the union of the PVC to the metal valve. The slip joint is welded to the PVC pipe with solvent and the threaded portion of the adaptor connects to the valve. When specifying PVC pipe, the designer should consider grade, type, internal operating pressure, and tensile pipe strength. The following discussion should help the designer make an appropriate pipe choice.

### Selecting PVC Piping

All PVC pipe which is delivered to the site will contain the following markings every 5 feet.[96]

| Markings | Explanation |
|---|---|
| 2″ | (A) |
| PVC 1220 | (B) |
| SDR 21 | (C) |
| 200 psi | (D) |
| D2241 | (E) |
| ABC Plastic Pipe Co. | (F) |
| NSF | (G) |

**(A)** The nominal size of the pipe (Example: 2 inches in diameter). Standard pipe sizes are normally expressed in nominal dimensions. The standard sizes are expressed in approximate outside dimensions.

**(B)** The type of plastic pipe material in accordance with the designated code (Example: PVC 1220). In this material designation (PVC 1220), PVC = polyvinylchloride, the first number (1) = type 1 pipe, the second number (2) = grade 2 and the last numbers (20) = the hydrostatic design pressure in multiples of 100 (2000 psi hydrostatic design stress).

Design stress is a designation of material strength rather than the allowable working pressure of the pipe. PVC 1220 and 1120 have higher design stresses than PVC 2110 and should be used where tensile stress may occur.

It should be noted that the first two numbers are a material designation rather than an indication of pipe quality. Materials are designated numbers in order of development.

Type 1, grade 2 material is one of three substances with the highest hydrostatic design stress. Type 1, grade 1 has a greater resistance to chemicals. In most applications, PVC 1120 or PVC 1220 is used.

**(C)** This will be an SDR designation or a schedule number (Example: SDR 21). SDR-PR is an abbreviation for standard dimension ratio-pressure rated. SDR is the ratio of pipe diameter to wall thickness. The ratio ensures that as pipe diameter increases, wall thickness will increase. This permits pipes with the same SDR number but different diameters to have equivalent internal working pressures (See Table 3.4).

When selecting an SDR rating for the pipe, the internal operating pressure of the pipe should be two times greater than the operating pressure of the fountain system. This will prevent pipe fatigue.

Smaller pipes are available in limited SDR ratings. Table 3.5 designates the availability of SDR ratings for each pipe diameter.

In some instances, a schedule number will be substituted for the SDR number. Schedule ratings will either be schedule 40 or 80. Care should be taken in specifying schedule rated PVC pipe.

Schedule number means that, whatever the pipe diameter, the wall thickness will remain the same. As the pipe diameter increases the pipe strength decreases. Therefore, pressure must be reduced in larger scheduled PVC pipes to prevent rupture.

**(D)** The operating pressure of the pipe in pounds per square inch for water at 23°C. This information is also provided in the SDR code (Example: 200 psi).

**(E)** The ASTM designation for type of pipe (Example: D2241 is for PVC SDR-PR plastic pipe).

**(F)** The manufacturer's name or trademark.

**(G)** A seal or mark of the laboratory evaluating the pipe (Example: NSF — National Sanitation Foundation. This rating is needed only for pipe transporting potable water).

Before selecting PVC pipe for fountain use, the designer should consider the following advantages and disadvantages:

### Advantages

1. Expensive tools are not required to install the pipe.

2. PVC pipe is more economical than other pipe materials.

3. PVC pipe is lightweight.

4. No heat is required to attach fittings. Heat transferred during soldering of copper pipe can damage electronic valves.

5. PVC pipe has a greater flow capacity than any other pipe material of a similar size.

**Table 3.2 Rated Internal Working Pressures (psi) for Tube for Service Temperatures up to 150°F.[94]**

| Nominal Pipe Size, inches | Type M | | Type L | | Type K | |
|---|---|---|---|---|---|---|
| | Annealed | Hard Drawn | Annealed | Hard Drawn | Annealed | Hard Drawn |
| ¼ | — — | — — | 810 | 1350 | 900 | 1595 |
| ⅜ | 475 | 840 | 675 | 1195 | 990 | 1745 |
| ½ | 430 | 760 | 625 | 1105 | 780 | 1375 |
| ⅝ | — — | — — | 545 | 965 | 640 | 1135 |
| ¾ | 350 | 610 | 495 | 875 | 750 | 1315 |
| 1 | 295 | 515 | 440 | 770 | 575 | 1010 |
| 1¼ | 295 | 515 | 385 | 680 | 465 | 820 |
| 1½ | 290 | 510 | 355 | 630 | 435 | 765 |
| 2 | 300 | 450 | 315 | 555 | 355 | 665 |
| 2½ | 235 | 410 | 295 | 520 | 355 | 520 |
| 3 | 220 | 385 | 275 | 490 | 340 | 605 |
| 3½ | 215 | 385 | 270 | 470 | 325 | 570 |
| 4 | 215 | 380 | 255 | 450 | 315 | 555 |
| 5 | 205 | 355 | 235 | 410 | 305 | 540 |
| 6 | 190 | 335 | 215 | 385 | 305 | 540 |
| 8 | 200 | 350 | 240 | 420 | 325 | 580 |
| 10 | 205 | 355 | 240 | 425 | 330 | 585 |
| 12 | 205 | 360 | 225 | 395 | 330 | 585 |

**Table 3.3 Rated Internal Working Pressures (psi) for Copper Tube Joints at Service Temperatures up to 100°F.[95]**

| Alloy Used for Joints | Tube Size K, L, and M (in inches) | | | | | |
|---|---|---|---|---|---|---|
| | ¼ to 1 Incl. | 1¼ to 2 Incl. | 2½ to 4 Incl. | 5 to 8 Incl. | 10 to 12 Incl. | |
| 50–50 Tin-Lead Solder | 200 | 175 | 150 | 130 | 100 | psi |
| 95–5 Tin-Antimony Solder* | 500 | 400 | 300 | 270 | 150 | psi |
| Brazing Alloys (Melting at or above 1000°F) | ** | ** | ** | ** | ** | |

* Not considered brazing material.
** Rated Internal pressure is that of tube being joined.
Reference: Copper Tube Handbook

**Table 3.4 Pressure Ratings* and SDR of Non-Threaded Pipe[97]**

| | SDR 64 | SDR 41 | SDR 32.5 | SDR 26 | SDR 21 | SDR 17 | SDR 13.5 |
|---|---|---|---|---|---|---|---|
| PVC 1120** | 63 | 100 | 125 | 160 | 200 | 250 | 315 |
| PVC 1220 | 63 | 100 | 125 | 160 | 200 | 250 | 315 |
| PVC 2116 | 50 | 80 | 100 | 125 | 160 | 200 | 250 |
| PVC 2112 | NPR*** | 63 | 80 | 100 | 125 | 160 | 200 |
| PVC 2110 | NPR | 50 | 63 | 80 | 100 | 125 | 160 |

* These pressure ratings do not apply for threaded pipe or account for surge pressures. (Most of the plastics industry does not recommend threaded PVC pipe with walls less than Schedule 80.)
** Code designations.
*** NPR = not pressure rated.

**Table 3.5 Availability of Pipe Diameters in SDR Ratings[98]**

| Nominal Pipe Size inches | Outside Diameter inches | Minimum Wall Thickness, inches | | | | | | |
|---|---|---|---|---|---|---|---|---|
| | | SDR 64 | SDR 41 | SDR 32.5 | SDR 26 | SDR 21 | SDR 17 | SDR 13.5 |
| ⅛ | 0.405 | * | ** | *** | — — | — — | — — | 0.060 |
| ¼ | 0.540 | — — | — — | — — | — — | — — | — — | 0.060 |
| ⅜ | 0.675 | — — | — — | — — | — — | — — | — — | 0.060 |
| ½ | 0.840 | — — | — — | — — | — — | — — | — — | 0.062 |
| ¾ | 1.050 | — — | — — | — — | — — | 0.060 | 0.062 | 0.078 |
| 1 | 1.315 | — — | — — | — — | 0.060 | 0.063 | 0.077 | 0.097 |
| 1¼ | 1.660 | — — | — — | — — | 0.064 | 0.079 | 0.098 | 0.123 |
| 1½ | 1.900 | — — | — — | — — | 0.073 | 0.090 | 0.112 | 0.141 |
| 2 | 2.375 | — — | — — | — — | 0.091 | 0.113 | 0.140 | 0.176 |
| 2½ | 2.875 | — — | — — | — — | 0.110 | 0.137 | 0.169 | 0.213 |
| 3 | 3.500 | — — | — — | 0.108 | 0.135 | 0.167 | 0.206 | 0.259 |
| 3½ | 4.000 | — — | 0.098 | 0.123 | 0.154 | 0.190 | 0.235 | 0.296 |
| 4 | 4.500 | — — | 0.110 | 0.138 | 0.173 | 0.214 | 0.265 | 0.333 |
| 5 | 5.563 | — — | 0.136 | 0.171 | 0.214 | 0.265 | 0.327 | 0.412 |
| 6 | 6.625 | 0.104 | 0.162 | 0.204 | 0.255 | 0.316 | 0.390 | 0.491 |
| 8 | 8.625 | 0.135 | 0.210 | 0.265 | 0.332 | 0.410 | 0.508 | — — |
| 10 | 10.750 | 0.168 | 0.262 | 0.331 | 0.413 | 0.511 | 0.632 | — — |
| 12 | 12.750 | 0.199 | 0.311 | 0.392 | 0.490 | 0.606 | 0.750 | — — |

*Available only in nominal pipe size diameters 6 to 12 inches.*

**Available only in nominal pipe diameters 3½ to 12 inches.*

***Available only in nominal pipe size diameters 3 to 12 inches.*

## Disadvantages

1. Most PVC pipe wil deteriorate when directly exposed to ultra-violet radiation.

2. PVC pipe has lower tensile strength and will shear more quickly than copper pipe. Accidental disturbance with a shovel or soil settlement, may shear the pipe. Resistance to shear can be increased by encapsulating the pipe in a concrete sleeve. When PVC pipe is installed under permanent objects like concrete slabs, a larger outside sleeve allows removal of the broken pipe without excavation of the slab.

3. PVC will stretch and only partially rebound when exposed to high pressures. This will cause thinning of a wall and may lead to a pipe break.

4. PVC pipe may fatigue when subjected to water hammer and eventually lead to pipe failure.

5. Thermal expansion of PVC pipe is greater than that of other pipe materials.

## Polyethylene Pipe

Polyethylene pipe is an extremely flexible plastic pipe which is occasionally used in fountains situated in lakes. Its ease of installation, bendability, and ability to withstand the pressure of freezing water left in the pipe make polyethylene pipe preferable for use in lake fountains.

Material flexibility allows pipe installation without the use of elbows to change directions. This reduces the required amount of pipe cutting. When using polyethylene pipe, fittings are only required at tee and valve locations and consist of an insert fitting and stainless steel hose clamp. When selecting "poly" pipe, pipe should be selected which is adequately pressure rated and of a material composition which will rebound to its original size after expansion from freezing water. The specification of "Ultra High Molecular Type" polyethylene pipe will ensure this rebounding capability.

## ECONOMIC PIPING

Current costs of copper pipe make its use prohibitive for some fountains. In applications where lower cost piping is required, the industry is currently employing schedule 80 PVC pipe. Its use is predicated on its wall thickness and ability to withstand pressure. When using PVC pipe care should be taken to prevent the following problems:

1. Solvent joints of PVC fittings and adaptors often leak.

2. Pipe risers extending up from concrete floors can be broken by vandals.

3. Pipes extending out from concrete footings can be sheared off due to settlement or improper pipe trench compaction.

Although these problems create some drawbacks in the use of PVC pipe, they can be alleviated through pressure testing of piping, construction detailing of metal pipe risers and through inspection and proper backfilling of pipe trenches.

## FILTER SYSTEMS

Filter systems are often included as part of a fountain. They prevent damage to the nozzle(s) and pump, and reduce maintenance requirements.

Tiny water particles, created by the fountain nozzle, trap lint and dust that are present in the air. The dirt held by the water particle is deposited into the basin when the water particle drops. In addition to this debris, airborne dirt can be blown directly into the fountain under adverse conditions. At this point, the material is either collected by a suction line, or is permitted to settle to the floor of the fountain. Dirt which settles to the bottom of the pool requires manual removal. Large dirt particles which enter a suction line may damage the impeller of the pump, or clog the fine orifice of a nozzle.

Leaves, cigarettes, and other litter are often blown or deposited into the fountain. This litter should be removed promptly. If allowed to sink to the bottom, it may enter the suction line of the pump, or may clog the suction screen. This flow restriction can decrease the pump's performance. Pipe restrictions allowed to continue for long periods of time may cause the pump to burn out.

Nozzle clogging and pump drainage and maintenance will be reduced if a filter system is employed. If suction lines of the filter system are numerous and located properly, sufficient underwater currents will prevent dirt from settling on the basin floor. Inherent movement of dirt into the filter system will reduce the amount of manual cleaning necessary.

Filter systems should be considered for medium to large fountains (3000 gallons or greater). Fountains retaining several hundred gallons are small enough to permit periodic drainage and water replenishment.[99] This eliminates the need for a filter. Before deciding against filter installation, the designer should consider water cost, the frequency of draining required to maintain clean water, and the possibility of local municipality water conservation.

## Filter System Components

A filter system requires a pump and motor, a filter media, a suction line, and a discharge line to operate properly.

## Filter Pump and Motor

The pump and motor used to operate the filter should be a separate unit from the water effects system. This will allow the filter to function when the water effects are not in operation. The water normally transverses a filter media at a low rate of 15 to 60 gallons/minute. Water effect pumps for large fountains operate at higher flow rates. These increased flow rates will force water through the media at a rate faster than the media can filter, thus reducing its effectiveness.

## Filter Media

Any filter media suited for swimming pools should be considered for use in a fountain system. Presently, three different media types are being used by the swimming pool industry: 1) cartridge filters, 2) diatomaceous-earth filters, and 3) permanent-media sand filters.

## Cartridge Filters

Cartridge filters require replacement or periodic manual cleaning to ensure proper performance. These filters are normally the most economical but require the most maintenance to keep clean. They should only be considered for small fountains.

## Diatomaceous-Earth Filters

Diatomaceous-earth filters contain siliceous shells of diatoms (unicelled plants) which remove dirt from the fountain water. These filters are able to screen out smaller particles much better than a permanent-media sand filter.

Pressurized water entering the filter passes through an earth layer which covers a permeable surface. Any dirt contained in the water is deposited in the earth. As the pores of the earth become clogged, water pressure through the media is lessened. Regular inspection of the pressure gauge will reveal when cleaning is necessary. To clean the media, the water direction is reveresed. This reversal in water flow backwashes the media and flushes the earth layer and dirt through the drain line of the filter. Before the filter is restarted, diatomaceous-earth must be manually replenished to the system.

## Permanent-Media Sand Filters

Permanent-media sand filters contain a silica sand filter media. These filters are similar in operation to the diatomaceous-earth filters because they require backwashing to clean the media. However, backwashing of a sand filter does not dissipate the media. The filter can thus be fitted

A. Cartridge

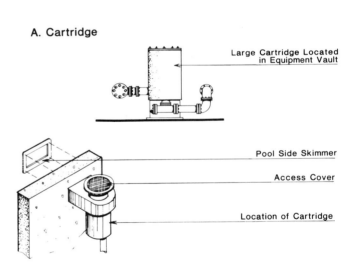

Large Cartridge Located in Equipment Vault

Pool Side Skimmer

Access Cover

Location of Cartridge

B. Diatomaceous Earth Media

Motor, Strainer & Filter Media

C. Sand Media

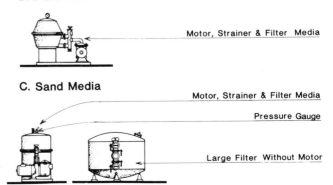

Motor, Strainer & Filter Media

Pressure Gauge

Large Filter Without Motor

**Figure 3.58**

with an electronic control device which automatically backwashes the system when the sand pores become clogged thus reducing the amount of maintenance required to operate the filter. Permanent-media sand filters are predominantly employed in fountain installations because of their reduced maintenance requirements.

## BIOLOGICAL FILTERS

In ponds or fountains where fish will be displayed, typical sand filters and swimming pool chemicals are not suitable water purification techniques. High rate sand filters are not designed to filter out algae by themselves. In addition, chlorine-based chemicals which remove algae are detrimental to the health of the fish.

Several alternate methods exist for controlling algae. The cheapest method involves pond aeration, high rate sand filters and Israeli carp.

The carp eat the algae while the sand filter removes dirt deposited in the water. In addition, the aeration maintains oxygen in the water, which can be depleted when algae blooms are created.

The optimal filter system for 'Koi' or other fountain fish employs a two-stage biological filter, air induction stones, settlement tank, and sand filter. When utilized, this system will adequately remove direct and algae from the fountain or lake.

The operation of this sytem employs a gravity fed settlement tank which removes mud and other large dirt particles from the lake. This water is then directed to a mechanical and biological filter. The biological filter contains filter trays consisting of bacteria which remove algae. Air stones are located in these filters to provide oxygen to the bacteria. Before the water returns to the fountain, or lake, the water passes through a high rate sand filter to remove suspended solids.

In some systems the biological filter is as simple as a gravity fed tank which is filled with bio-rings. This system is similar to biological filters used for public water systems or aquariums. The net result of the filter system is to remove algae without using chlorine or algaecide.

## OPERATION OF FILTER SYSTEMS

Most filter pumps are designed to operate 24 hours a day. In some commercial swimming pool applications, the pool filter and pump run non-stop, as required by code. Fountain filtration is less demanding due to the lack of human contact. In these instances, the filter system is manually operated or controlled by a timer. Typically, fountain and swimming pool filter systems are designed to turn over the total pool gallonage within a 6 to 8 hour period depending on health codes. In most instances, local health codes do not require fountains to have filter systems unless they are being used as wading pools. Filtering the same size pool or fountain in a 6 hour period versus an 8 hour period would require a larger diameter sand filter. The extra energy cost required by this larger filter system can be offset by allowing the pool

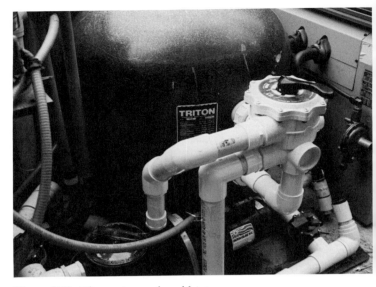

**Figure 3.59** *Filter system and pool heater.*

**Figure 3.60** *Multi-port or backwash valve.*

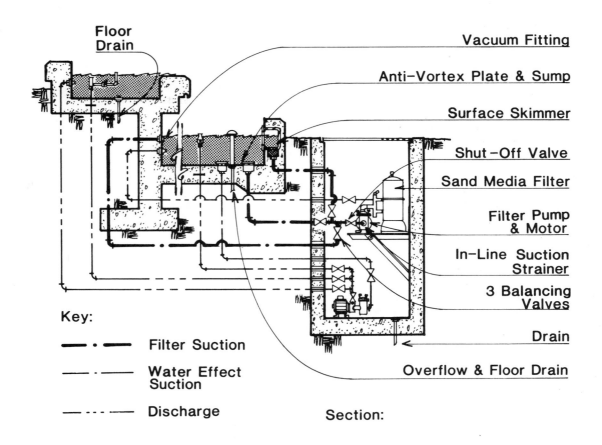

Floor Drain

Vacuum Fitting

Anti-Vortex Plate & Sump

Surface Skimmer

Shut-Off Valve

Sand Media Filter

Filter Pump & Motor

In-Line Suction Strainer

3 Balancing Valves

Drain

Overflow & Floor Drain

Key:

—— · —— Filter Suction

—— · —— Water Effect Suction

—— ·· —— Discharge

Section:

**Figure 3.61**      **Suction Line of Filter Pump**

operator to backwash less frequently and by providing the facility with clearer water.

### PURCHASE OF FILTRATION SYSTEMS

When specifying filter tanks and pumps, the designer should select equipment which is locally stocked or can be acquired within 2 to 4 days. Equipment failure, typically involves the pump and motor.

Pumps which have locally stocked replacement parts alleviate extensive downtime of the fountain. This is very critical in indoor applications or outdoor applications in summer. Filter system failure can cause algae or dirt accumulation in the fountain.

### Filter Suction Line

The suction line of a filter system will contain an anti-vortex plate and sump, a surface skimmer, a vacuum fitting, pipe, fittings, suction balancing valves, a suction shut-off valve, and an in-line strainer. In a multi-level pool, a surface skimmer or anti-vortex plate and sump should be installed in the basin with the lowest elevation. Bottom pools are normally larger than the combined upper pools and become

holding structures for the operating water of the upper pools when the fountain system is shut down.

On hot windy days, it may be necessary to shut down the fountain effects system and only operate the filter system. By locating the suction line of the filter system in the floor of the lowest pool (generally the largest), the greatest amount of water can be filtered. In upper level pools, where eyeballs or nozzles are required to feed weirs or spill lips, filter suction lines may reduce the amount of water designed to flow over the weir and diminish the desired water effect.

### Anti-vortex Plate and Sump

An anti-vortex plate and sump are used in a filter system to encourage proper circulation and to supply water to the filter. This device should be centrally located away from the anti-vortex plate and sump of the water effects system. Isolated locations will reduce competition between the two suction lines and ensure proper pump performance. One anti-vortex plate and sump should be installed for every 2,000 square feet of pool surface area. If trapped water areas exist, additional anti-vortex plates and sumps should be provided. Pools with a plan view shape of a capital 'E' or 'T' are particularly hard to circulate, and additional suction lines will be needed.

## Surface Skimmer

A surface skimmer is installed on the suction line of the filter pump. This device is used to collect surface debris before they sink to the bottom of the pool or enter the suction line. Skimmers operate with a suction capacity of about 30 gpm; they create enough suction to produce a slight surface movement towards the opening of the skimmer. Surface movement of the water will attract debris to the removable trash basket of the skimmer.

When installing skimmers, one skimmer should be provided for every 800 to 1000 square feet of pool surface area.[100]

By locating the skimmer in the direction of the prevailing wind, surface debris can be collected more quickly. Skimmer units are available with a front or top access to the trash basket. Top access units are easily reached but may be visually distracting to some designers. Periodic cleaning of the trash basket should be considered as part of the maintenance schedule.

Top access units are available in standard and deep-throated models. The deep-throated models are preferable in swimming pool construction because the access top can be located in the deck rather than the pool coping. Most top access models normally have a built-in adaptor which allows insertion of the vacuum tube. This alleviates the need for a separate vacuum fitting for pool vacuuming. Additional skimmers beyond recommendations will prevent dirt from settling to the bottom. This will ensure clearer water. An increase in pump size may be required to power the additional skimmers.

## Vacuum Fitting

A vacuum fitting is an optional device installed on the suction line of the filter to aid in removal of silt from the fountain floor. This fitting is normally centrally located and is placed 6 inches below the water level. A removable plug allows a portable hose and brush to be inserted into the plug. The suction created in this line allows floor cleaning without draining the pool.

Vacuum fittings are often incorporated into the skimmer. Check with the skimmer manufacturer before specifying a separate vacuum fitting.

## Suction Balancing Valves

A gate, butterfly or globe valve may be necessary to balance the capacity of each suction device. When separate lines are run from the pump to the fountain, the shortest pipe will be favored with the greatest amount of water.[101] The addition of a balancing valve will enable the proper proportioning of water entering a suction device.

## Suction Shut-off Valve and In-line Suction Strainer

As described in the fountain effects system, a suction shut-off valve and an in-line strainer will be needed in the

**Figure 3.62** *Rough-in of skimmer in gunite pool wall.*

suction line. Before specifying a separate in-line strainer to protect the pump impeller, check the manufacturer's data to see if the filter pump is already fitted with a built-in strainer.

## FILTER SHUT-OFF VALVES

Metal gate valves should not be used as shut off valves for filtration systems. Frequent operation during backwash operations tends to wear out these valves. PVC ball valves or PVC diversion type valves are best suited for this application. The plastic components of these valves allow continual use without evidence of wear.

## Filter Discharge Line

The discharge line of the filter and pump will consist of a discharge shut-off valve, pipe, fittings, and eyeball(s). The filtering systems of multi-level pools should have their discharge lines connected into the lowest fountain basin. The preferred practice is to recirculate filter water out of the lowest basin of a multi-level fountain. Typically, this is the largest body of water of the fountain and will provide the most benefit of filtration in situations where the water effects pump is not run in conjunction with the filter.

## Discharge Shut-off Valve and Eyeball

As described in the fountain effects system, the discharge line will contain a discharge shut-off valve and eyeball(s). Consult that section for further information on these devices.

## AUTOMATIC FLOOR SWEEPING SYSTEMS

Filter systems can be combined with automatic floor sweeping systems to alleviate or reduce the need to vacuum the pool or fountain floor. These systems are known in the trade as "Pool Valet," "Caretaker," and "Turbo Clean." All three systems consist of floor sweeping heads and a water valve or distribution head.

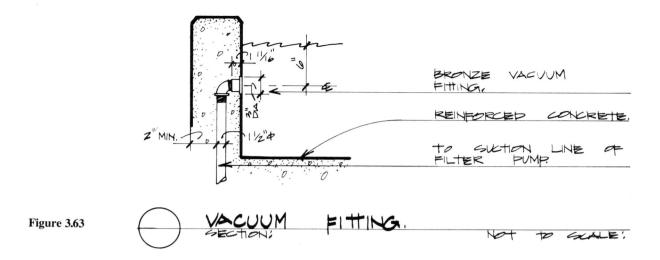

**Figure 3.63** VACUUM FITTING.
SECTION:                                    NOT TO SCALE:

BRONZE VACUUM FITTING.

REINFORCED CONCRETE.

TO SUCTION LINE OF FILTER PUMP.

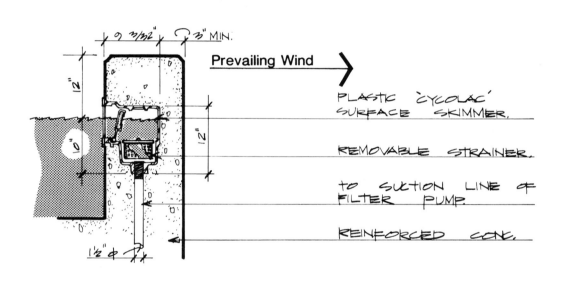

Prevailing Wind

PLASTIC 'CYCOLAC' SURFACE SKIMMER.

REMOVABLE STRAINER.

TO SUCTION LINE OF FILTER PUMP.

REINFORCED CONC.

**Figure 3.64** SIDE WALL SKIMMER
SECTION:                                    NOT TO SCALE:

When utilized, these systems return filtered water to the distribution head. This device contains a water rotor and four outlet pipes. When water enters the distribution head, water pressure moves the rotor and individually directs water to one of the outlet pipes. As water is individually directed to each outlet pipe, these pipes supply water to the floor sweeping heads. Each sweeping head elevates and sprays water against the floor. When the distribution head changes position, the floor sweep pops down and resets its position slightly to the right of its previous position. The outlet pipes of the distribution head are piped so that the floor sweeping heads are sequenced to push the floor dirt from the shallow end of the pool to the deep end of the pool. This dirt is then picked up by the main drain which is installed at this lower location.

### Sizing the Filter

Filter systems should be designed to recirculate the entire volume of the pool water in 6 to 10 hours.[102] If a pool contains 6000 gallons of water, and the whole volume is to be recirculated in 6 hours, the pump and filter must be able to circulate 1000 gallons per hour or 16.6 gallons per minute.

$$\frac{\text{Total pool gallons}}{\text{Number of hours to recirculate}} = \text{Gallons to circulate in one hour.}$$

$$\frac{6000 \text{ gallons}}{6 \text{ hours}} = 1000 \text{ gallons/hour}$$

$$\frac{\text{Gallons to circulate in 1 hour}}{60 \text{ minutes per one hour}} = \text{Gallons per minute to recirculate}$$

$$\frac{1000 \text{ gal./hour}}{60 \text{ min./hour}} = 16.6 \text{ gallons/minute}$$

Some texts and manufacturers recommend the sizing of the filter in respect to surface square footage. When using this method, 3 to 4 square feet of filter media should be supplied for every 1000 surface square feet of water.[103] The operating time required to filter the fountain water will be affected by the water temperature, geographic location, season, and dirt present in the air. Automatic controls should be provided on a filter system to account for the fluctuating length of filter operation.

## Additional Water Treatment

In addition to filtering, other water treatment may be required. Periodic maintenance is mandatory on all fountains. This requirement should not be neglected in the planning stages.

As exemplified by Roman Fountains, a good maintenance program for a fountain without a filter system may call for draining and restocking with fresh water every 3 to 6 weeks. This depends on the accumulation of dirt, season of the year, and the geographic location of the fountain.

## Sterilization Chemicals

Algae and bacteria can be a problem in water less than 3 feet deep. Water depths of 3 feet and over seldom contain algae.[104] Chlorine and algaecide are chemicals often used to prevent the algae growth. Chlorine needs to be replenished more quickly in fountains than in swimming pool applications. The water and chlorine mixture, which is propelled into the air by the nozzle, disseminates them into fine streams and releases the chlorine as a gas. If not replenished, algae will begin to grow.

Chlorine is extremely harmful to plant materials. When plant materials are adjacent to a fountain, they must be protected from chlorinated water. If splash and fountain mist cannot be restricted, plant-safe sterilization chemicals such as Consan should be substituted.[105]

Other suitable chemicals for water sterilization include ozone, bromine, chlorine dioxide, and metallic ions.

## SUPER CHLORINATING WATER

Clarity of water and algae infestation of fountain water can be improved by super-chlorinating the water. When this operation is performed, excess chlorine-based chemicals are added to the water to shock and kill the algae content and clarify the water. The increased parts per million of chlorine-based chemicals will eventually dissipate due to sun exposure or aeration. Over-chlorinated water typically has a burning chlorine smell which is unpleasant to the nose.

### Hard Water

As water evaporates, chemicals and minerals increase in concentration in the fountain basin. These elements are retained in solution in the remaining fountain water. If hard water is used to refill this lost water, the mineral concentration will increase. These dissolved minerals can build up in pipes and nozzles and reduce water flow or stain the basin. When hard water is used to fill the fountain, periodic draining and replenishing with fresh water will prevent these minerals from clogging the nozzles.

### Water pH

Water pH in fountains containing fish or water plants must be balanced. A pH of 7.0 to 7.2 is preferable.[106] If the pH climbs into the alkaline range, plants and fish will die. High water pH can be reduced by adding muriatic acid, sulfuric acid, hydrochloric acid, or sodium bisulfate. On the other hand, if water pH is too acid, soda ash, sodium carbonate, caustic soda or sodium hydroxide can be used to raise the pH. Care should be taken when pouring chemicals directly onto fish. If at all possible relocate fish while balancing water pH.

### Water Level Control Devices

Water level control and drainage devices are needed in fountains to replenish lost water, prevent basin overflow, and enable ease of drainage for cleaning and winterization.

### Water Level Controls

The water depth of a fountain will diminish because of surface evaporation and splash. This fall in the water level is detrimental to pool items such as lights, nozzles, and submersible pumps which require a minimum water cover for their proper operation. Small pools containing several hundred gallons of water can be manually replenished with a garden hose, but fountains containing large volumes of water should contain an automatic filling device.

Water level control devices are fed by a fresh water supply. This line is normally connected directly to a water meter on the main line or to a waterline of an adjacent building. These control devices are similar in concept to the filling system of a water closet. A float connected to a valve on the fresh water line allows the valve to open when the water level drops. When the pool level reaches a height set by the

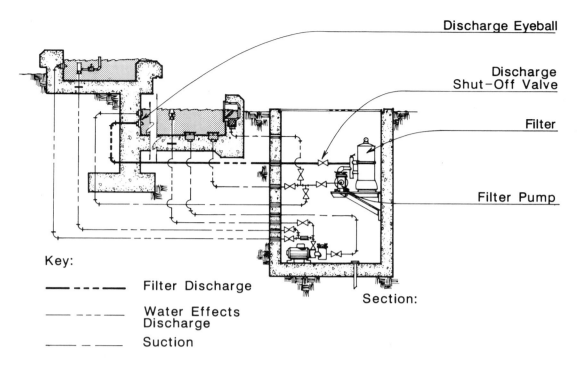

Discharge Eyeball

Discharge
Shut-Off Valve

Filter

Filter Pump

Key:

— — – – – — Filter Discharge

——— – – – —— Water Effects
Discharge

——— – – —— Suction

Section:

**Figure 3.65**     ## Discharge Line of Filter System

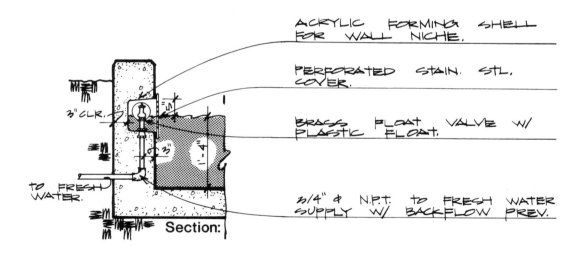

ACRYLIC FORMING SHELL
FOR WALL NICHE.

PERFORATED STAIN. STL.
COVER.

BRASS FLOAT VALVE W/
PLASTIC FLOAT.

3/4" ∅ N.P.T. TO FRESH WATER
SUPPLY W/ BACKFLOW PREV.

3" CLR.

to FRESH
WATER.

3"

4"

Section:

**Figure 3.66**     ## Float Valve Water Level Control

111

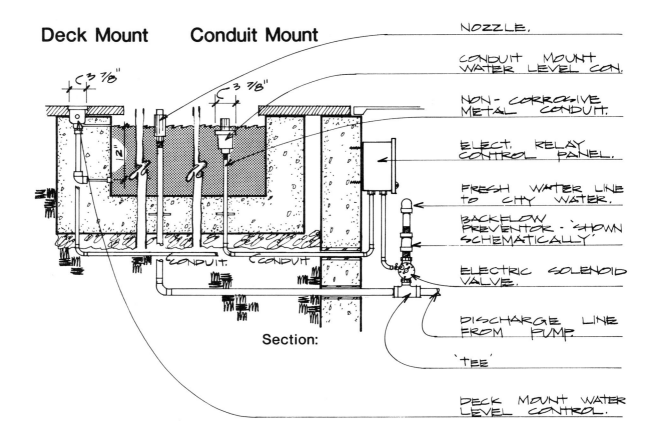

**Deck Mount**    **Conduit Mount**

NOZZLE.

CONDUIT MOUNT WATER LEVEL CON.

NON-CORROSIVE METAL CONDUIT.

ELECT. RELAY CONTROL PANEL.

FRESH WATER LINE TO CITY WATER.

BACKFLOW PREVENTOR - SHOWN SCHEMATICALLY.

ELECTRIC SOLENOID VALVE.

DISCHARGE LINE FROM PUMP.

'TEE'

DECK MOUNT WATER LEVEL CONTROL.

Section:

**Figure 3.67**    **Probe Type Water Level Control**

designer, the float closes the valve on the fresh water supply. The following devices are employed to maintain appropriate water levels:

*Float controls* are normally located in a concealed niche in the fountain wall. Float controls are constructed of plastic floats, acrylic, and brass valves. A fresh water connection needs to be run to the valve in the wall niche. These devices are normally not used in large fountains because they require a substantial water drop to open the valve. Pools having a surface area of over 700 square feet should not employ this device to maintain water levels.[107]

Turbulent water created by waterfalls and aerating nozzles may rock the float valve and continually open and close the supply valve. By providing a perforated cover over the wall niche, fluctuation of the water level is reduced. This cover also keeps the float out of sight and protected from vandals.

Float valves will allow minor adjustments after installation. The opening position of the valve should be installed in reference to the operating level instead of the static water level. This will prevent unnecessary pool filling when the fountain level drops due to pump initiation.

*Probe-type water level control devices* consist of a probe box, a relay control panel, and a solenoid fill valve. When the water level drops ½ of an inch, a probe sends a low

voltage current to the 110 volt relay panel. The panel in turn sends a low voltage current to an electrically operated solenoid valve. This current opens the valve, allowing fresh water to enter the fountain. When the water height reaches a prescribed height set by the designer, another probe set at a higher level signals the valve to close. In this type of installation, the probe box is located in or directly adjacent to the pool. The relay panel and electrical valve are located in the equipment vault. The electric fill valve is sized by the designer to achieve the proper water capacity. These valves, which introduce fresh water into the system, are normally hooked into the discharge line of the water effects system on the pump side of the balancing valve.

A recommendation by Kim Fountains is to incorporate the electric valve with a quick fill valve, a pipe by-pass, and a direct line into the fountain. This allows for automatic control and fast manual refilling of the fountain.

Both conduit and deck mount models allow for field adjustment of the probe heights. Conduit-mounted models should not be used in areas where vandalism is prevalent (See Figures 3.67 and 3.68).

*Mecury float switch control* consists of a hermetically sealed mercury float switch, a wall niche, and an electrical fill valve (See Figure 3.69).

112

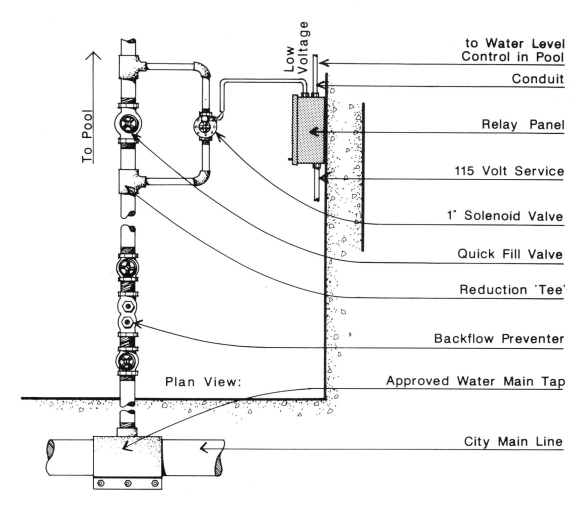

Low Voltage

to Water Level Control in Pool

Conduit

Relay Panel

115 Volt Service

1" Solenoid Valve

Quick Fill Valve

Reduction 'Tee'

Backflow Preventer

Approved Water Main Tap

City Main Line

To Pool

Plan View:

**Figure 3.68**

## Pump Vault Layout for Water Level Control Device

**Figure 3.69** *Mercury float switch.*

This system has the advantages of both the float control and the probe control and should be used where large bodies of dirty water are anticipated. As the water level changes, the float switch acts as a normal light switch and either opens or closes an electric circuit. As the water level drops, the mercury switch closes and supplies power to the electric valve. This allows the fresh water to flow into the pool until the float rises enough to open the mercury switch in the float.

**Backflow Prevention**

Since the water level control device is connected to the potable water supply of a city or other utility system, it is necessary to install a backflow prevention device. This device is regulated by local plumbing codes and prevents accidental siphoning of the fountain water into the potable water system.

Atmospheric vacuum breakers, pressure-type vacuum breakers, air gaps, double check assemblers, and reduced pressure principal devices are all used to prevent backflow. Local plumbing codes will dictate appropriate types and location.

## DRAIN DOWN PIPING

In multi-level fountains, providing piping associated with individual floor drains for each level can be costly. A cost effective method of draining each level can be provided by using a drain down line or a drain valve and line at the pump room.

In the application of the drain down line, a floor return and short pipe section are connected from the floor of the highest level to the wall of the level below. The wall outlet should be provided with a threaded screw cap or a threaded vacuum fitting. When draining is required, the fitting is unscrewed, allowing the upper basin to flow into the lower basin (See Figure 3.70). During this operation, care should be taken to prevent overflowing of the bottom basin.

If floor returns or anti-vortex plates are used to supply water to upper levels of a multi-level fountain, they can also be used to drain the fountain. A drain line and valve should be plumbed into the return line beyond the check valve. This line will allow the draining of the line and upper basin when the drain valve is opened. Care should be taken to place the drain line on the fountain side of the check valve so that positive flow will be created (See Figure 3.71).

This line should be connected into the sanitary sewer. In situations where back-up of this water would create damage to the pump room or adjacent habitable space other drainage methods should be used.

## Overflow Drains

Overflow drains are used to maintain a constant water level during heavy rains or excessive filling. One overflow drain is normally installed in a fountain.

When an overflow drain is installed in a multi-level pool, one overflow drain is located in every static basin (basin not containing a weir or other method to prevent uncontrolled overflow).

Multi-level pools, which empty water into lower basins by weirs or waterfalls, require only one overflow device as excessive water from rain will flow over the weir and be deposited into the lowest basin. The overflow device should be located at a height above the static water level. Once the fountain pumps are shut off, the level in the lowest pool will rise. This water increase permits operation of the pump and nozzles. If the overflow device is set at the operating level instead of the static water level, the operating water will be lost through the overflow device. When the pump is restarted, the lowered water level signals the control device to refill the basin. In instances where the pool will be frequently turned on and off, water will be wasted by this improper installation (See Figures 3.72, 3.73 and 3.74).

Overflow drains are constructed of brass, copper and/or cast bronze, and may contain a chrome-plated or stainless steel grill. Some manufacturers produce overflow drains which permit minor water level adjustments after the device is installed. Overflow devices are commercially available in two types.

*Overflow drain* contains a field adjustable standpipe which can be removed to drain the basin. This device extends above the water level and may be objectionable to some designers. Location of the standpipe should be away from turbulent water created by waterfalls or aerating nozzles.

*Sidewall Overflow Drain* is mounted flush with the side of the wall. This device requires a separate floor drain. Sidewall drains which allow level adjustments after installation are preferable. These consist of an interior shielded standpipe which allows water level adjustment after construction.

These pipes should be drained to a sanitary or storm sewer. Local plumbing codes should be checked to determine the appropriate connection.

## Floor Drain

All fountain basins which retain water must be provided with a floor drain or other drainage device. Fountains with pools on several levels will require a floor drain on each level enabling the basins to be drained for cleaning and/or winterizing.

The floor drain should be situated at the lowest elevation in the floor. A two percent floor slope towards the drain will ensure completely gravity drainage of the basin.

Pools, which are winterized to prevent damage during freeze-thaw cycles, should keep their floor drain in an open position. This will remove most of the free moisture (winter precipitation) and prevent water absorption by the basin material. Floor drains should be constructed of cast bronze and/or brass and include the following varieties:

*Floor drain* with removable closure cap or control valve. Drainage is to sanitary or storm sewer. (Check plumbing codes.)

*Overflow Drain* serves as a floor drain and overflow pipe. The standpipe is threaded and allows removal at the basin floor to permit drainage.

*Drain and Suction* or combined suction screen and drain. Water must flow through the suction line into the equipment vault to drain the pool. The suction line must be lower than the pool floor and must also slope towards the equipment vault. A drainage valve on the suction line empties the suction line into a drain line within the equipment pit.

## Backflow Preventors

Plumbing codes, height of the water table and elevation of the water basin being filled dictate the location of this device. Normally a backflow preventor is located above grade in an enclosure. Depending on the height relationship of the backflow preventor to the basin being filled, the device may be located below grade in a utility vault.

In all cases, the device must be located in an accessible and un-backfilled area which allows for drainage and testing of the device. Consult local plumbing codes to determine the proper location.

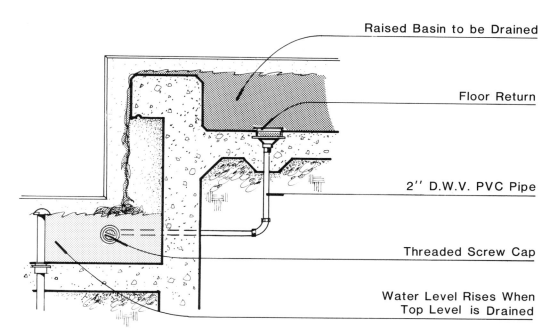

Raised Basin to be Drained

Floor Return

2'' D.W.V. PVC Pipe

Threaded Screw Cap

Water Level Rises When
Top Level is Drained

**Figure 3.70**        **Drain Down Line**

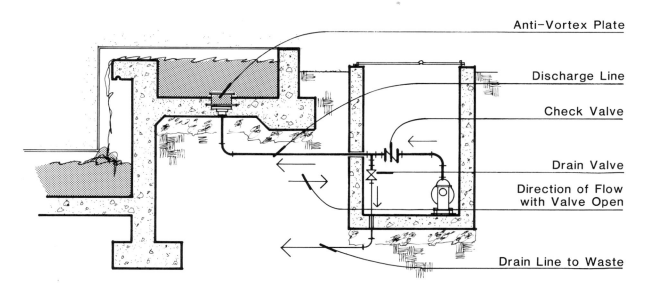

Anti-Vortex Plate

Discharge Line

Check Valve

Drain Valve

Direction of Flow
with Valve Open

Drain Line to Waste

**Figure 3.71**        **Drain Line**

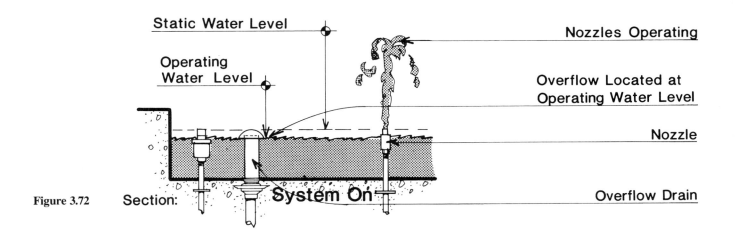

Static Water Level

Operating Water Level

Nozzles Operating

Overflow Located at Operating Water Level

Nozzle

**Figure 3.72** Section: System On

Overflow Drain

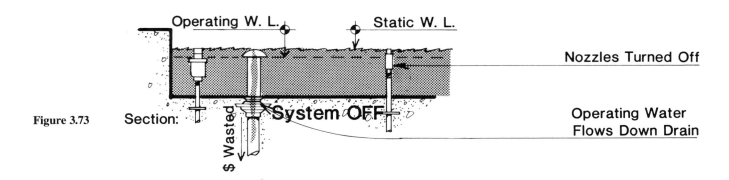

Operating W. L.

Static W. L.

Nozzles Turned Off

**Figure 3.73** Section: System OFF

$ Wasted

Operating Water Flows Down Drain

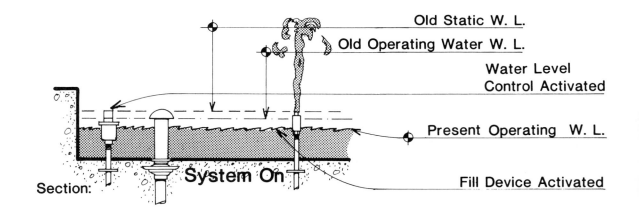

Old Static W. L.

Old Operating Water W. L.

Water Level Control Activated

Present Operating W. L.

**Figure 3.74** Section: System On

Fill Device Activated

## Improper Height Location of Overflow Drain

### Side Wall Mounted        Stand-Pipe Mounted

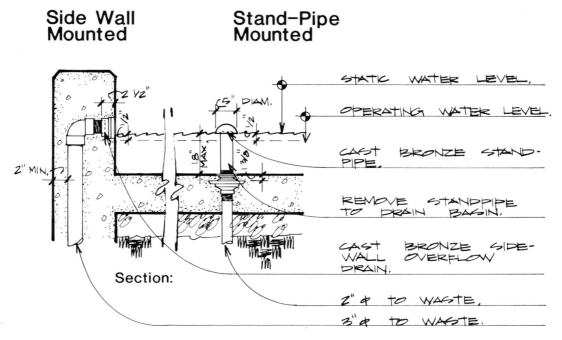

STATIC WATER LEVEL.

OPERATING WATER LEVEL.

CAST BRONZE STAND-PIPE.

REMOVE STANDPIPE TO DRAIN BASIN.

CAST BRONZE SIDE-WALL OVERFLOW DRAIN.

2" Ø TO WASTE.

3" Ø TO WASTE.

2 ½"

5" DIAM.

2" MIN.

Section:

**Figure 3.75**          **Types of Overflow Drains**

### Combination Anti-Vortex & Sump and Drain Valve

### Floor Mounted

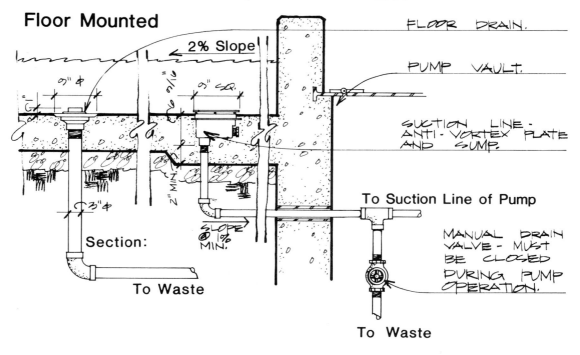

FLOOR DRAIN.

PUMP VAULT.

SUCTION LINE - ANTI-VORTEX PLATE AND SUMP.

2% Slope

To Suction Line of Pump

MANUAL DRAIN VALVE - MUST BE CLOSED DURING PUMP OPERATION.

Section:

To Waste

SLOPE @ 1% MIN.

To Waste

**Figure 3.76**          **Types of Floor Drains**

**Table 3.6  Appropriate Location for Fountain Mechanical Devices**

| | | | Multi-Level Fountains | | Single Level Fountains |
|---|---|---|---|---|---|
| | | | Highest Basin | Lowest Basin | |
| Water Efects System | Suction Line | Skimmer | No | No[2] | No[2] |
| | | Vacuum Fitting | No | No | No |
| | | Anti-vortex Plate or Suction Screen | No | Yes | Yes |
| | Discharge Line | Eyeball | Yes[3] | No | No |
| | | Nozzle | Yes | Yes | Yes |
| Filter System | Suction Line | Skimmer | No | Yes | Yes |
| | | Vacuum Fitting | 4 | 4 | Yes[5] |
| | | Anti-vortex Plate or Suction Screen | No[6] | Yes | Yes |
| | Discharge Line | Eyeball | No | Yes | Yes |
| | | Nozzle | No | No | No |
| Water Level Control Devices | | Water Level Controls | No | Yes | Yes |
| | | Overflow Drain | No | Yes[7] | Yes[7] |
| | | Floor Drain | Yes[8] | Yes[8] | Yes |

1. *Applies to fountains with level changes which empty into the lowest basin by weirs or water walls.*
2. *A skimmer should only be considered on the suction line of a water effects pump where the fountain is small and contains no filter devices; a skimmer will remove surface litter.*
3. *An eyeball or other discharge device may be needed to supply water for a weir.*
4. *An optional fitting used to sweep the pool floor. If installed, it should be centrally located for access to all basins.*
5. *Optional fitting — see above.*
6. *Consider only in situations where circulation is impaired by constricting shapes.*
7. *If this device is combined with a floor drain, no additional device is needed.*
8. *One floor drain for every basin.*

# 4

# ELECTRICAL SYSTEM

The installation of the fountain electrical system should conform to Article 680 of the National Electrical Code's latest printing. The following information should familiarize the designer with the terms and problems associated with the electrical system of a fountain. Additional research and technical help should be sought. The design of the electrical system should be carried out by a qualified person.

Electricity in contact with water is extremely dangerous consequently a ground-fault circuit interrupter (GFCI) should be installed in the branch circuit supplying fountain equipment. This will reduce the potential for electrical shock.

Electrical service is required for the:

1. Motor of the water effects pump.
2. Motor and timer of the filter system.
3. Timer or programmer to regulate the fountain or lighting.
4. Wind control panel.
5. Low water cut-offs.
6. Water level controls other than a float control.
7. Lighting.

## Ground-Fault Circuit Interrupter

A ground-fault circuit interrupter (GFCI) is designed to open an electrical circuit before an adult or child would receive energy sufficient for electrocution.[108] These devices open the circuit when there is a 5mA current between the ground and the electrical device.

In addition to a GFCI, a fuse system will be required on the circuit. A fuse protects the circuit in situations where two wires may cross but requires substantially more current than a GFCI senses to break the circuit. Normally, fuse systems are rated at 15 to 20 amps for a 120 volt system and at 30 to 200 amps for a 230 volt system. A fuse system should not be confused with the GFCI. The fuse system is intended for protection from accidental crossing of the positive and negative poles. When wires cross, a fuse system breaks the circuit before the wires generate enough heat to cause a fire. If a person touches the negative and positive poles of a fused circuit, the circuit will be completed, amperage is created; the electricity will seek a ground (earth); and the person will receive a shock. In this situation, if the person was standing in fountain water, the increased conductivity of the water would prevent the person from escaping the completed circuit.

When a circuit is protected by a GFCI, any minute current between a person and the ground will break the circuit. The effectiveness of a GFCI has been proven by many demonstrations of individuals wetting their fingers and inserting them into a light socket. Once witnessed, a person will not forget the GFCI's importance.

Because of the conductivity of water, it is necessary to include a GFCI in fountain installations. The location of a GFCI is regulated by the National Electric Code Article 680 which requires a GFCI in branch circuits supplying fountain equipment of 15 volts or more.[109]

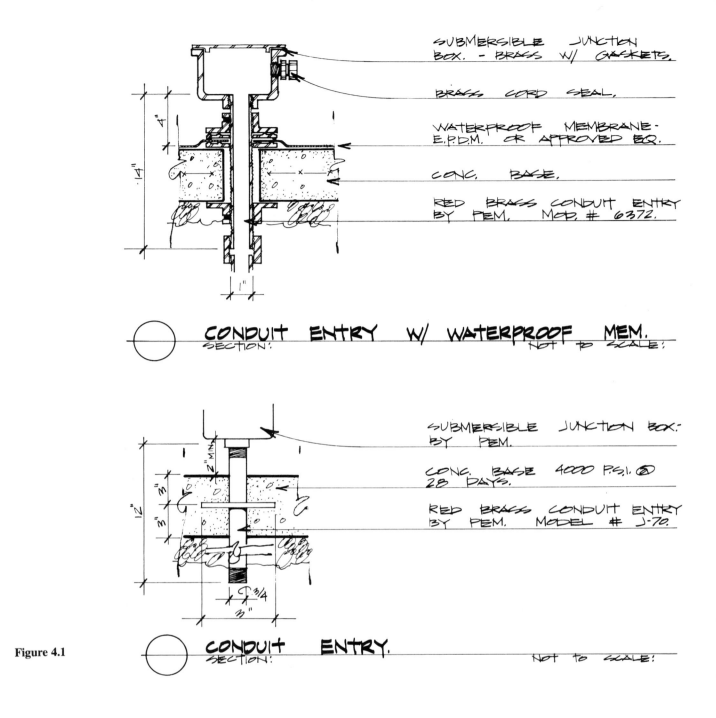

**Figure 4.1**

CONDUIT ENTRY W/ WATERPROOF MEM.
SECTION:
NOT TO SCALE!

SUBMERSIBLE JUNCTION BOX. - BRASS W/ GASKETS.

BRASS CORD SEAL.

WATERPROOF MEMBRANE - E.P.D.M. OR APPROVED EQ.

CONC. BASE.

RED BRASS CONDUIT ENTRY BY PEM. MOD. # 6372.

CONDUIT ENTRY.
SECTION:
NOT TO SCALE!

SUBMERSIBLE JUNCTION BOX: BY PEM.

CONC. BASE 4000 P.S.I. @ 28 DAYS.

RED BRASS CONDUIT ENTRY BY PEM. MODEL # J-70.

## Conduit

Conduit which penetrates the fountain wall should be of a corrosive-resistant material (PVC or corrosive-resistant metal). Conduits which penetrate the wall are normally of red brass or copper alloy and must have pipe collars around them to prevent water seepage.

The following examples are several commercially available entry conduits (See Figure 4.1).

All metal conduit and other metal equipment must be grounded to a common bonding grid (steel reinforcing) and will comply with Article 680 of the National Electrical Code. Provide a corrosion-resistant coating on brass or copper alloy conduit when the conduit will be in contact with concrete.

## Submersible Junction Boxes

All underwater junction boxes and other underwater enclosures should comply with Article 680 of the National Electrical Code. When a fountain is incorporated into a swimming pool, the total project is considered a swimming pool, and requires junction boxes and other devices to meet the requirements outlined for swimming pool installations. (Swimming pool standards vary from fountain standards.)

All junction boxes should be of brass, copper, or other

**Figure 4.2** *Submersible junction box.*

approved corrosion-resistant material. These junction boxes are to be equipped with provisions for threaded conduit entries, compression glands, or seals for cord entry. When the junction box is supported by the conduit, the conduit should be copper, brass, or other approved corrosion-resistant metal. To prevent accidental entry of moisture, the junction box should be filled with an approved potting compound. When installing a junction box, the position and location should comply with Article 680 of the National Electrical Code.

## DOUBLE ENTRY JUNCTION BOXES

Freestanding submerged junction boxes with more than one conduit entry require thought and consideration before constructing the fountain floor. Threaded conduit connections on multiple pipes make it impossible to thread the conduit into the junction box after pouring of the concrete floor.

Proper material purchase schedules and/or installation of a threaded slip fitting into the J-box and then brazing this assembly to the vertical conduit will alleviate any problems.

### Centrifugal Pumps

The motors of centrifugal pumps in water effects or filter systems should be wired into an approved junction box in the pump room.

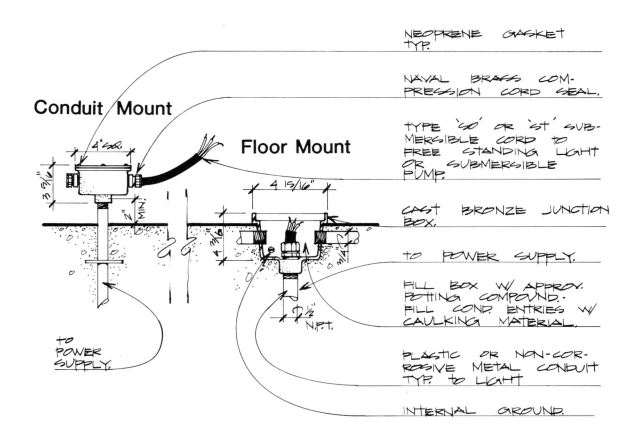

**Figure 4.3**    **Types of Submersible Junction Boxes**

121

In addition to the junction box, proper shut-off switches, timers, switch relays, contactors and/or motor starters should be specified as required to complete the electrical system.

## Submersible Pumps For Water Effects Systems

Motors of submersible pumps should be supplied with a water-resistant, flexible, grounded cord of 10 feet maximum length. This cord should be of the "SO" or "ST" type and should not be operated at greater than 300 volts.[110] This flexible cord should be wired into an approved submersible junction box. The end of the flexible cord jacket and the conductors of the flexible cord should be covered or encapsulated in a suitable potting material. Potting materials and threaded cord seals will prevent water from entering the junction box.

## Timers and Programmers

Timers can be employed to regulate the fountain's water effects, filter and lighting systems. Timers can be set to turn the fountain system on in the morning and off at night. Substantial energy savings are possible by running the fountain during peak pedestrian hours. Timers also free a manager or maintenance man from the daily routine of starting the fountain systems. As a means of ensuring safety, a timer can also be used to regulate the starting hours of the fountain lighting system.

Programmers are similar to timers in that they operate with a mechanical or electronic clock. However, programmers operate for shorter intervals of time and are traditionally used to frequently change various lighting patterns or water effects of the fountain.

When employed to regulate lighting, the programmer activates various color schemes for the fountain. A red light may stay on for only 2 minutes, then the programmer may turn on a blue light for a prescribed time interval, thus creating a volatile nighttime mood.

As a water effects regulator, the programmer is used in conjunction with a low voltage transformer and electric solenoid valves. As the programmer goes through its sequence, the valves are instructed to open or close, changing the water display.

## Wind Control Devices

Two-stage wind control devices include a wind speed sensor head, a control panel, and an electric solenoid valve.

The wind sensor head is mounted on a building or pole at the maximum height of the water effects,[111] while the control panel is located in the equipment vault. This panel allows the designer to program two wind speeds into the panel's memory.

When the sensor detects a moderate wind speed, the low voltage sensor head sends an impulse to the control panel. At this time, the control panel activates an electrical solenoid valve which reduces the discharge capacity. The reduced discharge will lower splash outside the basin.

**Figure 4.4** *Submersible pump.*

**Figure 4.5** *Sequence of water heights controlled by a programmer. Ponca City, Oklahoma.*

**Figure 4.6** *Sequence of water heights controlled by a programmer. Ponca City, Oklahoma.*

**Figure 4.7** *Sequence of water heights controlled by a programmer. Ponca City, Oklahoma.*

**Figure 4.8** *Low water cut-off and submersible junction box.*

As the wind speed increases and reaches the higher velocity set by the designer, the control panel will interrupt the circuit operating the fountain effects. This turns the system off until wind speeds diminish to the rate at which splash will not be transported out of the basin.

A one-stage wind control unit is similar to a two-stage device, except that it only allows one wind speed setting. When the wind reaches this velocity, the system is either interrupted or the discharge rate is restricted by a solenoid valve.

### Low Water Cut-offs

Low water cut-offs are required in fountains which contain lights, submersible pumps or other equipment which depend on submersion for their safe operation. These devices are required by Article 680 of the National Electrical Code.

Low water cut-offs consist of a 10 to 12 volt probe box and a 120 volt relay box. The probe box is inserted into the pool wall or onto a conduit mount from the pool floor. All materials should be of a noncorrosive material. Material employed for the conduit construction is predominantly red brass.

When the PVC conduit is employed as a mount for the probe box, additional noncorrosive metal supports must be provided.[112] This is necessary because of the brittleness of the PVC pipe.

In the event of a drop in water level, the low voltage probe sends a message to the 120 volt relay panel which in turn shuts the system off. By turning the system off, overheating of equipment can be prevented (See Figure 4.8).

In lake fountains and other applications where dirty water exists, traditional low water cut-off probes are unsuitable for use. Dirty water tends to foul the probes or floats associated with these devices. Alternate low-water cut-offs such as mercury float switches should be used.

### Electric Low Water Control Device

A low voltage electric water level control consists of a control panel, solenoid valve, and a sensing probe. The control panel is normally located in the equipment vault and has a primary current of 120 volts. The sensing probe is located in the fountain wall or on a conduit mount from the fountain floor and operates at 10 to 12 volts.

All materials used for construction should be noncorrosive. If PVC conduit is used to install the conduit-mounted model, additional noncorrosive metal supports must be provided.

As the water level drops, the probe closes the circuit and instructs the control panel to open a solenoid feed valve on the potable water system. The electrical valve is operated by 10 to 24 volts and will stay in an open position as long as current is flowing through the solenoid.

### Lighting

Lighting for use in fountains is normally constructed from a noncorrosive metal such as bronze. Lights are available in high voltage and low voltage models.

High voltage models are normally operated by a 120 volt current. The National Electrical Code (Article 680-51b) limits the current to 150 volts maximum and requires the circuit to be protected by a GFCI.

Low voltage fountain lights normally operate at 12 volts of current. These lamps require a 120 volt transformer to step the current down to 12 volts. Lamps with less than 15 volts current do not require a GFCI (Article 680-51a).

Lights which are designed for underwater installation should be located below the water level (normally 2 inches). Underwater lights are normally sealed to prevent water from entering the lamp.

Although these seals are watertight, substantial heat is generated. By maintaining watercover over the lamp, overheating can be prevented. To prevent a drop in water level while the lamp is on, it is necessary to provide a low water cut-off (Article 680-51d) to turn off the system when the water level drops. Lighting fixtures that face upward shall have an adequate guard over the lens to prevent contact with any person. This cast bronze grill also protects the lens and lamp from breakage.

Lights for fountains are normally installed using one of three methods: free standing, wet niche, or dry niche.

*Freestanding lights* have a flexible cord which connects the watertight body of the lamp to a submersible junction box. The lamp body is mounted on an adjustable yoke and base which allow adjustment in all directions. Freestanding lights permit the designer to field adjust the lighting after installation. Once the adjustment has been made, the light base should be anchored to the fountain floor with a noncorrosive anchor.

*Wet niche lights* are installed in a recessed niche that is flush with the floor or wall. These lights consist of a non-corrosive forming niche which is mounted into the wall or floor of the pool, a watertight flexible cord, and a noncorrosive watertight lamp body. The watertight body which conceals the lamp is connected to the niche by a flexible cord and cord seals. The flexible cord allows relamping of the watertight body without draining of the fountain. Because the lamp body, cord, and niche are all watertight, water is admitted between the niche and lamp body.

Wet niche lights are installed while the fountain basin is being constructed, and permit less field adjustment. When using this type of installation, select the basin location with care.

*Dry niche* lights are also installed in a recessed niche in the floor or wall of the fountain. This type of installation requires a watertight seal between the lamp body and niche. No water is permitted between the niche and the lamp body. A dry niche differs from a wet niche in that it requires a niche drain to remove water. Dry niche lights are somewhat of an inconvenience because they normally require fountain draining to relamp a fixture (See Figure 4.12).

**Figure 4.9** *Night lighting of a large spray ring. Boston, Massachusetts.*

**Figure 4.10** *Free-standing lights.*

**Figure 4.11** *Maze of electrical lines visible in the fountain basin.*

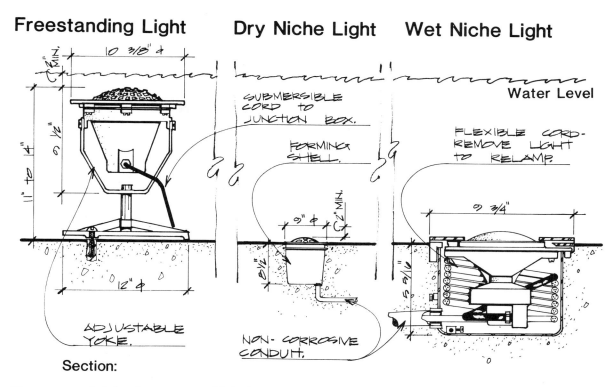

## Freestanding Light    Dry Niche Light    Wet Niche Light

Water Level

SUBMERSIBLE
CORD TO
JUNCTION BOX.

FORMING
SHELL.

FLEXIBLE CORD-
REMOVE LIGHT
TO RELAMP

ADJUSTABLE
YOKE.

NON- CORROSIVE
CONDUIT.

Section:

**Figure 4.12  Types of Underwater Lights**

**Figure 4.13** *Freestanding lights with plexiglass rock guard.*

## ROCK GUARDS

Glass lenses of vertically directed fountain lights are covered with rock guards to prevent accidental breakage of the glass. Rock guards are constructed of non-corrosive metal grilles or Plexiglas shields and are used to help prevent lens breakage and exposure of the interior light wires to the fountain water. In areas of high vandalism, stones can be thrown through the openings of some rock guards. In this application, a Plexiglas shield is more suited in preventing breakage of the light lens. Although Plexiglas shielding is more vandal-resistant, regular maintenance will be required to clean off chemical deposits (See Figure 4.13).

### Lamp Bulbs

The bulb selection for a light fixture will depend on light color, type, and height of the water effect.[113] Bulbs selected for use in fountains are normally incandescent or quartz. Incandescent and quartz bulbs create a white or off-white color. By providing a colored lens over the bulbs, various hues can be created. As a rule, colored lenses produce less candlepower than a clear lens, and will require higher wattage bulbs to provide the same footcandles as a clear lens.

As the height of the water increases, it is necessary to increase the candlepower output of the bulb. This is achieved by raising the bulb wattage. Table 4.1 gives general candlepower requirements for water heights. By comparing the required candlepower with the manufacturer's bulb specifications, the correct bulb wattage can be chosen.

**Table 4.1 Candlepower Required for Water Effects Height**

| Height of water effect in feet | Candlepower of bulbs[115] |
|:---:|:---:|
| 5 | 4000 |
| 10 | 11000 |
| 20 | 34000 |
| 30 | 69000 |
| 40 | 115000 |
| 50 | 170000 |

*For colored lenses, the required candlepower should be multiplied by the following conversion factors: Blue & Green x 3.5; Red x 2; Amber & Turquoise x 1.5.*

## ILLUMINATING NOZZLES

Nozzle water acts like fiber optics and draws light up the water coming from the nozzle. When the light is moved closer to the surface, a more intense lighting effect is achieved. In most applications, a freestanding light creates a better lighting effect than a floor-mounted light because there is less water for the light to pass through.

Bulbs should be selected so that beam spread complements the water spread from the nozzle. Wide, fluffy nozzles should be lighted with flood-type bulbs, while smooth bore nozzles should be lighted with spotlights. In situations where tall aerating type nozzles are used, combining spotlights with floodlights is extremely successful. By using both types of bulbs, the height and width of the nozzle water can be illuminated properly.

Each water display requires a different lighting method to achieve the desired effect. Spray rings and waterfalls require one wide-angle flood (per color) spaced at 4 to 5 increments for heights up to 15 feet.

For heights over 15 feet, medium floods should be spaced 2½ to 3 feet apart.[114] Lights should be directed so that the light will travel up the stream of water. Single nozzles require two spot lamps (per color) aimed in a vertical direction.

## WET NICHE WALL LIGHTS

Area lighting or basin illumination can be achieved by installing wet niche wall lights. These lights should be equally spaced along the basin wall and sized to provide one watt of light per square foot of surface water. This recommendation provides sufficient light to see the bottom of pools or fountains up to a 5-foot depth. Where subdued lighting is preferable, less bulb wattage should be specified.

Wall light location should be selected so the lights are not pointed towards the person viewing the fountain. High wattage bulbs create a hot spot which is very disturbing when directly viewed. A more subdued effect can be achieved by specifying additional lights of lower wattage. This should reduce the potential of bulb glare (See Figure 4.14).

## LIGHTING OF SWIMMING POOL FOUNTAINS

Several specific problems occur related to lighting of these installations. Area lighting of the swimming pool is preferable and is achieved through wall-mounted lights

**Figure 4.14** *Wet niche wall lights behind waterfall.*

pointed away from viewing areas. Waterfalls that empty directly into the fountain cannot be adequately or legally lighted from the pool with floor-mounted uplights. This is in violation of the electrical code and is best achieved through spotlights located away from the water's edge. Traditional fountain lights which incorporate freestanding lights and floor-mounted lights are best suited for illuminating the fountain feature itself.

National and local code research should be done prior to electrical design. Each municipality interprets the electrical code differently and may require the specific design application to comply with electrical standards for swimming pools and/or fountains. Each section of the electrical code has specific regulations with respect to allowable lights, junction boxes and methods of providing low-water cut-off protection. Each device is regulated differently. Interconnection of the swimming pool with the fountain does not alleviate your responsibility in complying with each individual code. In most uses, wall-mounted, low-voltage lighting will create fewer problems with code compliance and personal injury.

126

**Table 4.2 Electrical System Components**

| Device | | Operating voltage | G.F.C.I. needed | Water cover needed for operation | Device location | Location of wire connections |
|---|---|---|---|---|---|---|
| Submersible Pump-Motor | | 120 230V | Yes | Yes[9] | 2 | Submersible Junction Box |
| Centrifugal Pump-Motor | | 120 230–460V | Yes & No | No | 3 | Junction Box |
| Programmer or Timer Clock | Panel | 120 240V | Yes | No | 3 | Junction Box or in programmer |
| | Electric[10] Valve | 10 to 24V | No Yes | No | 3 | Direct Wire or Junction Box |
| Wind Control | Panel | 120/240V | Yes | No | 3 | Junction Box or in Panel |
| | Sensor | 24V | No | No | 4 | Junction Box |
| | Electric Valve | 10 to 24V | No Yes | No | 3 | Direct Wire or Junction Box |
| Low Voltage Water Level Control | Relay Panel | 120V | Yes | No | 3 | Junction Box or in Panel |
| | Probe Box | 10V | No | No[7] | 5–6 | In Probe[8] |
| | Electric Valve | 10 to 24V | No Yes | No | 3 | Direct Wire or Junction Box |
| Low Water Cutoffs[1] | Relay Panel | 120V | Yes | No | 3 | Junction Box |
| | Probe Box | 10V | No | No[11] | 5–6 | In Probe[8] |
| Wet Niche & Freestanding Lighting | High Voltage Models | 120V | Yes | Yes[9] | 2–12 | Junction Box[8] |
| | Low Voltage Models | 12V | No | Yes[9] | 2–12 | Junction Box[8] |
| | 12 Volt Transformer | 120V | Yes | No | 3 | Junction Box |
| Dry Niche Lighting | High Voltage Models | 120V | Yes | Yes[9] | 2–12 | Junction Box[8] |
| | Low Voltage Models | 12V | No | Yes[9] | 2–12 | Junction Box[8] |
| | 12 Volt Transformer | 120V | Yes | No | 3 | Junction Box |

1. Fountains will require a low water cut-off device in each basin that equipment is located.
2. Locate in water of fountain basin.
3. Locate in equipment vault or adjacent building.
4. Locate sensor on building or pole at maximum height of water effect.
5. Locate in pool deck and extend probe through pool wall.
6. Locate on vertical conduit in fountain basin.
7. Intended to fill pool when water level drops.
8. Depends on location and code. A submersible junction box may be required.
9. Requires a low water cut-off device.
10. When programmer is used to change lighting display, no valve is needed.
11. When water level drops, this device shuts system off.
12. Locate in pool wall.

# 5

# BASIN SIZING AND HYDRAULIC CALCULATIONS

**Fountain Basin Sizing**

Fountain basins should be sufficient in surface area to contain water splash from nozzles and weirs, and deep enough to ensure proper circulation and equipment operation.

When a single nozzle is installed in the center of a basin, the horizontal dimension should be twice the height of the water effect above the water surface[116] (See Figure 5.1). These dimensions create an exact 45° angle between the top of the water and the basin edge and apply to site conditions containing still air. Additional basin area must be provided for windy locations. Wind-blown water travels substantial horizontal distances. By providing a basin with a horizontal dimension four times the water height, wind-blown splash can usually be retained in the basin.[117]

**Example:** A fountain is located on a windy site. The overall height of the water effect from the nozzle is 10 feet. How big should the basin be? [Water effect height] × [4] = [minimum horizontal dimension of basin] 10 feet × 4 feet = 40 feet minimum diameter or 20 feet minimum radius.

On sites where prevailing wind patterns persist, it is possible to maintain the minimum radius only on the windward side of the nozzle. The leeward side can be of a lesser distance.

In windy locations, the horizontal dimension of a fountain basin can be reduced by installing a two-stage wind control device. These systems can reduce the height of the water during moderate wind speeds.

Lower fountain basins which have weirs emptying into them must contain the water splash from the falling water. The horizontal dimension of the basin must be equal to the height of the weir above the lower water surface[118] (See Figure 5.3).

In addition to providing forward space to contain water splash from weirs, this same dimension must be respected at both weir sides parallel to the face. Detailing side walls next to the weir or designing a weir with side restrictions will reduce water splash (See Figure 5.4).

**Fountain Depth**

Much disparity exists over the proper water depth for fountains. McCulley recommends 14 to 24 inches. Roman Fountains suggests that 8 to 12 inches is the minimum depth, while Kim Lighting specifies that 16 inches be the water depth.

Outdoor fountains which are designed to contain fish may require a depressed area of additional depth to protect fish during winter. As the water cools, the fish's metabolism slows. Fish will survive in the fountain as long as some water remains unfrozen. The appropriate depth will depend on the lowest temperature of the region.

Excessive fountain depths may be dangerous to children entering the basin. By providing shallow depths at the basin edge and increased depths at the center and over equipment,

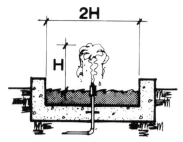

Figure 5.1 **Basin Sizing for Non-Windy Locations**

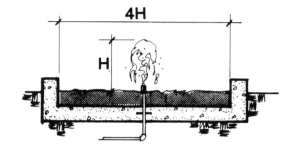

Figure 5.2 **Basin Sizing for Windy Locations**

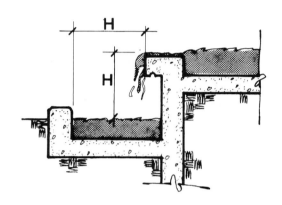

Figure 5.3 **Basin Sizing for Weirs**

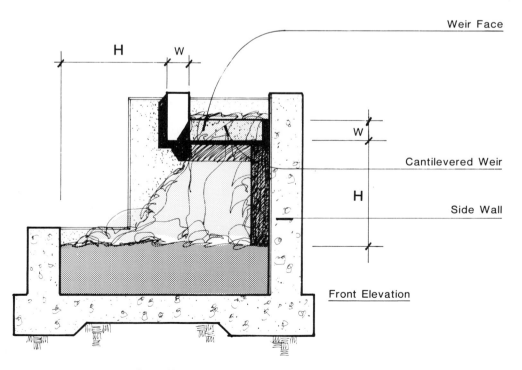

Figure 5.4 **Basin Sizing for Cantilevered Weirs**

a safer environment can be created. In no situation should there be floor slopes in excess of 8.33 percent. The proper choice of water depth will depend on the following conditions:

1. Are there any weight restrictions which will require a reduction in water depth? One cubic foot of water weighs 62.366 pounds.

2. Will children enter the pool? If so, is the depth appropriate to prevent accidental drowning?

3. Is proper water cover provided over the top of lights, nozzles, and submersible pumps? In most cases, a 2-inch minimum cover is needed.

4. Do local codes restrict maximum depths of fountains? Fountains with excessive depths may be considered swimming pools and will be regulated as such.

5. Is the water deep enough to cushion the fall of the nozzle water? Aerating nozzles located in shallow depth basins will create excessive surge.

**Static and Operating Water Levels**

Nozzles and weirs displace water into the air and lower the water level of the basin during operation. The water used by these devices is called the operating water; the reduced depth of water is termed the operating level.

Multi-level pools, which contain weired, upper-level basins, will only have a reduction in the level of the lowest pool during operation. Once the pool is shut off, the circulating water volume will raise the water level of the lowest pool which is labeled the static water level.

Normal practice is to design the lowest pool larger in surface feet than the total surface area of the pools which empty into it. When the system is shut off, it allows for storage of the water layers, which are built-up behind the weirs. Excessive rising of the water level in the bottom basin will be prevented by providing this large surface area. The inclusion of a large bottom basin will prevent continual activation of the water-level control devices.

To determine the static water level of the bottom pool of a weired fountain, it will be necessary to ascertain the volume of water which is built-up behind the weirs. By multiplying the design depth over the weir by the width and length of the basin, the operating volume can be calculated. This will be computed for each basin which empties into the lower basin. By dividing the operating volume of all upper pools by the square footage of the lowest basin, the rise in operating level (static level) can be calculated.

**Example:** (See Figure 5.6) The design depth of water over the top weir is ½ inch. The top basin is 8 x 30 feet in surface area. The bottom basin is 10 x 30 feet in surface area. Determine the rise in the operating level in the lowest basin under static conditions.

1. Change weir operating depth from inches to feet.

$$\frac{.5 \text{ inch}}{12 \text{ inch}} = \frac{x \text{ feet}}{1 \text{ foot}}$$

$$x \text{ feet} = .0417 \text{ over weir.}$$

2. Determine total operating volume.

$$\frac{.0417 \text{ feet x 8 feet}}{\text{x 30 feet}} = \frac{10.01 \text{ cu. ft. operating}}{\text{volume top pool}}$$

3. Divide operating water volume by surface square footage of lower pool.

$$\frac{10.01 \text{ ft}^3}{(10 \text{ ft})(30 \text{ ft})} = \text{Rise in lowest pool}$$

$$\frac{10.01 \text{ ft}^3}{300 \text{ ft}^2} = .0334 \text{ feet}$$

4. Convert rise in water level from feet to inches.

$$\frac{.0334 \text{ ft.}}{1 \text{ foot}} = \frac{x \text{ inches}}{12 \text{ inches}}$$

$$x \text{ inches} = .4008 \text{ inches}$$

$$\frac{40}{100} = \frac{x}{32}$$

Rise in lower pool = 13/32 of an inch

If the operating depth of the lower pool is 16 inches, then the static water level equals 16-13/32 inches. As a rule of thumb, the following time periods are required to drain the water built-up behind the weir crest. Dimension A-B is the basin measurement in the direction of water flow over the weir (See Figure 5.7 and Table 5.1).

When a fountain is shut off, the airborne water generated by a nozzle is somewhat insignificant, and will only marginally raise the water level in the basin. A nozzle which reaches a height of 40 feet and operates at 285 gpm will raise the level of an 80 x 80 foot basin 0.0148 inches when the fountain is turned off. Normally the operating water required for nozzle operation is so insignificant that it is not included in the static water calculation.[119] Although individually insignificant, it may be necessary to calculate the water

**Table 5.1 Drainage Time for Weired Basins**

| Dimension A-B | Time |
| --- | --- |
| 10 ft. | 12 sec. |
| 16 ft. | 14 sec. |
| 25 ft. | 19 sec. |
| 36 ft. | 22 sec. |
| 49 ft. | 28 sec. |
| 64 ft. | 30 sec. |
| 81 ft. | 33 sec. |

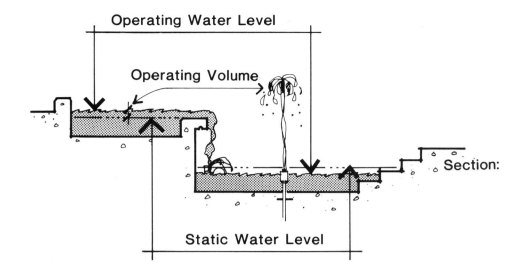

**Figure 5.5** **Static and Operating Levels of Fountains**

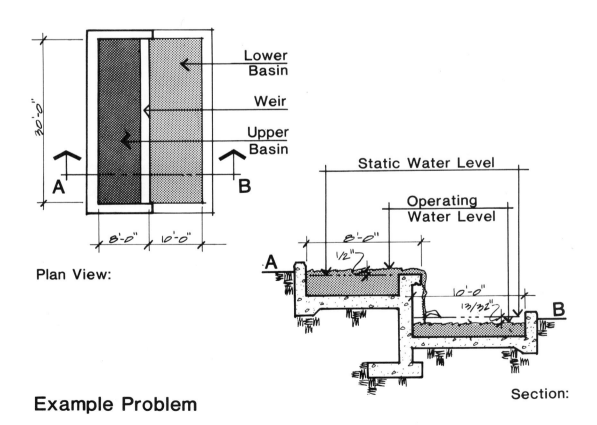

Plan View:

**Figure 5.6** **Example Problem**

Section:

rise from operating water of many high capacity nozzles. This climb in water level can be calculated by determining the time that is required for the water to completely fall after the nozzle is shut off. The time in seconds is then multiplied by the required nozzle capacity in gallons per second (gallons per minute divided by 60 seconds per minute).

Total gpm's
suspended in air = (Seconds for water to fall) x
(Required nozzle capacity) x
(1 min./60 sec.) x
(2)

This means that after the nozzle is activated, water will be ascending and descending at this gpm. The factor of (2) in the equation accounts for the amount of water which falls under its own energy. By multiplying the total operating gallons by .13368 cu.ft./gal., cubic feet of water can be found. By dividing the cubic feet of nozzle operating water by the surface square footage of the receptacle, the rise in depth can be found.

1 gallon = .13360 cu.ft.
1 gallon = 231 cu.in.

## Weirs

A weir is a notch of regular form through which water flows.[120] The edge or surface of the weir is called the crest of the weir, while the overflowing sheet of water is defined as the nappe. The depth of water producing the discharge over the weir is defined as the weir head or "H" (See Figure 5.8).

Weirs are generally classified by the shape of the notch through which water flows. The various weir types include: rectangular, triangular, v-notch, trapezoidal, and parabolic. These basic shapes can be further classified as sharp-crested, round-crested or broad-crested weirs. A sharp-crested weir contains a sharp upstream corner, which physically springs the nappe free of the crest.[121] In this weir type, the crest is normally narrow and has a machined 90 degree angle on the upstream edge of the crest (See Figure 5.10).

A round-crested weir is one containing rounded edges on the crest. The rounding of edges reduces friction of the surface water layer creating a smoother nappe flowing over the crest.

A broad-crested weir is defined as a weir which contains a crest of sufficient length, in the direction of the water flow over the weir, to support the nappe. Because of the sharp upstream edge of a broad-crested weir, there is a contraction in the nappe at the crest. Figure 5.10 illustrates the various weir shapes.

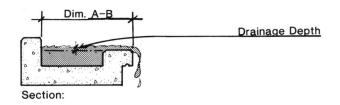

**Weir Drainage**

**Figure 5.7**

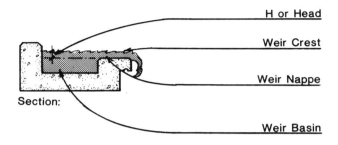

**Definition of Terms**

**Figure 5.8**

**Figure 5.9** *A broad-crested weir, 3 feet in breadth, ''V'' shaped, in plan view. Tulsa, Oklahoma.*

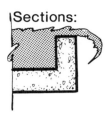
Sections:

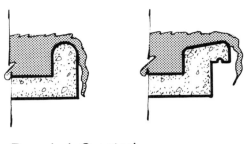

Sharp–Crested

Rounded–Crested

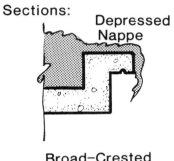
Sections: Depressed Nappe

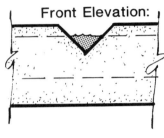
Front Elevation:

Broad–Crested

Triangular–Crested

'V' Notched

**Figure 5.10**     **Weir Types**

**Figure 5.12** *Sharp crested weir. Virginia Beach, Virginia.*

**Figure 5.11** *Sharp crested weir. Virginia Beach, Virginia.*

133

**Figure 5.13** *Rustic granite broad crested weir with metal height adjustment.*

**Figure 5.16** *Granite broad crested weir. Washington, District of Columbia.*

**Figure 5.14** *Polished granite rounded crested weir. Washington, District of Columbia.*

**Figure 5.17** *Broad crested weir. Virginia Beach, Virginia.*

**Figure 5.15** *Curved rounded crested weir. Washington, District of Columbia.*

**Figure 5.18** *Broad crested weir. Virginia Beach, Virginia.*

Photo by Theodore D. Walker

**Figure 5.19** *Vertically stacked broad-crested weir, Kansas City, Missouri.*

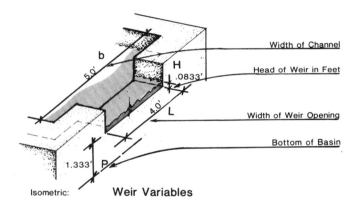

Isometric:  **Weir Variables**

**Figure 5.20**

## Weir Capacity

A general purpose method for determining the capacity of a sharp-crested weir would employ the following formula:

Using the equation $Q = CLH^{3/2}$

where:

Q  =  the flow in C.F.S.

L  =  the width of the weir opening in feet

C  =  the discharge coefficient

H  =  the head above the weir in feet.

> The equation can be used to establish the capacity required to operate the weir in Figure 5.20. C is established from Figure 5.21. To find the discharge coefficient (C), the intersection of L/b and H/P must be found on the graph.

L  =  width of the weir opening in feet

b  =  width of channel (in feet) where the weir is located. When L < b, the weir is said to have end contractions.

P  =  depth of water retained by weir in feet, measured from the top of the horizontal crest to the basin bottom.

H  =  the head above the weir in feet.

### Example:

L  =  4 ft.

b  =  5 ft.

P  =  1.333 ft. (16 inches)

H  =  .0833 feet (1 inch)

L/b  =  4/5 =  .80

H/P  =  .0833/1.33 =.063.

By locating these two factors on the graph, we find that:

C  =  3.15

Inserting these values into the equation, we find that:

Q  =  $(3.15) (4.0) (.0833^{3/2})$

=  (12.6) (.024)

=  .302 C.F.S.

**Table 5.2  Values of C for Broad-Crested Weirs**

| Measured Head In feet, H | Breadth of Crest of Weir in Feet, B | | | | | | |
|---|---|---|---|---|---|---|---|
| | .50 | .75 | 1.0 | 1.5 | 2.0 | 2.5 | 3.0 |
| Up to 0.2 | 2.80 | 2.75 | 2.69 | 2.62 | 2.54 | 2.48 | 2.44 |

*Adapted from King and Brater, 1963*[124]

By using the following equation, cubic feet per second can be converted into gallons per minute. This assumes that 60 seconds equal 1 minute and 7.4805 gallons equal 1 cubic foot.

$$\frac{(cu.ft./1\ sec.)\ (60\ sec./1\ min.)}{(7.4805\ gal./1\ cu.ft.)} = gpm$$

$$\frac{(.302\ ft^3/sec.)\ (60\ sec./min.)}{(7.4805\ gal./ft.^3)} = gpm$$

$$135.55 = gpm$$

These additional formulas can be used to determine weir capacity.

### Sharp-Crested Weirs — Rehbock Formula[123]

$$Q = Ce\ L\ He^{3/2}$$

$$He = H + 0.004$$

$$Ce = 3.22 + 0.44\ H/P$$

### Broad-Crested Weirs

$$Q = CLH^{3/2}$$

### V-Notch Weir[125]

$$Q = 2.48H^{5/2} \tan \theta/2$$
$$Q = 2.48\ H^{5/2}$$

If $\theta = 90°$
$$Q = 1.43\ H^{5/2}$$

If $\theta = 60°$

### Quick Method for Determining Weir Capacity

General rules of thumb exist for establishing the water capacity needed to operate a weir. To induce a ¼-inch depth of water to flow over a weir, it is necessary to input 10 gallons per minute for every 1-foot width of weir. A water depth of 1 inch over the weir requires 30 gallons per minute per 1 foot width of weir.[126]

**Example 1:** (See Figure 5.24) A weir of 10 feet in width is required to have a water depth of 1 inch falling over the crest. What water capacity is needed to operate the weir?

$$(10\ feet)\ (30\ gpm/ft.) = 300\ gpm.$$

**Example 2:** (See Figure 5.25) A sculptural basin has a continual weir along the edge. This weir is designed to have a water depth of ¼ inch cascade over the entire edge. A bubbler nozzle of 50 gpm is located in the center of the basin. Will an additional discharge device like an eyeball be needed to supply the weir? Each side of the weir is 5

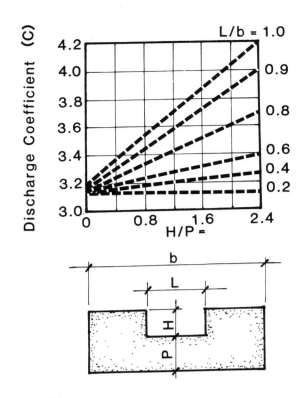

**Figure 5.21**

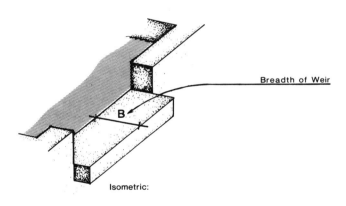

Weir Variables

**Figure 5.22**

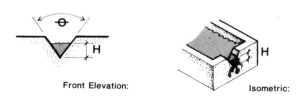

'V' Notch Weir

**Figure 5.23**

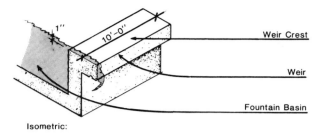

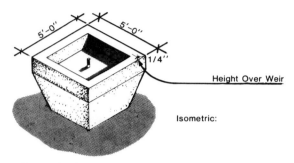

Isometric:

**Example 1**

**Figure 5.24**

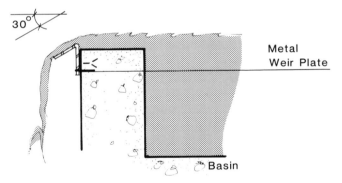

Isometric:

**Example 2**

**Figure 5.25**

**Figure 5.26    Efficient Weir**

feet in length. The total weir length is 20 feet (4 sides × 5 feet = 20 feet).

$$20 \text{ feet} \times 10 \text{ gpm/ft.} = 200 \text{ gpm}$$

$$\text{Total discharge} - \text{nozzle discharge}$$
$$= \text{supplemental discharge}$$

$$200 \text{ gpm} - 50 \text{ gpm} =$$
$$150 \text{ gpm} = \text{eyeball discharge}$$

An additional discharge device of 150 gpm will be needed.

## SOUND CREATED BY WEIRS AND WATERFALLS

As a rule of thumb, as the height and volume of water from a weir increases, the sound is amplified. In addition to increasing the sound, an increase in weir volume will reduce the effect of wind on the waterfall and may reduce splash in some applications. The most cost effective use of water volume can be achieved by constructing a weir face as illustrated in Figure 5.26. This weir configuration creates less surface tension and friction and allows the water to form a smooth, vertical water curtain. Contrary to belief, this weir configuration is more effective than a rounded, crested weir in creating a smooth waterfall. The rounded weir top tends to create various water velocities along the weir surface. The difference in water velocity tends to make the water spring back under the weir face and cause disturbance. In addition to height, a general rough texture applied to the weir face will create more sound for the water effect. By introducing a sand-blasted finish or exposed-aggregate finish to concrete and other applicable materials, more sound can be created. Although more sound is created, a coarser aerated effect is produced.

## SCALLOPED WEIRS

Periodic blocking along the face of a weir or basin can considerably reduce the water requirements of a water feature. This blocking can be ground or cast into the weir. Each raised element along the weir face impedes water and reduces the total required gallonage. To calculate the water requirements of this scalloped weir, the total openings between the blocking are measured and multiplied by the multiplier as described in this chapter. This altered weir creates an effect which is similar to rain and is very soothing (See Figures 5.27 and 5.28).

## WATER STEPS

Water steps consist of small interconnected concrete steps which simulate a series of waterfalls. In this design, water flows over the top step and each successive step into a collection basin. As it flows, the water pattern changes from a smooth to a turbulent sheet, to an aerated water sheet. Typically, three or more successive steps will create an aerating effect. More than three steps typically do not increase the quality of aeration. Water depth over the top weir or step should be sized to provide an ⅛-inch depth of water for each inch of step height. For a turbulent, foamy effect, a minimum of ½-inch depth of flow over the top step should be supplied. Care should be taken so that the riser (step height) and tread (step length) are equivalent, or that the riser is not more than 125 percent of the tread. Variations of these proportions will create acceptable results which provide less aeration (See Figures 5.29 to 5.35).

## WATER CHANNELS

Water channels are often used in participatory and large-scaled fountains. McCulley describes the various effects created by channels.[127] To determine the amount of discharge required to operate the channel, it is necessary to know the cross-sectional area, wetted perimeter, roughness, and gradient of the channel.

Standard procedures for the design of storm drainage channels should be used to establish the gpm needed to create the desired water effect. The equation $Q = Va$ will determine the volume of flow in cubic feet per second (CFS). By using the conversion factor above, CFS can be changed to gpm. Consult the Handbook of Landscape Architectural Construction, published by the Landscape Architecture Foundation, for further information on sizing channels.

*Example:* What is the discharge in gpm to operate this fountain channel?

1. The channel will be constructed of cut rock and will have a friction coefficient of n = .033.

2. The gradient of the channel will equal 10 percent.

3. Cross-sectional area will be as follows:

$Q = Va$

Velocity (V) can be found by using the Manning formula:

$V = (1.486/n) \, r^{.67} \, s^{.5}$

"r" or the hydraulic radius is the only unknown variable. The following equation will determine "r" for this specific channel section:

$$r = \cfrac{d}{\cfrac{1 + 2d}{w}}$$

**Figure 5.27** *Scalloped stone weir. London, England.*

**Figure 5.28** *Scalloped weir. Charlottesville, Virginia.*

**Figure 5.29** *Brick watersteps at lake. Tulsa, Oklahoma.*

138

**Figure 5.30** *Watersteps with nozzles and cover plates. Cheltenham, England.*

**Figure 5.31** *Concrete watersteps and pump vault. Richmond, Virginia.*

**Figure 5.32** *Tile watersteps. Norfolk, Virginia.*

**Figure 5.33** *Stone water steps. Chatsworth, England.*

**Figure 5.34** *Waterfall and watersteps. Kew Gardens, England.*

**Figure 5.35** *Waterfall and watersteps. Kew Gardens, England.*

The following variables are redefined and shown in Figure 5.39.

$$r = \frac{\dfrac{.08 \text{ ft.}}{1 + 2\,(.08) \text{ ft.}}}{4.0 \text{ ft.}}$$

$$= 0.08 \text{ ft.}/1.16 \text{ ft.}/4 \text{ ft.}$$

$$r = 0.08/0.29$$
$$= .276 \text{ ft.}$$

$$V = (1.486/.033)\,(276^{.67})\,(.1^{.5})$$
$$= (45.030)\,(.422)\,(.316)$$
$$= 2.534 \text{ ft./sec.}$$

The cross-sectional area for this channel is:

$$a = wd$$
$$= (4.0)\,(0.08)$$
$$= .32 \text{ ft.}^2$$

$$Q = Va$$
$$= (2.534 \text{ ft./sec.})\,(.32 \text{ ft.}^2)$$
$$Q = .811 \text{ ft.}^3/\text{sec.}$$

$$gpm = (.811 \text{ ft.}^3/\text{sec.}) \times (60 \text{ sec./min.})$$
$$(7.4805 \text{ gal./ft.}^3)$$

$$Q = 364.00 \text{ gpm.}$$

To operate this channel, the combined capacity of nozzles and eyeballs should add up to 364.00 gpm.

## SIZING PIPES

The primary function of the pipe is to transport the appropriate capacity of water (gpm) and pressure to the fountain nozzle. When choosing pipe diameter, it is necessary to consider water capacity, friction loss per 100-foot length, and water velocity. Manufacturers will rate nozzles by the gpm and water pressure required to achieve a certain water height. When the water reaches the nozzle, the water must meet these prescribed specifications. This can be achieved by properly sizing the pipe. Water capacity or gpm will be fairly consistent throughout the length of pipe. The pipe diameter should be sized to provide the required gpm's below a prescribed velocity. As gpm's are increased through the same diameter pipe, the velocity in feet per second and pressure loss due to friction (pressure loss per 100 feet of pipe) increase. By putting this same water capacity through a larger diameter pipe, velocities and friction can be reduced. This is known as up-sizing of pipe and is often employed in the industry. Often, pipe diameter is reduced as an attempt to increase pressure in the system. This is an improper practice which actually creates lower pressures at higher velocities.

Along with water capacity, water pressure is required at each nozzle. Water pressure is lost by pipe friction, fitting friction, and losses due to rises in elevation.

**Figure 5.36** *Water channel. Tulsa, Oklahoma.*

**Figure 5.37** *Water channel. Denver, Colorado.*

Photo by Theodore D. Wa

**Figure 5.38** *Water channel. Fort Worth, Texas.*

140

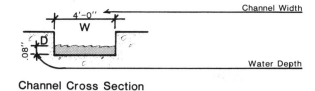

Channel Cross Section

**Figure 5.39**

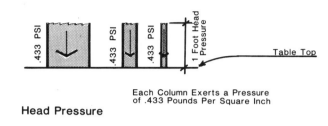

Each Column Exerts a Pressure
of .433 Pounds Per Square Inch

Head Pressure

**Figure 5.40**

## Pressure Loss Through Pipe Friction

The inside diameter of a pipe is somewhat rough and creates friction between the pipe material and water. As the water moves from the pump to the nozzle, the friction robs the water of some of the pressure generated by the pump. Water pressure in the pipe continually lessens due to the friction. Pipe diameters should be chosen to meet the described pressure at the nozzle. Different piping materials carrying the same gpm's will have different friction-loss rates per 100-foot length. Check the Appendix for various pipe specifications.

Pressure required by nozzles and generated by the pump is normally rated in head feet pressure. Pressure lost through pipe friction is rated in psi (pounds per square inch). See Appendix for Tables. Feet head refers to the pressure created by a column of water 1 foot high. This pressure is consistent for any diameter cylinder of 1-foot height (See Figure 5.40).

When determining pressure loss through pipe, psi is normally converted to head feet to establish head feet required by the pump. Pumps are generally specified and sold by head feet capacity. One head foot of pressure = .433 pounds per square inch.

**Example:** (See Figure 5.41) Find the head foot pressure lost due to friction in an 80-foot length of level 2 inch diameter Type "K" copper pipe (C=140) having a flow capacity of 30 gpm's. By looking at Figure 5.41, we see that 100 feet of pipe has a psi loss of 1.04 psi per 100 feet of length.

$$1.04 \text{ psi}/100 \text{ feet} = x \text{ psi}/80 \text{ feet}$$
$$x = .83 \text{ psi}$$

$$\frac{1 \text{ head foot of pressure}}{.433 \text{ psi}} = \frac{x \text{ head feet lost due to friction}}{.83 \text{ psi}}$$

$$x = 1.92 \text{ head feet lost}$$

Gpm's are somewhat independent of water pressure. In Figure 5.42, both water streams provide the same gpm's but have different psi ratings. The smaller diameter pipe would require more energy to produce the same flow rate.

Generally speaking, pipes used for discharge lines should have velocities of less than 8 feet per second and friction losses of less than 10 head feet (4.33 psi) per 100 feet length of pipe.[128] In some applications, friction losses will be in excess of 4.33 psi per 100 feet, while velocity will be less than 8 feet per second. This should not affect nozzle performance or pipe longevity, but will necessitate a pump with a larger head feet requirement. Suction lines should have water velocities which do not exceed 6 feet per second and friction losses less than 6 head feet (2.6 psi) per 100 feet.[129] Velocities exceeding this should be avoided to prevent water scour, turbulent water flow and cavitation.

Certain nozzle types require non-turbulent (laminar) water flow for proper operation. Turbulent or twisted water will deform delicate water displays and create a distorted

141

# Abbreviated Friction Loss Table for Type 'K' Copper Pipe

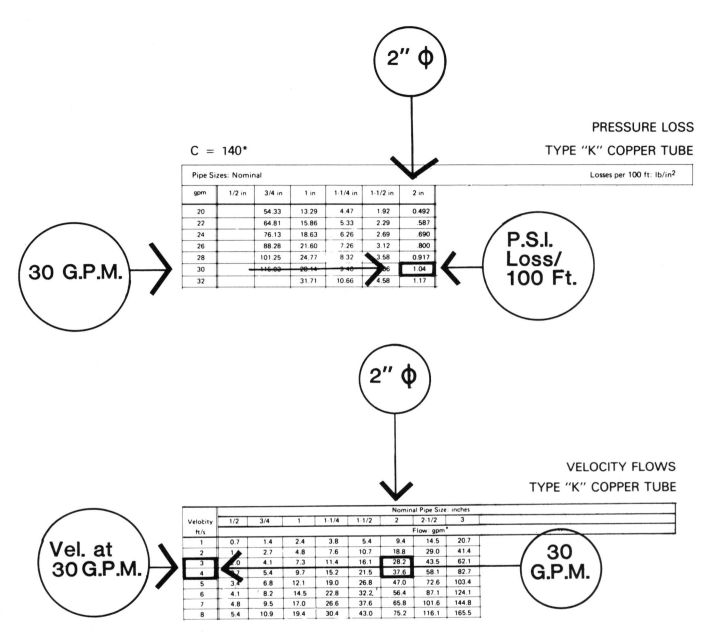

Adapted from:
*Turf Irrigation Manual*
by J.A. Watkins

**Figure 5.41**

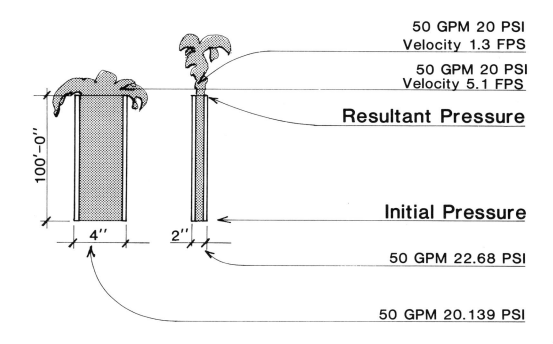

**Figure 5.42**          **GPM'S and Pressure**

effect. The degree of turbulence in a pipe is a function of velocity and the length of the riser between the nozzle and elbow. Traditionally, short runs of risers create more turbulence than long runs. By inserting a flow vane in the pipe at the nozzle base, non-twisted water can be provided.[130] Flow vanes should be constructed from noncorrosive sheet metals in the shape of a solid "V." The length of the "V" is to be four times the diameter of the pipe and appropriately positioned so that the point is directed away from the nozzle.

As a means of reducing construction costs, pipe diameters should be selected which closely meet the prescribed maximum standards above.

**Steps for Sizing Pipe**

1. Select appropriate pipe material to be used in the fountain. Acquire the appropriate friction loss table for this pipe material.

2. Consult manufacturers' literature on the desired fountain nozzle to determine nozzle gpm and size of female or male pipe threads at the nozzle base. Pipe threads are often specified by the NPT designation. In most cases, the pipe

size specified at the nozzle base is appropriate. This pipe diameter should be checked in the friction loss chart to ensure that the pipe will carry the required gpm's to the nozzle with desirable velocities and friction losses. In some cases, larger-than-necessary pipe threads are provided at the base of the nozzle. This is intended to reduce water turbulence and create laminar water flow. In this situation, smaller diameter pipe should not be connected to the nozzle.

Sometimes, nozzles operated at their maximum designed height require a discharge pipe larger than the specified size of the nozzle base. Use of larger pipe reduces water velocity and pressure demand on the pump. In this situation, a reducer is required and should be located at the base of the riser. Locating the reducer too close to the nozzle will create turbulent water flow and distort the water pattern.

3. As additional water capacity is required by other nozzles or eyeballs on the circuits, the pipe must be increased in diameter to account for the additional gpm's.

4. Proceed to sizing of the pump. It may be economical to increase pipe diameter in order to reduce pressure output of the pump.

**Example:** The discharge circuit of the fountain in Figure 5.43 is to contain four nozzles. The manufacturer's literature supplies the information shown in Table 5.3. By checking Figure 5.44 we find that a 1½-inch diameter pipe will carry the prescribed gpm's to the nozzle with velocities of less than 8 fps. Table 5.4 has been filled in for pipe segments AB, CD, EF, and GH. By cumulatively adding the total gpm required to pass through the pipe, gpm has been filled in for pipe segments BD, DF, FH, and HI. Pipe segment BD supplies water to nozzle number 1 and equals 50 gpm. Segment DF supplies water to nozzles numbers 1 and 2 and equals 50 + 35 gpm = 85 gpm. Segment FH supplies water to nozzles numbers 1, 2 and 3 equals 50 + 35 + 35 gpm = 120 gpm. Segment HI supplies water to all nozzles and equals 50 + 35 + 35 + 27 gpm = 147 gpm. By referring to Figure 5.25 we can find the appropriate pipe diameters which have also been listed in Table 5.4. BD = 1½", DF = 2", FH = 2½", and HI = 3".

## Pressure Loss Through Pipe Fittings

Elbows, tees and valves all generate friction and reduce water pressure. The more water diverted or restricted, the more friction generated.

Long-sweep elbows will generate less friction than a standard elbow, while a side outlet of a tee will generate more friction than a standard run of tee (see Figure 5.45).

Tables A-1 and A-2 (See Appendix) specify friction losses of various pipe fittings per diameter. Friction loss through pipe fittings is rated in equivalent length of pipe. By referring to friction loss tables for pipe, equivalent pipe length can be converted to psi, then head feet.

**Example:** Pipe to be PR SDR 21
Looking at Table A-2 we find that a 2-inch diameter standard elbow is equal to 6.81 feet of pipe.

Conversion factor x equal
pipe length of 90 degrees  = equal pipe length

$$1.31 \times 5.2 = 6.81$$

This means that the friction loss through the elbow is equal to the friction loss through 6.81 feet of pipe. If the

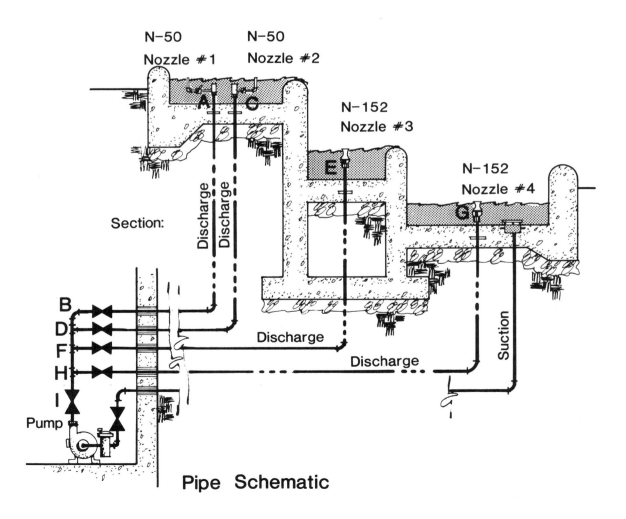

**Figure 5.43**

**Pipe Schematic**

# Abbreviated Friction Loss Table for P.V.C. PR SDR 21

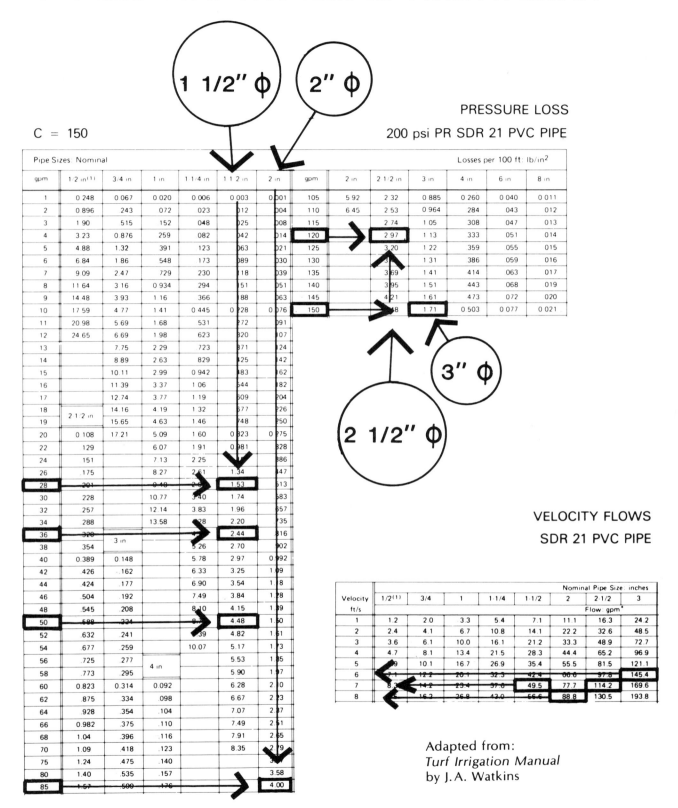

**Figure 5.44**

flow rate is 50 gpm and the pipe is PVC 1120 PR SDR 21, psi loss through the elbow would be .102 psi. This is obtained by interpolating the following:

$$\frac{1.50 \text{ psi (from Friction Loss Table)}}{100 \text{ ft.}} = \frac{x \text{ psi}}{6.81 \text{ ft.}}$$

$$x = .102 \text{ psi}$$

Converting to feet head

$$.102 \text{ psi} = .102 \text{ psi} \times \frac{.433 \text{ psi}}{\text{hd. ft.}}$$

$$= .24 \text{ head feet}$$

### Pressure Loss and Gain Through Change in Elevation

Water pressure is often generated for municipal water systems by storing water in an elevated tank. The higher the top of the water source above the water outlet, the more pressure available at that outlet (discounting pressure loss due to friction). In Figure 5.46, nozzle A has 0 head feet pressure, nozzle B has 40 head feet pressure, and nozzle C has 60 head feet pressure. In all these situations, there is a cumulative gain in pressure due to the weight of the water column above the nozzle. When water goes uphill, there is a cumulative loss in head pressure generated by the water tank.

To better understand this concept, consider the following analogy: Two boys are in a wagon. They are required to go downhill, then uphill. The wagon can be considered the water in the pipe, while the energy exerted by the two boys to push the wagon can be considered the energy generated by the weight of the water column (the higher the water column, the more water pressure available). As the boys go downhill, no additional energy is required to power the wagon. Also, the further they go on the same incline, the more energy the wagon accumulates. When the boys reach the uphill portion of their ride, the wagon starts to lose its gained energy. The further they go, the less energy the wagon will have. Eventually, the boys will have to get out and push the wagon.

To establish pressure loss or gain due to elevation, the vertical measurement of the uphill rise should be subtracted from the vertical measurement of downhill run of the pipe (See Figure 5.47 and Table 5.5).

## SIZING PUMPS

When specifying a fountain pump, it is necessary to determine the water pressure (head feet) and water capacity

**Table 5.3 Nozzle Specifications**

| Nozzle # | Model # | gpm | Nozzle N.P.T. | Water effects height |
|---|---|---|---|---|
| 1 | N-50 | 50 | 1½″ diam. | 18″ |
| 2 | N-50 | 35 | 1½″ diam. | 12″ |
| 3 | N-152 | 35 | 1½″ diam. | 4′ |
| 4 | N-152 | 27 | 1½″ diam. | 2′ |

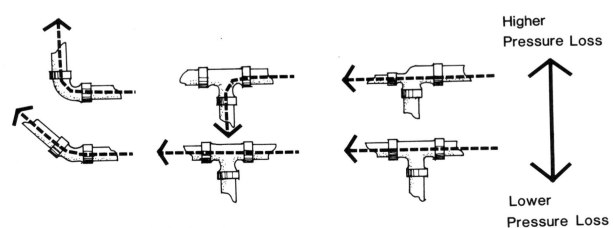

Higher Pressure Loss

Lower Pressure Loss

## Comparative Friction Loss
## Through Fittings

**Figure 5.45**

**Table 5-4  Pipe Diameter for Pipe Segments**

| Pipe segment | Pipe gpm | Pipe diameter |
|:---:|:---:|:---:|
| AB | 50 | 1½" |
| CD | 35 | 1½" |
| EF | 35 | 1½" |
| GH | 27 | 1½" |
| | | |
| BD | 50 | 1½" |
| DF | 85 | 2" |
| FH | 120 | 2½" |
| HI | 147 | 3" |

**Table 5.5  Elevation Pressure for Figure 5.47**

| Pipe segment | Head pressure gain | Head pressure lost |
|:---:|:---:|:---:|
| AB | 50 ft. | |
| BC | 15 ft. | |
| CD | 0 | 0 |
| DE | | −10 ft. |
| EF | 0 | 0 |
| FG | | −20 ft. |
| | 65 ft. | −30 ft. |

*Total pressure at nozzle "G" is 65 feet − 30 feet = 35 feet.*

(gpm) that the pump must supply to the nozzles.

### Determining Pump Pressure

When determining head feet requirements for the pump, it is essential to determine the pipe route with the greatest pressure requirement. This would include the discharge pipe route originating at the pump and continuing to the nozzle. Calculation of pressure requirement of a pump should not be confused with calculations of water capacity. This is "not" a summation of pressure requirements of all nozzle and pressure losses through all discharge pipes and fittings. The worst pressure requirement means the single pipe route with the highest cumulative pressure requirement. Pump pressure requirement would include the following:

*Pump head feet requirement = single nozzle head feet requirement + pressure loss due to rises in the discharge line + pressure loss due to pipe friction in the discharge line + pressure loss through fittings and valves on the discharge line + pressure required by the suction line.
*(*Pipe route from nozzle to pump with worst pressure requirement.*)

The ultimate pump choice should have a head feet rating in excess of 10 percent. This safety margin is required to compensate for reduction in pump and pipe performance.

Pressure lost through the suction line is a function of:

1. Pressure loss through pipe and fittings.

2. Pressure loss at the water intake of the suction line.

3. Pressure loss due to elevation changes in the suction line.

4. Pressure loss due to atmospheric pressures.

5. Pressure loss due to the vapor pressure of water.

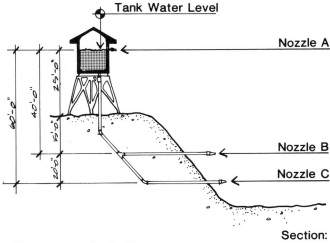

## Pressure Gain Due to Elevation Change

**Figure 5.46**

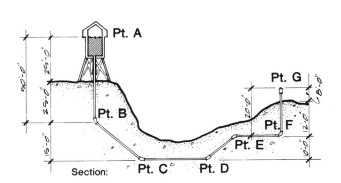

**Pressure Lost Through Elevation Change**

**Figure 5.47**

147

Pressure requirements of the suction line should be established by a trained pump engineer. In addition to these calculations, the engineer should be asked to verify that:

1. The available pump Net Positive Suction Head (NPSH) is higher than the required pump NPSH. NPSH is the pressure required at the suction entrance (anti-vortex plate) to provide a consistent water flow into the suction intake at the pump. Without proper external pressures generating pressure in the suction line, water is not forced into the suction impellers of the pump at a proper rate. As a result the pump will draw air and produce no discharge.

2. Cavitation of pump will not occur. Cavitation is a condition which arises from reduced vapor pressure in the suction line. In this situation, pressure differences at the pump and at the suction line entrance force air bubbles towards the pump impellers. When air bubbles hit the impellers, they break and gouge holes in the metal impellers.

Both problems are a function of altitude, suction velocity, suction line size, water height above or below the center of the suction intake at the pump and pump performance. Improper handling of these potential problems will result in pump failure.

Normally, the pipe route from the nozzle to the pump is figured for each individual nozzle. The route with the highest pressure requirement is then chosen as the pump pressure.

With experience, most designers can determine which route contains the highest pressure requirement. Often, the nozzle with the highest pressure requirement is chosen as the route with the worst pressure. When using this technique, make sure elevation changes and pipe lengths are considered.

**Determining Pump Capacity**

Water capacity of pumps must equal the total gpm's of all nozzles and eyeballs located on the discharge line.

Pumps gpm's = total gpm's of nozzles and eyeballs.

Common practice is to add 10 percent to this sum when specifying the pump. This is a safety factor which accounts for a decrease in performance due to pump wear.

Pump pressure is somewhat limiting in fountain design. As the head feet requirement of the pump increases, the gpm's which the pump can transport water will reduce. This will require a larger pump which will carry equal capacity at a higher pressure. This concept is better understood through the following analogy:

A worker is required to carry water up a stairwell to various floors. The water which he carries can be compared to the gpm's which the pump moves, while the distance he travels up the steps is comparable to the energy the pump produces to create water pressure. When the worker is required to travel only one flight of steps, he can carry many buckets. If he must transport water to the tenth floor, he can carry only a few buckets. To carry the same quantity of water to the tenth floor as to the first floor, it would be necessary to employ several workers.

**Example:** Establish the gpm and discharge head feet requirement for a dry centrifugal pump illustrated in the fountain in Figure 5.48. The pipe will be type "K" copper pipe with wrought tube fittings and angle globe valves.

1. Determine the discharge capacity for nozzles and eyeballs. The fountain will employ three nozzles as shown in Table 5.6

2. Establish required pump capacity.

    Pump Capacity = sum of all nozzles and eyeballs
    $$+ 10\% \text{ of total}$$
    $$= 20 + 20 + 104 + (10\% \text{ of total})$$
    $$= 158 \text{ gpm required by pump}$$

3. Establish pump head feet requirement. Pump head feet requirement equals the pump-to-nozzle pipe route with the highest head feet requirement.

    Pump Head Feet = A + B + C + D + E where:

    A = Nozzle head feet required
    B = Head feet lost through pipe friction
    C = Head feet lost through fitting pressure
    D = Head feet lost through rises in discharge pipe elevation
    E = Head feet required by suction line

3.1 Required nozzle head is specified by nozzle manufacturer and is shown in Table 5.6

3.2 Because friction loss is a function of gpm's and pipe diameter, it will be necessary to establish gpm and diameter for each pipe segment. The following pipe routes exist for the three nozzles. Pipe gpm is designated for each pipe segment.

3.3 After referring to the friction loss table for copper pipe, pipe diameter is filled in for Figures 5.49, 5.50 and 5.51. Diameter is established by finding a pipe size which will handle the required gpm's at a velocity less than 8 fps and, ideally, a friction loss of less than 4.33 psi or 10 head feet per 100 feet length.

3.4 Pipe length for Figures 5.49, 5.50 and 5.51 are established from Figure 5.48.

    Friction loss through a pipe varies as the gpm's or the pipe diameter changes. To determine friction loss through pipe segments, pipes of equal gpm's and diameter "must" be segregated. In Figure 5.49 pipe segments AB, BC, CD, DL all operate at the same gpm and have the same diameter. These pipe segments are grouped together.

    As stated previously, friction loss through fittings and valves is expressed in equivalent pipe lengths. Pressure loss through fittings = pressure loss through "x" feet of pipe of same diameter and gpm. For convenience, equivalent lengths of pipe calculated from the fittings are added to pipe lengths to determine

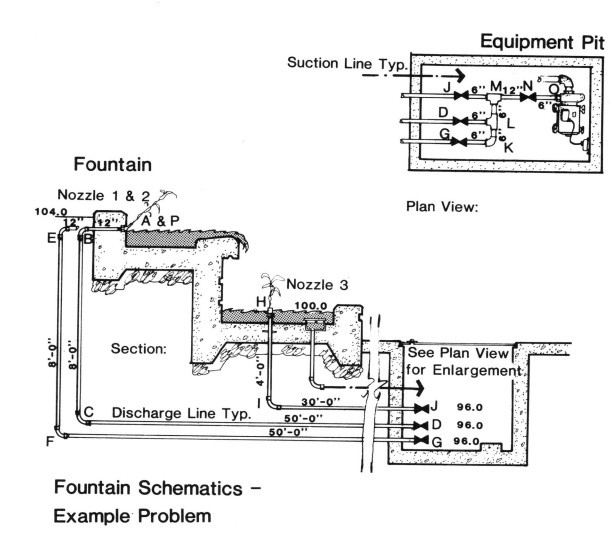

Figure 5.48

## Fountain Schematics –
## Example Problem

**Table 5.6 Nozzle Specifications for Figure 5.48**

| Nozzle # | Nozzle model | Water spray height | Operating head ft. of nozzle | Eyeball and nozzle gpm | N.P.T. |
|---|---|---|---|---|---|
| 1 | KIM N-111 | 5 | 7 | 20 | 1½″ diam. |
| 2 | KIM N-111 | 5 | 7 | 20 | 1½″ diam. |
| 3 | KIM N-146 | 10 | 30 | 104 | 3″ diam. |

*The information above comes from the manufacturer's literature on fountain nozzles.*

**Table 5.7 Pipe Routes for Nozzles**

| Nozzle # | Pipe route | Pipe gpm |
|---|---|---|
| 1 | AB | 20 |
| | BC | 20 |
| | CD | 20 |
| | DL | 20 |
| | LM | 40 |
| | MN | 144 |
| | NO | 144 |
| 2 | PE | 20 |
| | EF | 20 |
| | FG | 20 |
| | GK | 20 |
| | KL | 20 |
| | LM | 40 |
| | MN | 144 |
| | NO | 144 |
| 3 | HI | 104 |
| | IJ | 104 |
| | JM | 104 |
| | MN | 144 |
| | NO | 144 |

friction loss. This summation is shown in the pipe length subtotal column. Equivalent pipe lengths of fittings must be added to pipe lengths having similar diameter and gpm's.

3.5 Pipe velocity for the tables is established by comparing pipe gpm's with pipe diameter on the friction loss table.

3.6 Equal pipe lengths for Figures 5.49, 5.50 and 5.51 are filled in from Tables A-1 and A-2 (See Appendix). Pipe fittings B, C, D all operate at 20 gpm. Equal pipe length of these fittings is added to the length of pipe segments AB, BC, CD, and DL of Figure 5.49.

Pipe fitting B is 1½ inch in diameter and operates at 20 gpm. Looking at Table A-1 we see that the friction through fitting B equals the friction through 2.5 feet of 1½-inch diameter pipe at 20 gpm's. Figure 5.49 is appropriately completed. Pipe lengths (pipe & fittings) of similar gpm's and diameter are totaled. This summation is shown in the "length subtotal" column of Figure 5.49.

3.7 By referring to the friction loss tables for type K copper pipe, psi loss for that diameter and gpm can be found. In most instances, it will be necessary to interpolate.

3.8 Total psi loss through pipe length and fittings for Figure 5.49 is totaled (psi loss column) to convert psi to head feet, divide by .433. (1 head foot pressure = .433 psi).

Moving to the friction loss table for type K copper pipe, we find the total psi loss to be 2.79 psi.

$$\frac{1 \text{ head foot}}{.433 \text{ psi}} = \frac{x \text{ head feet}}{2.79 \text{ psi}}$$

$$x \text{ head feet} = \frac{2.79 \text{ psi head foot}}{.433 \text{ psi}}$$

$$x = 6.44 \text{ head feet}$$

Follow the same procedure until all columns are completed.

3.9 Friction loss or gain due to changes in pipe elevation comes from Figure 5.48 and is shown in Figure 5.52

Rise in pipe elevation = additional head feet pressure which pump exerts.

Fall in pipe elevation = reduction in head feet pressure which pump exerts.

Pipe segment BC rises 8 feet above the discharge center line of the pump. Eight additional head feet of pressure will be required by the pump. Figure 5.52 is filled in appropriately.

3.10 The elevation of the center line of the pump suction is lower than the pool floor. Consult with a pump engineer for head feet required by the suction line.

3.11 Total head requirement for pipe routes of nozzles is achieved by summing up the vertical columns in Figure 5.52. Nozzle No. 3 has the pipe route with the highest head feet requirement, so the total head feet requirement for the pump will equal 37.44 head feet, while gpm's will equal 144.

4. Preliminary selection of a pump should be made at this time. Pump manufacturer's data should be consulted to select an appropriate pump. Looking at Table 5.8 we see that model KP4-50-3 will produce 158 gpm's at 43 feet head. Only 158 gpm's at 37.44 feet of head are required for the fountain in Figure 5.48. This excess will provide about a 12 percent safety margin for pump pressure. In most applications a safety margin of 10 percent is desirable for pump pressure.

Final pump gpm and head feet pressure can be established after a pump engineer's calculations for pressure demand of the suction lines are completed.

**Short-Cut Methods**

Various short-cut methods are available to bypass the chore of performing hydraulic calculations for dry pumps. One manufacturer suggests that pump pressure is equal to the nozzle with the highest single head-pressure requirement plus an additional 30 feet head pressure.[131] Water capacity is equal to the total gpm's of all nozzles and eyeballs on the discharge line. This shortcut method can only be used when the following requirements are met:

1. The pump shall be located less than 75 feet from the fountain basin.

2. The water level in the fountain basin is a minimum of 16 inches deep.

3. The center line of the suction outlet on the pump is at or below the floor level of the basin containing the anti-vortex plate.[132] See manufacturer's literature for additional restrictions. This information applies to a specific manufacturer and should be appropriately adapted when using different products.

When using the quick method to size a submersible pump, employ the same method as above but add 20 instead of 30 head feet.[133] This reduction accounts for the decrease in pipe lengths associated with submersible pumps.

**Table 5.8  Pump Specifications**

| Model Number | HP | Head feet pressure output | | | | |
| --- | --- | --- | --- | --- | --- | --- |
| | | 30 | 40 | 50 | 60 | 70 |
| KP4-30-3 | 3 | 250 | 150 gpm | | | |
| KP4-50-3 | 5 | 375 | 250 gpm | | | |
| KP4-75-3 | 7½ | 625 | 450 gpm | | | |
| KP4-100-3 | 10 | 750 | 600 | 400 gpm | | |
| KP4-150-3 | 15 | 950 | 850 | 725 | 575 | 300 gpm |

*Specifications for 230-460 volts/3 phase/60 hertz dry centrifugal pump. Table adapted from manufacturer's literature by Kim Lighting.*

## Friction Loss of Pipe Route for Nozzle #1

| Pipe Segment | Pipe Length (FT.) | G.P.M. | Vel. (F.P.S.) | Pipe Diam. | Pipe Fitting | Fitting Diam. | G.P.M. | Equal Pipe Length | Length Sub-Total | P.S.I. Lost | Head FT. Lost |
|---|---|---|---|---|---|---|---|---|---|---|---|
| AB | 1.0 | 20 | 3.7 | 1 1/2" | B-90° Elb. | 1 1/2" | 20 | 2.5 | | | |
| BC | 8.0 | 20 | 3.7 | 1 1/2" | C- 90° Elb. | 1 1/2" | 20 | 2.5 | | | |
| CD | 50.0 | 20 | 3.7 | 1 1/2" | D-Gt. Val. | 1 1/2" | 20 | (+) 1.1 | | | |
| DL | (+) 0.5 | 20 | 3.7 | 1 1/2" | | | | 6.1 | → 6.1 | | |
| | 59.5 | | | | | | | | (+) 59.5 | | |
| | | | | | | | | | 65.6 → | 1.26 | |
| LM | 0.5 | 40 | 4.3 | 2" | L-Red. | 1 1/2"-2" | 40 | 3.9 | | | |
| | | | | | L-Sid. Out. Tee | 2" | 40 | (+) 5.0 | | | |
| | | | | | | | | 8.9 | → 8.9 | | |
| | | | | | | | | | (+) 0.5 | | |
| | | | | | | | | | 9.4 → | .17 | |
| MN | 1.0 | 144 | 7.0 | 3" | M- Sid. Out. Tee | 3" | 144 | 7.5 | | | |
| NO | (+) 0.5 | 144 | 7.0 | 3" | M-Red. | 3"-2" | 144 | 12.5 | | | |
| | 1.5 | | | | N-Glb. Val. | 3" | 144 | (+) 27.5 | | | |
| | | | | | | | | 47.5 → | 47.5 | | |
| | | | | | | | | | (+) 1.5 | | |
| | | | | | | | | | 49.0 → | (+) 1.36 | |
| | | | | | | | | | | 2.79 → | 6.44 |

Circled references at bottom: 3.4 | Table 5.7 | 3.5 | 3.3 | 3.6 | 3.7 | 3.8

**Figure 5.49**

## Friction Loss of Pipe Route for Nozzle #2

| Pipe Segment | Pipe Length (FT.) | G.P.M. | Vel. (F.P.S.) | Pipe Diam. | Pipe Fitting | Fitting Diam. | G.P.M. | Equal Pipe Length | Length Sub-Total | P.S.I. Lost | Head FT. Lost |
|---|---|---|---|---|---|---|---|---|---|---|---|
| PE | 1.0 | 20 | 3.7 | 1 1/2" | E-90° Elb. | 1 1/2" | 20 | 2.5 | | | |
| EF | 8.0 | 20 | 3.7 | 1 1/2" | F-90° Elb. | 1 1/2" | 20 | 2.5 | | | |
| FG | 50.0 | 20 | 3.7 | 1 1/2" | G-Gt. Val. | 1 1/2" | 20 | 1.1 | | | |
| GK | 0.5 | 20 | 3.7 | 1 1/2" | K-90° Elb. | 1 1/2" | 20 | (+) 2.5 | | | |
| KL | (+) 0.5 | 20 | 3.7 | 1 1/2" | | | | 8.6 | → 8.6 | | |
| | 60.0 | | | | | | | | (+) 60.0 | | |
| | | | | | | | | | 68.6 → | 1.31 | |
| LM | 0.5 | 40 | 4.3 | 2" | L-Red. | 2"- 1 1/2" | 40 | 3.9 | | | |
| | | | | | L-Str. Run Tee | 2" | 40 | (+) 1.0 | | | |
| | | | | | | | | 4.9 | → 4.9 | | |
| | | | | | | | | | (+) 0.5 | | |
| | | | | | | | | | 5.4 → | .10 | |
| MN | 1.0 | 144 | 7.0 | 3" | M-Sid. Out. Tee | 3" | 144 | 7.5 | | | |
| | | | | | M-Red. | 3"-2" | 144 | 12.5 | | | |
| NO | (+) 0.5 | 144 | 7.0 | 3" | N-Glb. Val. | 3" | 144 | (+)27.5 | | | |
| | 1.5 | | | | | | | 47.5 → | 47.5 | | |
| | | | | | | | | | (+) 1.5 | | |
| | | | | | | | | | 49.0 → | (+)1.36 | |
| | | | | | | | | | | 2.77 → | 6.40 |

**Figure 5.50**

152

## Friction Loss of Pipe Route for Nozzle #3

| Pipe Segment | Pipe Length (Ft.) | G.P.M. | Vel. (F.P.S.) | Pipe Diam. | Pipe Fitting | Fitting Diam. | G.P.M. | Equal Pipe Length | Length Sub-Total | P.S.I. Lost | Head FT. Lost |
|---|---|---|---|---|---|---|---|---|---|---|---|
| HI | 4.0 | 104 | 5.0 | 3″ | I–90° Elb. | 3″ | 104 | 5.0 | | | |
| IJ | 30.0 | 104 | 5.0 | 3″ | J–Gt. Val. | 3″ | 104 | (+)2.5 | | | |
| JM | (+)0.5 | 104 | 5.0 | 3″ | | | | 7.5 →→ 7.5 | | | |
| | 34.5 ————————————————————→ | | | | | | | | (+)34.5 | | |
| | | | | | | | | | 42.0 →→ .64 | | |
| MN | 1.0 | 144 | 7.0 | 3″ | M–Str. Run Tee | 3″ | 144 | 1.5 | | | |
| NO | (+) 0.5 | 144 | 7.0 | 3″ | N– Glb. Val. | 3″ | 144 | (+)27.4 | | | |
| | 1.5 —————┐ | | | | | | | 28.9 →→ 28.9 | | | |
| | └————————————————————→ | | | | | | | | (+) 1.5 | | |
| | | | | | | | | | 30.4 | | |
| | | | | | | | | | | (+).85 | |
| | | | | | | | | | | 1.49 →→ 3.44 | |

**Figure 5.51**

## Head Feet Requirement of Pipe Route

| | | Nozzle # | | | | | |
|---|---|---|---|---|---|---|---|
| | | **1** | | **2** | | **3** | |
| | Head Feet Required at Nozzle | 7.00 | Table # 5.6 | 7.00 | Table # 5.6 | 30.00 | Table # 5.6 |
| 3.9 → | Head Feet Lost Through Pipe and Fittings | 6.44 | Figure # 5.30 | 6.40 | Figure # 5.31 | 3.44 | Figure # 5.32 |
| | Head Feet Lost Through Pipe Elev. Rise (+) | 8.00 | Pipe Segment BC | 8.00 | Pipe Segment EF | 4.00 | Pipe Segment HI |
| | Head Feet Gain Through Drop in Pipe Elev. (−) | 0.00 | – | 0.00 | – | 0.00 | – |
| 3.10 → | Head Feet Lost Through Suction Lift (+) | – | – | – | – | – | – |
| | Total Head Ft. | 21.44 | | 21.40 | | 37.44 | |

**Figure 5.52**

3.11

Head Feet Required of Pump Excluding Safety Factor    37.44

Note: Safety Factor Must be Included.

# CONSTRUCTION DETAILING

Now that materials, components and design factors have been discussed, the specific detailing of fountains can be addressed.

Concrete is the predominant building material for fountains. Cost of material, ease of construction, waterproof quality, and relative durability are all factors which contribute to its popularity. The details in this chapter elaborate on the construction of fountains using concrete.

## BASIN CONSTRUCTION

Singular fountain basins can be constructed using the following methods. Wall thickness and depth will be determined by soil type, interacting forces, depth to frost line, and visual scale. Design of footings and wall thickness should be carried out in accordance with Chapter 2.

### Method No. 1

Method No. 1 requires the following construction techniques:

1. Forming and pouring of a wall footing.

2. Forming and pouring of the wall.

3. Filling and compaction of the subgrade.

4. Pouring of the floor slab.

Because the floor is physically keyed into wall, the floor acts as a structural beam. Any soil disturbance under the

floor may lead to unanticipated tensile floor stress. This stress, in turn, can cause floor cracking.

Soil compaction to 95 percent of Standard Proctor Density under the floor slab is imperative when the floor slab is keyed into the wall. This will reduce cracking from tensile stress.

Keys should be of sufficient depth to support the weight of the water and floor slab in the event of a subgrade failure. In no instance should the key be deleted. This would require the steel reinforcing to support the total weight of the floor and water. By providing a key, a structurally sound condition exists. Both the reinforcing and key seat support the total weight (See Figure 6.2).

The floor key location is somewhat independent of the footing and will allow the floor to be located above the exterior grade. This method of floor-to-wall connection permits a variety of basin elevations, while the footing rests below the frost line.

When the water is suspended above grade, a cantilevered wall may be required to prevent horizontal thrust. Thus the footing must be designed to prevent wall overturning. The physical condition of all walls in a fountain situation will somewhat mitigate the typical forces associated with wall overturning.

Waterstops should be located on the top side of the reinforcing which keys the floor into the wall. By specifying a split bulb type waterstop, appropriate positioning can be facilitated. As shown in Figure 6.1, this permits key and vertical waterstops positioning without pouring the wall, using a split wall form.

## Method No. 2

This construction process is better known in the building trades as a floating slab method. Building procedures are similar to Method No. 1 except for the pouring of the floor.

Because the wall is somewhat independent of the floor, separate settling of the floor and walls can occur.

In rigid situations where the floor is physically connected into the wall, soil settlement affects the whole fountain. A slight settlement in the wall may crack the basin floor. A floating slab will allow for differential settlement and may reduce cracking due to soil settlement.

No wall-to-floor key is required to support the floor weight. The weight of the floor and water is supported by the footing. The floor is physically "pulled down" to allow its weight to be transmitted to the footing.

Since no key is employed to support the floor, the floor elevation is somewhat dependent on the wall footing. When utilizing this building technique, the designer will be required to position the floor at an elevation near the top of the wall footing. Due to the depth of the wall footing (depth of frost), this method will prevent an above-grade positioning of the basin floor.

Because of anticipated soil movement, the floor may be subjected to tensile stress which is generated when the floor spans a depressed area. The floor slab should be appropriately reinforced to account for tensile strength.

Waterstops should be selected to allow for joint movement. The joint should be caulked with an appropriate joint filler and backer rod.

This method has specific application for building in expansive soils. A grade beam footing can be substituted for the typical footing shown in Figure 6.5. Both grade beam and floating slab will allow for soil movement with undue stresses.

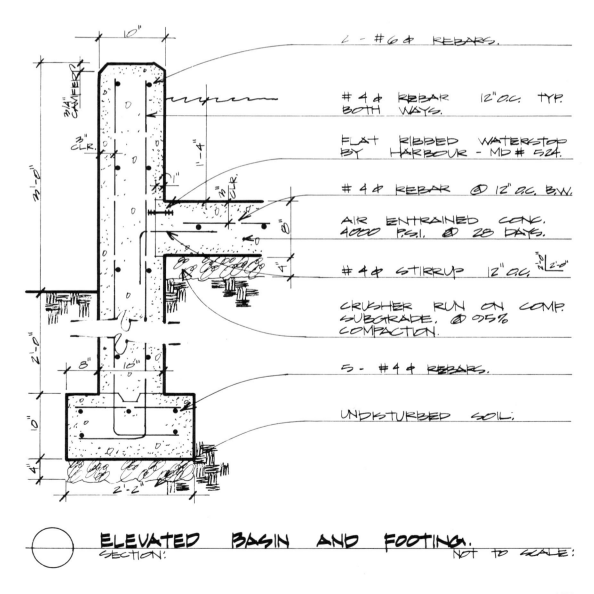

**Figure 6.1**  ELEVATED BASIN AND FOOTING. SECTION.  NOT TO SCALE.

155

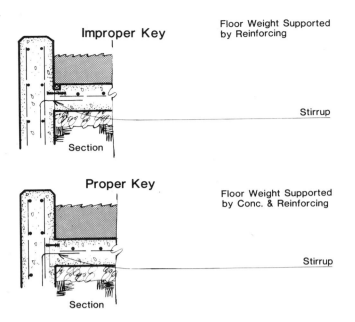

**Improper Key**

Floor Weight Supported by Reinforcing

Stirrup

Section

**Proper Key**

Floor Weight Supported by Conc. & Reinforcing

Stirrup

Section

Proper Floor to Wall Key

Figure 6.2

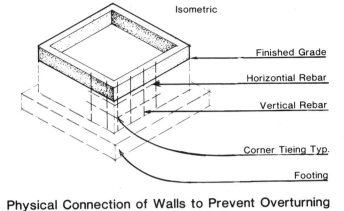

Isometric

Finished Grade

Horizontial Rebar

Vertical Rebar

Corner Tieing Typ.

Footing

Physical Connection of Walls to Prevent Overturning

Figure 6.3

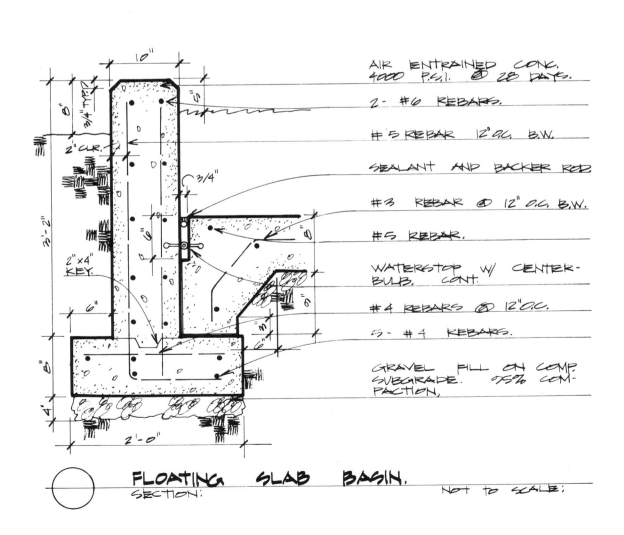

AIR ENTRAINED CONC. 4000 P.S.I. @ 28 DAYS.

2 - #6 REBARS.

#5 REBAR 12" O.C. B.W.

SEALANT AND BACKER ROD

#3 REBAR @ 12" O.C. B.W.

#5 REBAR.

WATERSTOP W/ CENTER-BULB. CONT.

#4 REBARS @ 12" O.C.

5 - #4 REBARS.

GRAVEL FILL ON COMP. SUBGRADE. 95% COMPACTION.

FLOATING SLAB BASIN.

SECTION:

NOT TO SCALE:

Figure 6.4

156

## Method No. 3

Method No. 3 requires the following construction procedures:

1. Compaction and preparation of subgrade.

2. Side forming and pouring of floor.

3. Forming and pouring of walls.

When compared to the other basin construction methods, this procedure requires the least forming to build the fountain.

This technique utilizes the floor as a footing for the wall. In some situations it may be necessary to "pull down" the floor and increase its thickness under the wall. This will increase friction between the floor and soil and prevent sliding of the fountain. This increment in thickness under the wall

will also give added support to the wall weight and reduce the chance of cracking (See Figure 6.7).

Incorporation of the footing into the floor slab prohibits the location of the basin floor above grade. The floor and footing should be appropriately located to prevent fountain movement due to freeze-thaw conditions. Locating the floor below the frost line will prevent fountain movement caused by freeze-thaw.

In some regions with a high depth to frost line a depressed basin will occur. If visually unacceptable, select an alternate construction process. Waterstops designed for vertical, non-moving applications should be specified.

Reusable concrete wall-forming systems require vertical bracing (strong backs), horizontal braces (walers), and diagonal bracing which ties the top of the wall to the ground. Strong backs and walers prevent the walls from

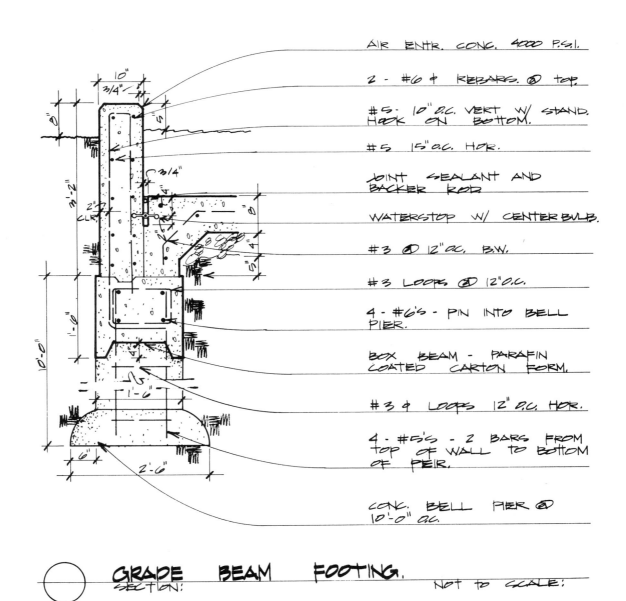

**Figure 6.5**  ◯  GRADE BEAM FOOTING.
SECTION:                                    NOT TO SCALE:

157

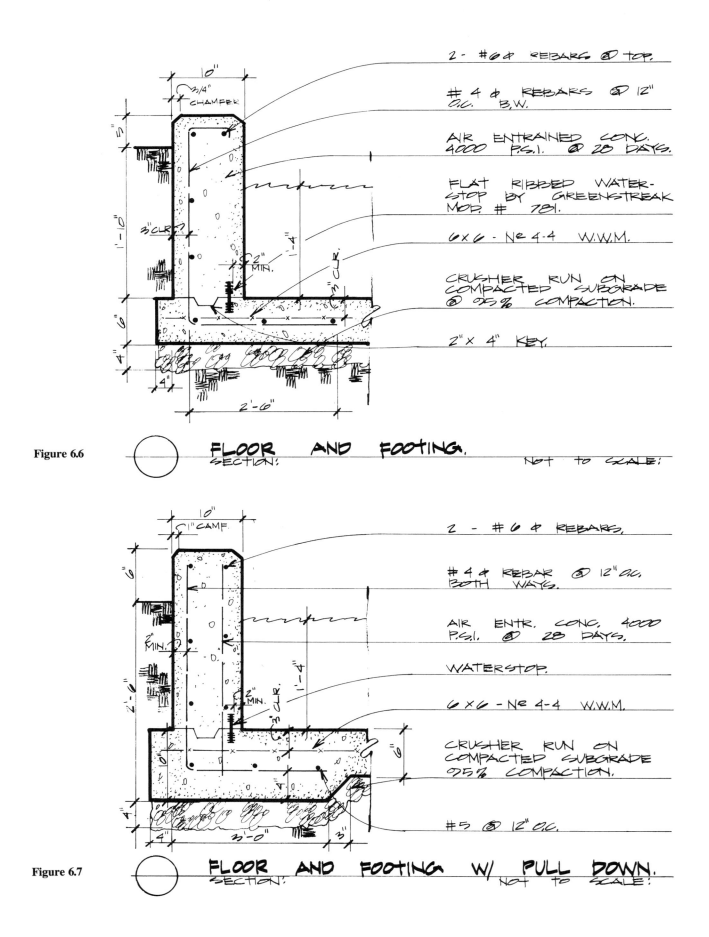

**Figure 6.6**

2 - #6 ⌀ REBARS @ TOP.

#4 ⌀ REBARS @ 12" O.C. B.W.

AIR ENTRAINED CONC. 4000 P.S.I. @ 28 DAYS.

FLAT RIBBED WATER-STOP BY GREENSTREAK MOD. # 781.

6 × 6 - N⁰ 4-4 W.W.M.

CRUSHER RUN ON COMPACTED SUBGRADE @ 95% COMPACTION.

2" X 4" KEY.

10"

3/4" CHAMFER

3" CLR.

2" MIN.

3" CLR.

2'-6"

4"

FLOOR AND FOOTING.
SECTION:                                    NOT TO SCALE!

**Figure 6.7**

2 - #6 ⌀ REBARS.

#4 ⌀ REBAR @ 12" O.C. BOTH WAYS.

AIR ENTR. CONC. 4000 P.S.I. @ 28 DAYS.

WATERSTOP.

6 × 6 - N⁰ 4-4 W.W.M.

CRUSHER RUN ON COMPACTED SUBGRADE 95% COMPACTION.

#5 @ 12" O.C.

10"

1" CAMF.

2" MIN.

2" MIN.

3" CLR.

2'-0"

4"

3'-0"

3"

FLOOR AND FOOTING W/ PULL DOWN.
SECTION:                      NOT TO SCALE!

bulging under the weight of the poured concrete. Diagonal braces hold walls of considerable height in a plumb position and ensure stability during concrete curing. When the floor and footing is poured in one piece, it will be necessary to temporarily anchor these braces into the basin floor. Care should be taken in patching these blemishes. Latex-based grouts should be used to ensure good bonding strength.

## REBAR

Traditionally, deformed steel (ASTM, A-615, Grade 60) has been used as reinforcing steel for fountains. This steel tends to rust when surface cracks allow water to penetrate and attack the steel or when steel is accidentally placed too close to the concrete face. The advent of epoxy-coated rebar alleviates this problem. The increased cost of this coating can offset some long-term maintenance costs. Care must be taken when specifying expoxy-coated rebar. Cuts and bends must be performed in the fabrication shop prior to shipment to the job site. Any field cuts must be recoated to prevent rusting.

## CONCRETE COVER

Proper concrete cover must be provided over steel rebar to prevent deterioration of the steel. Steel type and wall thickness dictate the proper concrete cover required over the rebar. In most applications, the rebar should be located 2 to 3 inches back from an exposed face of the concrete.

## Reinforcing and Footing Keys

The reinforcing which extends from the footing into the wall should be located to prevent gapping of the key joint. Gapping of the key joint should be prevented to reduce stressing on the waterstop and reinforcing steel. Normal practice is to position the vertical rebar on one side of the key in the footing. In a keyed joint, a single vertical reinforcing bar will act as a hinge. When located on the key side closest to the predominant force, the exerted pressure forces the wall into the key and prevents gapping of the wall and floor at the key joint. In this situation, the force exerted is transferred to the concrete key instead of the sparsely spaced reinforcing. When reinforcing steel is located on the key side, away from the predominant force, gapping will occur. In this case, all exerted force is transferred to the reinforcing steel (See Figure 6.9).

In situations where the direction of the force may vary, it will be necessary to alternate the location of the vertical rebar so that hinging of the key joint is prevented. Rebars would be alternately located on each side of the key.

Vertical reinforcing is often located in the center of the key to allow for uneven forces exerted on each wall side. Although this prevents gapping at the key, it requires excessive cutting of the wood key void to allow for protrusion of the vertical rebars. Figure 6.10 illustrates situations of predominant force.

In some instances two rows of vertical steel are used to prevent surface cracking of concrete (See Figure 6.7). In addition, no hinging will occur at the key joint.

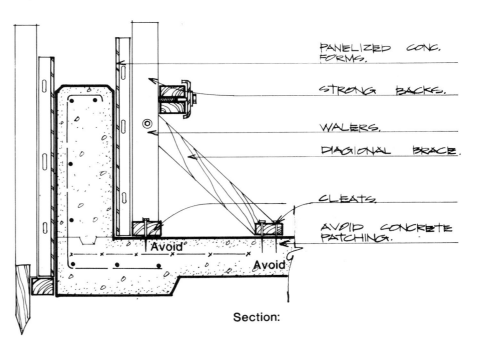

**Figure 6.8**  **Panelized  Reuseable Concrete Forms**

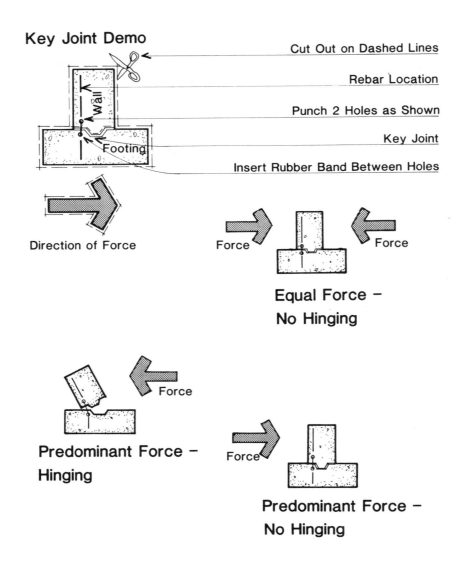

Key Joint Demo

Cut Out on Dashed Lines

Rebar Location

Punch 2 Holes as Shown

Key Joint

Insert Rubber Band Between Holes

Wall

Footing

Direction of Force

Force — Force

Equal Force –
No Hinging

Force

Predominant Force –
Hinging

Force

Predominant Force –
No Hinging

Figure 6.9     Hinging of Wall at Key Joint

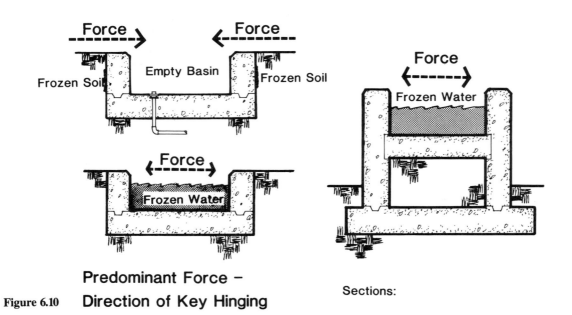

Force → ← Force

Frozen Soil    Empty Basin    Frozen Soil

Force

Frozen Water

Force

Frozen Water

Predominant Force –
Figure 6.10    Direction of Key Hinging

Sections:

**Figure 6.11** *Temporary steel edge at Weir. Virginia Beach, Virginia.*

**Figure 6.12** *Finished weir with steel edge removed. Virginia Beach, Virginia.*

### Chamfers

All exposed wall edges, weir edges or column edges should have the edges chamfered. Chamfers should be a minimum of ¼ inch and will enable the contractor to create a better finished product. By providing a chamfer on all concrete edges, chipping of edges due to wear and tear can also be reduced.

### TEMPORARY STEEL EDGES

Temporary steel edges can be bolted to weir edges or walls to ensure exact tolerances and heights. Steel plates are bolted to forms or existing concrete. This edge acts as a guide for concrete finishing. Steel guides do not warp or bow like typical wood forms (See Figure 6.11).

### Broad Rims for Basins

Broad rims are utilized to reduce splash created by wave action, as a mechanism to amplify the splashing sounds of water and to hide floating debris (See Figure 6.13). By extending the pool rim above the water level, water-like motions will be directed back into the pool, instead of over the basin rim. This same protrusion of the rim creates an echo-like chamber that amplifies sound.

Because of the cantilevered position of the rim, reinforcing needs to be situated to prevent key gapping, support the weight of the cantilevered rim, and prevent tensile stress in the floor.

### Multi-leveled Pools

Multi-leveled pools may incorporate a combination of basin construction techniques to achieve the end results. These fountains are typified by multi-leveled basins or the progressive layering of basins which relate to topography, and weired basins which fall into lower-leveled pools. Proper detailing of these fountains will consider the following:

1. When situated on sloping topography, sliding of the fountain must be prevented.

2. Elevated basins create a cantilevered wall application and will require footings to account for forces associated with cantilevered walls.

3. Due to the interconnected nature of the basins, larger fountains need to deal with the expansion and contraction of the concrete.

4. Because of the interconnected nature of the basins, settlement of the subgrade must be prevented. Any subgrade movement under the fountain will affect the whole fountain and may lead to structural cracking.

5. When the floors of lower basins are attached to the walls of basins of greater height, the lower basin floor is keyed into the support wall of the higher basin. Proper keying, reinforcement ties, and waterstops will be required at this connection.

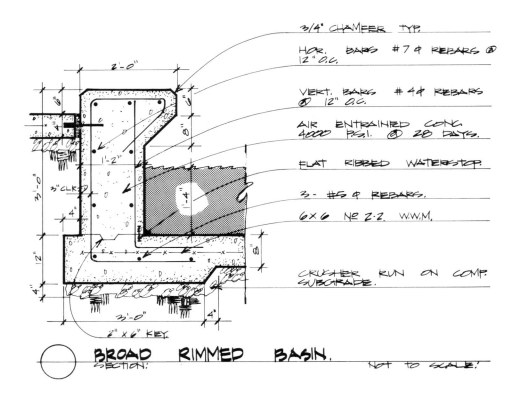

3/4" CHAMFER TYP.

HOR. BARS #7 ⌀ REBARS @ 12" O.C.

VERT. BARS #4 ⌀ REBARS @ 12" O.C.

AIR ENTRAINED CONC. 4000 P.S.I. @ 28 DAYS.

FLAT RIBBED WATERSTOP.

3- #5 ⌀ REBARS.

6×6 № 2·2. W.W.M.

CRUSHER RUN ON COMP. SUBGRADE.

2'-0"

3'-0"

1'-2"

3"CLR.

4"

12"

4"

3'-0"

4"

2"×6" KEY.

**Figure 6.13**    ⊙ BROAD RIMMED BASIN.
                    SECTION!                    NOT TO SCALE!

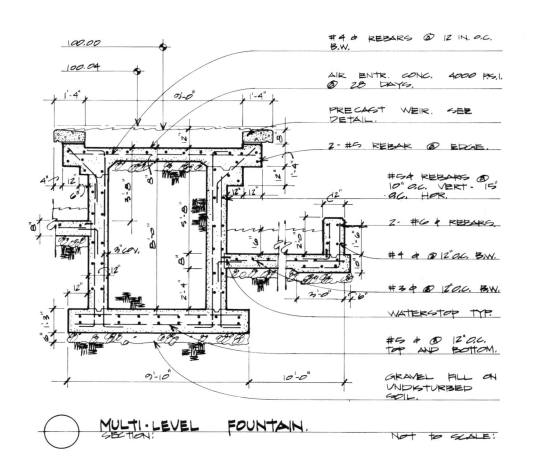

#4 ⌀ REBARS @ 12 IN. O.C. B.W.

AIR ENTR. CONC. 4000 P.S.I. @ 28 DAYS.

PRECAST WEIR. SEE DETAIL.

2- #5 REBAR @ EDGE.

#5⌀ REBARS @ 10" O.C. VERT - 15" O.C. HOR.

2- #6 ⌀ REBARS.

#4 ⌀ @ 12" O.C. B.W.

#3 ⌀ @ 12" O.C. B.W.

WATERSTOP TYP.

#5 ⌀ @ 12" O.C. TOP AND BOTTOM.

GRAVEL FILL ON UNDISTURBED SOIL.

100.00

100.04

1'-4"    0'-0"    1'-4"

4" 12"

8"

12"

3'-0"

5'-0"

8'-0"

2'-4"

1'-3"

0'-10"    10'-0"

**Figure 6.14**    ⊙ MULTI·LEVEL FOUNTAIN.
                    SECTION!                    NOT TO SCALE!

**Figure 6.15** *Multi-level fountain on flat terrain. Kansas City, Missouri.*

**Figure 6.16** *Multi-level river fountain. Tulsa, Oklahoma.*

**Figure 6.17** *Multi-level river fountain. Tulsa, Oklahoma.*

6. When walls of lower basins intersect with walls of higher basins, vertical application of keys, reinforcement ties, and waterstops are also required.

7. Keys and waterstops will be logically located to ensure waterproofing and expedite the construction process. These will be required in walls and floors. In elevated basins, it may be easier to pour a support wall and then pour a one-piece basin rim and floor on top of the support wall (See Figure 6.14).

## Weirs

Cantilevered weir crests constructed of *in situ* concrete should support the weight of the cantilevered portion of the weir. This is achieved by extending the vertical rebars to ensure added strength in the cantilevered portion. Additional strength is produced by physically tying the weir into the adjacent basin wall. The tying is achieved by connecting an "L" stirrup from the vertical reinforcement of the wall to the horizontal reinforcement of the weir. Weirs will be required to have a linear drip or reglet on the bottom of the downstream side of the weir crest.

## Drips and Reglets

Drips or reglets will be required on the bottom side of a cantilevered broad or rounded-crested weir to reduce surface tension and spring the nappe free of the weir crest. These are constructed by installing a void material in the concrete form prior to pouring. Void shapes include V-notches, ½ circles, and trapezoids. Square void shapes should be avoided because of their difficult removal from the cured concrete.

Wood or plastic void materials are easily formed and are anchored to the form prior to pouring. Void shapes having a cross-sectional area of ½ x ½ inch will be sufficient to break the surface tension.

"V"-shaped void located too close to the weir edge can create problems during concrete pouring. If located too near the edge, large aggregate will lodge between the form and the void of the drip. This lodging will prevent concrete paste from reaching the form edge, resulting in a honeycombing of the drip. This occurrence is prevalent when employing architectural form liners to articulate the surface of concrete with closely spaced "V"-shaped ribs. For proper operation and ensured strength, the drip should be located a minimum of ½ inch from the front edge of the weir chamfer.

An alternate method for drip construction would be to permanently embed a non-corrosive drip into the weir bottom. Many pre-shaped drips are available from manufacturers. These products are produced from metal and plastic sheets and are appropriately formed to provide anchorage.

A roughening of the weir crest will entrain air and create a nappe of white color. Roughening can be achieved by raking or troweling the crest before the concrete cures. As an option to this process, fiberglass form liners can be used to texture the crest surface. When excessive surface texture exists, the crest should be backsloped at ½ inch per foot to ensure drainage of the crest when the pool is drained.

Textures which run in a parallel direction to the water flow will tend to segregate the nappe and form many separate trickles over the crest.

## DRIPS AND REGLETS FOR STONE AND METAL CONSTRUCTION

In fountains constructed of metal or stone, weirs should also be supplied with drips or reglets. In stone applications, the drip can be sawn cut into the underside of the weir with a carbide saw (See Figure 6.21). When metal weirs are used, the metal can be extended to create a sharp lip or "L" configuration which will also reduce the surface tension of the water.

When a blunt, blade-like configuration is ground to the backside of an extended metal lip or weir, the water tends to drop straight down into the basin.

### Broad-crested Weirs

Broad-crested weirs of considerable length require special consideration to achieve a level crest. Normal execution tolerances associated with *in situ* concrete create longitudinal variances which produce a nappe of variable depth. In fountains employing nappes of shallow depths and considerable lengths, additional crest detailing will be required.

Installation of a stainless steel or aluminum angle on the forward edge of the crest will provide a level nappe. The angle must be supplied with anchors to adhere it to the concrete. Before the concrete is poured, the angle will be leveled and attached to the concrete form (See Figure 6.24).

Another acceptable process to assure a thin, level nappe is to form a raised triangular form on the weir crest. Once the concrete has cured, the point of the triangle can be ground to achieve a level edge for water to flow over (See Figure 6.24).

### Pre-cast Weirs

Pre-cast weirs are yet another means of achieving a long level crest. Construction accuracy typical of precast concrete allows for weir construction with minimum tolerances from level. The earlier discussion on pre-cast concrete describes a pre-cast weir utilizing stainless steel anchor pins to attach it to the basin. The following detail employs a non-corrosive anchor bolt to attach the weir to the basin. In the event of a grout failure, galvanic action can occur. Additional surface coatings will prevent galvanic action between the zinc used for galvanizing and the copper or brass nozzle equipment.

Grout, used as a leveling bed or as a plugging material for the bolt void, should contain a latex admix to increase bonding strength. The anchor bolt must be manufactured from a non-corrosive material to prevent bolt corrosion in the event of a loosening at the grout joint. Lead shims are soft and allow the weir to be beaten slightly until a level position is reached. At this point in execution, the pre-cast weir is removed and properly coated with a grout coat. The weir is then lifted onto the grout bed and the bolts are tightened.

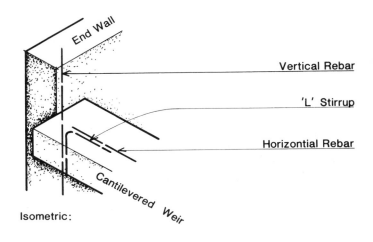

Isometric:

## Weir Support

**Figure 6.18**

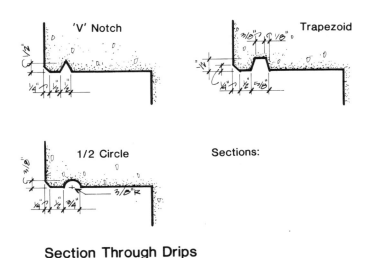

## Section Through Drips

**Figure 6.19**

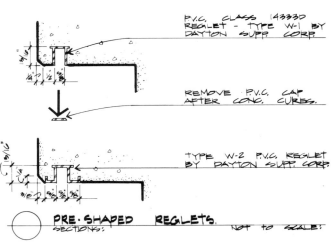

**Figure 6.20**

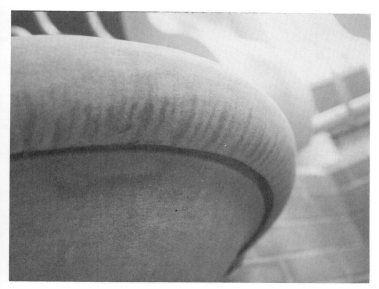

**Figure 6.21** *Ground or saw cut drip in stone construction. Washington, District of Columbia.*

**Figure 6.23** *Roughening of weir crest to achieve white water. Tulsa, Oklahoma*

Anchor or "J" bolts used to secure the weir should maintain a minimum of 2-inch clearance between all exterior faces. In the event that galvanized "J" bolts are substituted for stainless steel, this minimum clearance provides protection from corrosion or galvanic action.

The grout leveling bed may need to vary in depth to ensure a level crest. Grout thickness should not exceed ½ of an inch or be less than ¼ of an inch.

Detailing of the bolt void will be provided by the pre-cast manufacturer. The void must be large enough to allow for insertion of a wrench to tighten the nut, and to facilitate the ease of construction and removal of the void after curing. Cardboard void tubes used by the concrete industry will provide a suitable void. These materials are available precoated on the interior or exterior to ensure ease of removal after curing. This allows for the formation of a void or column.

A permanently inserted pipe sleeve creates a shaft for the anchor bolt. This facilitates ease of weir construction and ensures additional strength when the bolt is tightened. The sleeves must be of a noncorrosive material and should be located no closer than 10 inches from the weir edge. The number and location of bolts should allow for proper anchoring without weakening the edges.

Pre-cast weir panels should be from 4 to 8 feet in length. Lengths in excess of 8 feet are somewhat difficult to position and level. Difficulty arises when the heavy weir panels must be lifted for positioning or application of grout.

Back slope of the weir top and the rounded edges of the weir make the water fall almost vertically into the lower basin. Other weir configurations often create surface tension which springs the water outward, away from the weir.

Pre-cast weirs designed to cantilever considerable distances will require anchor bolts instead of stainless steel dowels to attach the weir to the basin. Single rows of anchors arranged in a straight line will create a hinge-type situation and encourage rocking.

In some instances, it may be necessary to jog the location of the anchors to prevent rocking of the precast panel. When utilizing lead shims, spread them out to create a stable base and prevent rocking.

### Elevated Basins or Spill Lips

Centrally located, elevated basins are nice additions to small gardens or courtyards. The basin stem should be supported by a slab footing to create stability and sustain the weight of the basin and stem.

Once the basin footing has cured, the basin stem is poured into a keyed footing. The key should form a circle around the pipe chase (See Figure 6.28).

The cantilevered portion of an elevated basin should be supported by the horizontal reinforcing to ensure proper strength. This reinforcing should be tied to the vertical reinforcement of the basin stem. The addition of a key between the stem and elevated basin will reduce the potential of shearing at the joint. By providing a concrete key, any stress which is imposed on the steel reinforcement will be applied

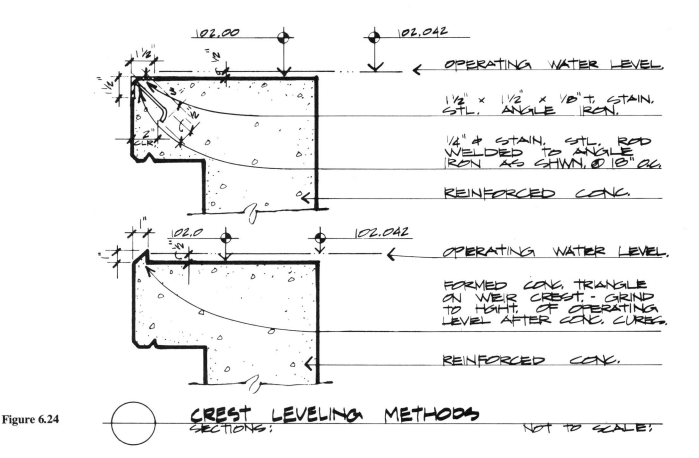

102.00     102.042

OPERATING WATER LEVEL.

1½" × 1½" × ⅛" t. STAIN.
STL. ANGLE IRON.

¼" ⌀ STAIN. STL. ROD
WELDED TO ANGLE
IRON AS SHWN, @ 18" O.C.

REINFORCED CONC.

102.0     102.042

OPERATING WATER LEVEL.

FORMED CONC. TRIANGLE
ON WEIR CREST. - GRIND
TO HGHT. OF OPERATING
LEVEL AFTER CONC. CURES.

REINFORCED CONC.

**Figure 6.24**    ◯   **CREST LEVELING METHODS**
SECTIONS:             NOT TO SCALE!

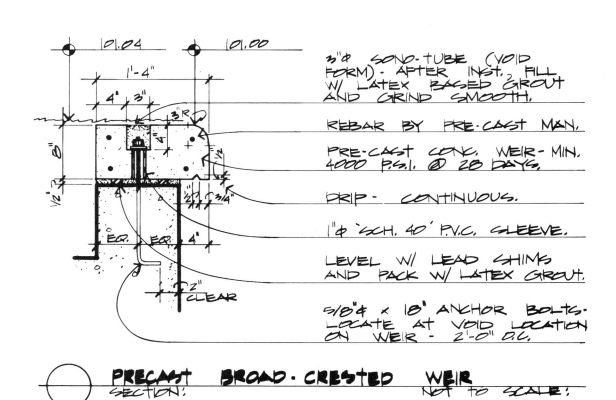

101.04     101.00

3" ⌀ SONO-TUBE (VOID
FORM) - AFTER INST., FILL
W/ LATEX BASED GROUT
AND GRIND SMOOTH.

REBAR BY PRE-CAST MAN.

PRE-CAST CONC. WEIR - MIN.
4000 P.S.I. @ 28 DAYS.

DRIP - CONTINUOUS.

1" ⌀ "SCH. 40" P.V.C. SLEEVE.

LEVEL W/ LEAD SHIMS
AND PACK W/ LATEX GROUT.

5/8" ⌀ × 18" ANCHOR BOLTS -
LOCATE AT VOID LOCATION
ON WEIR - 2'-0" O.C.

**Figure 6.25**    ◯   **PRECAST BROAD-CRESTED WEIR**
SECTION:             NOT TO SCALE!

166

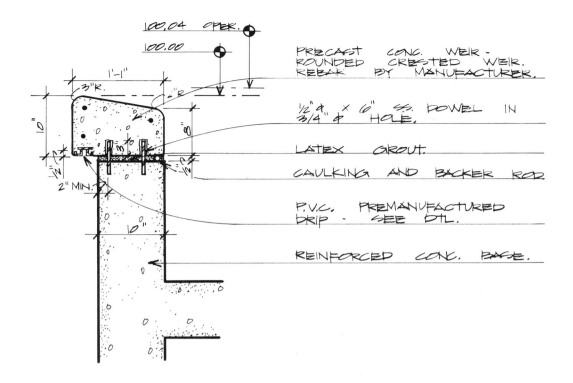

100.04 OPER.

100.00

1'-1"

3"R.

10"

2" MIN.

10"

PRECAST CONC. WEIR - ROUNDED CRESTED WEIR. REBAR BY MANUFACTURER.

1/2" ø X 6" SS. DOWEL IN 3/4" ø HOLE.

LATEX GROUT.

CAULKING AND BACKER ROD

P.V.C. PREMANUFACTURED DRIP - SEE DTL.

REINFORCED CONC. BASE.

**Figure 6.26**

PRECAST ROUNDED-CRESTED WEIR.

SECTION: NOT TO SCALE:

**Figure 6.27** *Elevated spill lip. Stillwater, Oklahoma*

to the key. Once the stem has cured, the elevated basin can be poured.

The weight of the basin floor slab must be supported by the basin stem or elevated basin footing. This is achieved by pulling down the floor slab to the footing or by keying the floor into the stem. In both situations, a waterstop will be required.

The remaining basin walls will be poured into the key of the cured floor slab.

As an alternative to this construction method, a one-piece floor and footing can be poured for the entire fountain. The floor under the elevated basin will employ a key and waterstop to connect the fountain stem. Additional floor depth, created by a pulled-down floor, will give added support to the elevated basin (See Figure 6.29).

This method of construction is best suited for small, elevated basins. Basins of considerable weight and size will require an independent footing as shown in Figure 6.28.

167

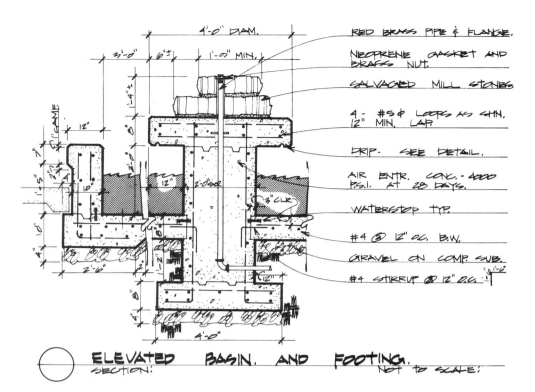

RED BRASS PIPE & FLANGE.

NEOPRENE GASKET AND BRASS NUT.

SALVAGED MILL STONES.

4 - #5∅ LOOPS AS SHN, 12" MIN. LAP.

DRIP. SEE DETAIL.

AIR ENTR. CONC. - 4000 P.S.I. AT 28 DAYS.

WATERSTOP TYP.

#4 @ 12" O.C. B.W.

GRAVEL ON COMP. SUB.

#4 STIRRUP @ 12" O.C.

**Figure 6.28**  ELEVATED BASIN. AND FOOTING.
SECTION.                    NOT TO SCALE.

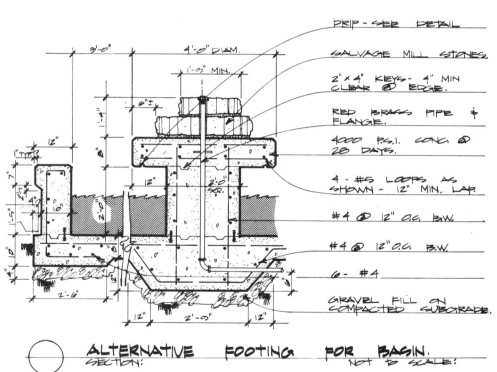

DRIP - SEE DETAIL

SALVAGE MILL STONES.

2" X 4" KEYS - 4" MIN CLEAR @ EDGE.

RED BRASS PIPE & FLANGE.

4000 P.S.I. CONC. @ 28 DAYS.

4 - #5 LOOPS AS SHOWN - 12" MIN. LAP.

#4 @ 12" O.C. B.W.

#4 @ 12" O.C. B.W.

6 - #4

GRAVEL FILL ON COMPACTED SUBGRADE.

**Figure 6.29**  ALTERNATIVE FOOTING FOR BASIN.
SECTION.                    NOT TO SCALE.

# 7

# SPECIALTY ITEMS

### Sculptural Elements

Single basins are somewhat unattractive when the water features are turned off. By providing a sculptural element within the basin, additional interest can be created for the non-operating fountain.

When designing the footing for a sculptural element, it will be necessary to consider object weight, wind loads, and durability of the artwork.

**Figure 7.1** *Fountain basin is somewhat unattractive during down time of pump. Wilmington, Delaware.*

Noncorrosive metal elements of sufficient stability can be directly anchored to the floor. Art objects of sufficient weight will require the thickening of the floor slab at this connection. Fasteners should be manufactured from a non-corrosive metal with low galvanic action (See Figure 7.5).

Sculptural elements built from stone, brick, concrete or combined materials will require a separate footing which is independent of the floor (See Figure 6.29).

In the event that a tall sculptural element is installed into the basin, the footing depth will need to be sufficient to prevent overturning.

Sculptural elements constructed from nondurable materials or slightly corrosive metals should be elevated above the water level. Materials like Cor-Ten steel are not intended for submersible applications and will require a base support which is higher than the water level.

### Kinetic Sculpture

The main thrust of these features is to encourage water to operate some moving part of the sculpture.

Movement is permitted by use of axles, sleeves or bearings or by using water as a natural lubricant.

When axles and sleeves are used, they must be fabricated from noncorrosive metals. Bearings must be specified of stainless steel casings containing sealed, watertight bearings (See Figure 7.15).

**Figure 7.3** *Sculptural hands (60 feet tall) in fountain. Tulsa, Oklahoma.*

**Figure 7.2** *Sculptural elements require footings to counteract wind loads. Philadelphia, Pennsylvania.*

**Figure 7.4** *Granite and cast iron sculptural element. Charlottesville, Virginia.*

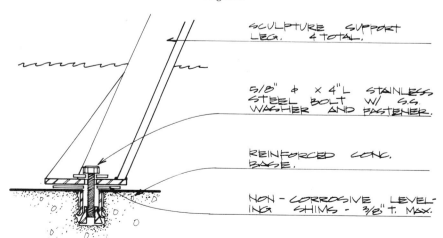

SCULPTURE SUPPORT LEG. 4 TOTAL.

5/8" ⌀ × 4"L STAINLESS STEEL BOLT W/ S.S. WASHER AND FASTENER.

REINFORCED CONC. BASE.

NON-CORROSIVE LEVELING SHIMS - 3/8" T. MAX.

**Figure 7.5**

SCULPTURE SUPPORT LEG
SECTION:          NOT TO SCALE:

170

**Figure 7.7** *See Figure 7.6*

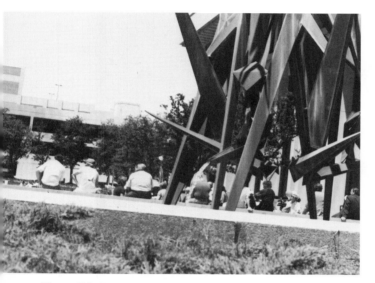

**Figure 7.8** *See Figure 7.6*

**Figure 7.6** *Water scoops of the sculptural element fill, and then empty the water into the fountain basin. Oklahoma City, Oklahoma.*

To ensure continual operation, lubrication and corrosion protection will be required (See Figure 7.12).

Water can be used as a natural lubricant to propel large spheres fabricated from stone (See Figures 7.9 to 7.11). In this application, a socket and sphere are carved so that the sphere is slightly smaller than the socket. Water is piped into a water sump located at the bottom of the socket. The pipe to the sump is located off center from the sphere. Because of this eccentric situation, more lubricating water flows around one side of the ball than the other, thus causing the ball to spin.

Because the water film between the ball and socket is approximately .005 inches, any dirt deposited in the water will act as grit and prevent the ball from spinning. Care must be taken to provide a sufficient filter media to remove grit from the circulating water.

### Brick Waterwall

A waterwall is a wetted vertical plane comprised of undulating surfaces. These nonplumb surfaces create a white, fluffy water effect which is similar to a waterfall. Waterwalls are typically designed with a slight batter so water will adhere to the surface rather than fall freely. This greatly reduces water splash which can be a problem in waterfalls.

Photo by R. John Summers

**Figure 7.9** *Water powered sculpture. Wilmington, Delaware.*

Photo by R. John Summers

**Figure 7.10** *Water powered sculpture. Wilmington, Delaware.*

**Figure 7.11** *Spinning granite sphere. Wilmington, Delaware.*

Photo by R. John Summers

## Fountains without Retained Water

Fountains without retained water are urban fountains in which nozzles are set flush with the pavement. When the fountain pumps are activated, the water sprays on the pavement and flows into a collection grate around the perimeter of the paving. Although these fountains have no visible basin, a water basin is still provided. This basin is located underneath a reinforced plaza floor and meets the water demand for the suction line.

The increased popularity of these fountains can be attributed to the following:

1. Low water depths allow children to interact with the water without liability problems.

2. By turning the pumps off, the space can be used for parades and other public gatherings.

3. Floating trash, which makes traditional fountains unsightly, is retained underground.

In applications where water level dependent aerating nozzles are used, each nozzle must be supplied with sufficient water cover. Individual water sumps, concealed under the pavement, provide the nozzles with the required cover (See Figures 7.20 to 7.22).

## Summary

Combining some creative genius with the technical data in this book should create an exciting and well-constructed fountain. Special attention to material selection and construction techniques will ensure a water feature of lasting value, instead of a maintenance nightmare.

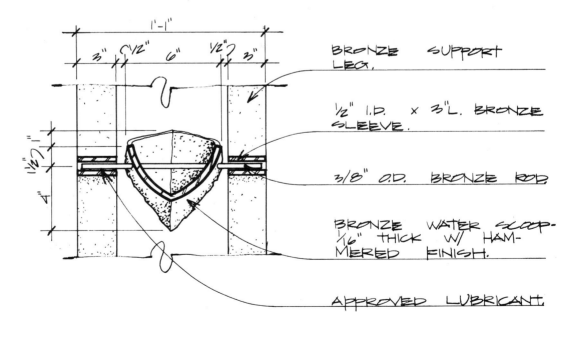

**Figure 7.12**

BRONZE SUPPORT LEG.

1/2" I.D. × 3"L. BRONZE SLEEVE.

3/8" O.D. BRONZE ROD

BRONZE WATER SCOOP- 1/16" THICK W/ HAMMERED FINISH.

APPROVED LUBRICANT.

MOVING WATER SCOOP
SECTION                    NOT TO SCALE

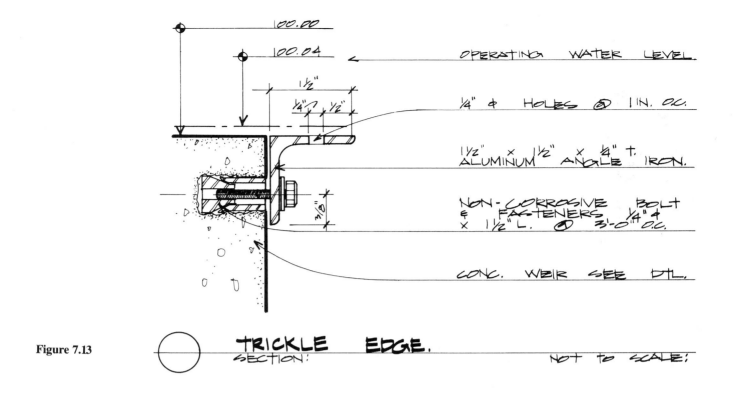

100.00

100.04 ← OPERATING WATER LEVEL.

1½"

¼" ½"

¼" ∅ HOLES @ 1 IN. O.C.

1½" × 1½" × ¼" t.
ALUMINUM ANGLE IRON.

³/₈"

NON-CORROSIVE BOLT
& FASTENERS ¼" ∅
× 1½" L. @ 3'-0" O.C.

CONC. WEIR SEE DTL.

TRICKLE EDGE.
SECTION:

NOT TO SCALE!

Figure 7.13

**Figure 7.14** *Waterproof bearings of an acrylic waterwheel. Oklahoma City, Oklahoma.*

**Figure 7.15** *Waterproof bearings of an acrylic waterwheel. Oklahoma City, Oklahoma.*

174

**Figure 7.16** *Trickle edge weir. Kansas City, Missouri.*

**Figure 7.17** *Brick waterwall. Kansas City, Missouri.*

**Figure 7.18** *Concrete waterwall. Denver, Colorado.*

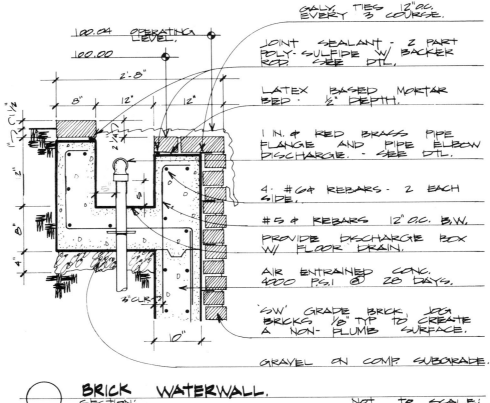

GALV. TIES 12" O.C.
EVERY 3 COURSE.

100.04 OPERATING LEVEL.

100.00

JOINT SEALANT - 2 PART POLY-SULFIDE W/ BACKER ROD. SEE DTL.

LATEX BASED MORTAR BED - ½" DEPTH.

1 IN. ⌀ RED BRASS PIPE FLANGE AND PIPE ELBOW DISCHARGE. - SEE DTL.

4 - #6⌀ REBARS - 2 EACH SIDE.

#5 ⌀ REBARS 12" O.C. B.W.

PROVIDE DISCHARGE BOX W/ FLOOR DRAIN.

AIR ENTRAINED CONC. 4000 P.S.I @ 28 DAYS.

'SW' GRADE BRICK, JOG BRICKS ⅛" TYP TO CREATE A NON-PLUMB SURFACE.

GRAVEL ON COMP. SUBGRADE.

**Figure 7.19**

**BRICK WATERWALL.**
SECTION:                                          NOT TO SCALE:

**Figure 7.20** *Granite fishscale pattern waterfall. Washington, District of Columbia.*

**Figure 7.21** *Granite fishscale pattern waterfall. Washington, District of Columbia.*

**Figure 7.22** *Fountains without retained water, New Orleans, Louisiana.*

**Figure 7.23** *Fountain without retained water.*

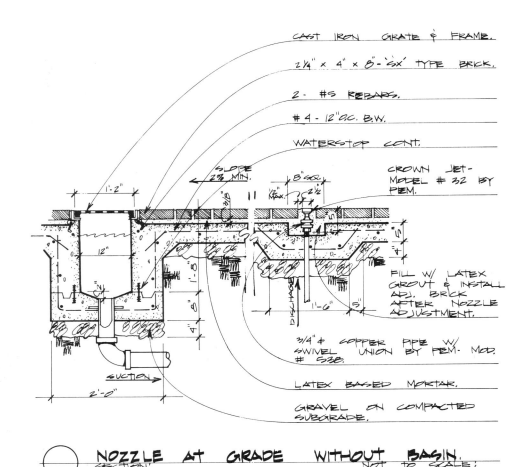

CAST IRON GRATE & FRAME.

2¼" × 4" × 8" - 'SX' TYPE BRICK.

2 - #5 REBARS.

# 4 - 12"O.C. B.W.

WATERSTOP CONT.

CROWN JET - MODEL # 32 BY PEM.

SLOPE 2% MIN.

FILL W/ LATEX GROUT & INSTALL ADJ. BRICK AFTER NOZZLE ADJUSTMENT.

3/4"∅ COPPER PIPE W/ SWIVEL UNION BY PEM. MOD. # 538.

LATEX BASED MORTAR.

GRAVEL ON COMPACTED SUBGRADE.

SUCTION

**Figure 7.24**   NOZZLE AT GRADE WITHOUT BASIN. SECTION: NOT TO SCALE:

**Figure 7.25** *Frozen fountains. Oklahoma City, Oklahoma.*

# END NOTES

[1]Craig S. Campbell, *Water in Landscape Architecture* (New York, NY: Van Nostrand Reinhold Co., 1978), p. 76.

[2]Kent and Pamela Jacobs Keegan, *Swimming Pools* (Passaic, NJ: Creative Homeowner Press, 1981), p. 34; Harlow C. Landphair and Fred Klatt, Jr., *Landscape Architecture Construction* (New York, NY: Elsevier North Holland, Inc., 1979), p. 290.

[3]Sidney Mindness and Jay Francis Young, *Concrete* (New York, NY: Prentice-Hall, 1981).

[4]Philip H. Perkins, *Swimming Pools,* 2nd ed (Essex, England: Applied Science Publishers Ltd., 1978), p. 145.

[5]*Ibid.*

[6]*Ibid.,* p. 146.

[7]*Ibid.*

[8]"Factors Influencing Temperature of Concrete — Means of Attaining Low Temperature Concrete," *Concrete Topics.* Bulletin of Kaiser Cement and Gypsum Corporation, No. 11 (1965), p. 3.

[9]Perkins, p. 147.

[10]*Ibid.,* p.113.

[11]*Ibid.*

[12]"Designing Concrete for Special Uses," *Concrete Topics.* Bulletin of Kaiser Cement and Gypsum Corporation, No. 15 (1965), p. 2.

[13]*Ibid.*

[14]L. C. Porter, "Some Surface Treatments Increase Concrete Durability," in *Durability of Concrete* (Detroit, MI: American Concrete Institute, Table 1, 1975), p. 219.

[15]*Behavior of Concrete Under Temperature Extremes,* Pub. #SP-39 (Detroit, MI: American Concrete Institute, 1973), p. 2.

[16]Carl Bergwanger and A. Farque Sarker, "Effect of Temperature and Age on Thermal Expansion and Modulus of Elasticity of Concrete," in *Behavior of Concrete Under Temperature Extremes,* Pub. #SP-39 (Detroit, MI: American Concrete Institute, 1973), p. 10.

[17]"Silicone Construction Sealants," *General Electric Technical Bulletin* (Waterford, NY: General Electric Corporation, January 1983), p. 2.

[18]*Ibid,* p. 4.

[19]Keegan and Keegan, p. 39.

[20]E. Byron McCulley, "Waterpools and Fountains" *Handbook of Landscape Architectural Construction,* Ed. Jot D. Carpeter (McLean, VA: The Landscape Architecture Foundation, 1976), p. 491.

[21]Perkins, pp. 155–156.

[22]"Floors and Pavements," *Technical Notes on Brick and Tile Construction,* No. 14 (Washington, D.C.: Structural Clay Products Inst., June 1962), p. 1.

[23]"Chemical-Resistant Materials; Vitrified Clay, Concrete Fiber-Cement Products; Mortars; Masonry," *1982 Annual Book of A.S.T.M. Standards,* ed., XVI (Philadelphia, PA: American Society for Testing and Materials, 1982), pp. 140–144.

[24]"Floors and Pavements," p. 6.

[25]"Portland Cement-Lime Mortars for Brick Masonry," *Technical Notes on Brick and Tile Construction,* Bulletin of Structural Clay Products, No. 8 (McLean, VA: September 1972), p. 7.

[26]Personal Interview with Technical Aid Staff, Laticrete International, Inc. (Bethany, CT: 15 May 1983).

[27]"Reinforced Brick Masonry Swimming Pools," *Technical Notes on Brick and Tile Construction,* Bulletin of Structural Clay Products, No. 17K, Table 1 (August 1967), p. 4.

[28]"Brick Paver Specifications," *Hastings Technical Bulletin* (Lake Success, NY: Hastings Pavement Co., Inc., 1983).

[29]L & M Surco Mfg., Inc., *A Complete Product Line for Installing Grouting, Sealing and Cleaning Ceramic Tile, Slate, and Clay Products.* Pamphlet Sweet's 6-81 (South River, NJ: L & M Surco, June 1981), pp. 1–4.

[30]Laticrete International Inc., *The Laticrete System,* Brochure Corbett 70M (Bethany, CT: Laticrete International, 1982), p. 4.

[31]*Ibid.*

[32]*Ibid.*

[33]*Ibid.*

[34]*Ibid.,* p. 5.

[35]Conference for 1982/83 Handbook for Ceramic Tile Installation, *1983 Handbook for Ceramic Tile Installation* (Princeton, NJ: Tile Council of America, Inc., 1982), p. 10.

[36]"Standard Specification for Portland Cement-Lime Mortar for Brick Masonry," *Technical Notes on Brick Construction,* Bulletin of Structural Clay Products, No. 8A (Oct–Nov., 1972), p. 1.

[37]Conference for 1982/83 Handbook for Ceramic Tile, p. 27.

[38]*Ibid.*

[39]*Ibid.,* p. 5.

40Laticrete International Inc., *Ceramics and Mosaics: Tiles and Veneer,* Pamphlet 230.3–230.6 (Bethany, CT: Laticrete International, May 1982), pp. 1–2.

41*Ibid.*

42*Ibid.*

43*Ibid.*

44*Ibid.*

45Personal Interview with Henry C., Technical Aid Staff, Laticrete International Inc., (Bethany, CT: 17 May 1983).

46"Soil and Rock; Building Stones," *1982 Annual Book of A.S.T.M. Standards,* ed. XIX (Philadelphia, PA: American Society for Testing and Materials, 1982), pp. 34–35.

47*Ibid.,* pp. 36–37.

48Nelson Miller, "Pouring Life into a Landscape: Water Gardens," *The Construction Specifier,* April 1983, p. 35.

49"Soil and Rock; Building Stones," p. 37.

50"Don A. Watson, *Construction Materials and Processes,* 2nd ed (New York, NY: McGraw-Hill, Inc., 1978), p. 93.

51"Soil and Rock; Building Stones," pp. 38–39.

52*Ibid.,* pp. 28–29.

53Copper/Brass/Bronze Design Handbook, p. 4.

54*Ibid.*

55*Ibid.,* p. 6.

56*Ibid.,* p. 8–9.

57*Ibid.,* pp. 55–56.

58Letter and Drawings Received from J. Scott Howell, Vice President, General Manager of Robinson Iron Works (Alexander City, AL: 27 May 1983).

59*Ibid.*

60Watson, p. 114.

61*Ibid.*

62*Ibid.*

63*Ibid.,* pp. 115–116.

64*Ibid.,* pp. 124–131.

65*Ibid.,* pp. 139–140.

67Uniroyal-U.S. Rubber, Waterproof Rubber Surfaces, Pamphlet 3619 (Mishawaka, IN: Uniroyal, no date), p. 3.

68Laticrete International Inc., *The Laticrete System,* p. 5.

69Perkins, p. 156.

70Landphair, pp. 390–391.

71Perkins, p. 200.

72*Ibid.,* pp. 319–339.

73*Ibid.*

74Campbell, p. 109.

75Kim Lighting, Inc., *Architectural Fountain Equipment.* Brochure P1 (City of Industry, CA: Kim Lighting, 1981), p. 39.

76James A. Watkins, *Turf Irrigation Manual: The Complete Guide to Turf and Landscape Sprinkler Systems.* ed. H. Gene Johnson, 3rd ed (Dallas, TX: Telsco Industries, 1978), p. 16.

77Campbell, p. 102.

78Campbell, pp. 102–105; McCulley, pp. 483–484.

79Kim Lighting, p. 37.

80Peter Micha, *Pem Equipment.* 15th ed (Ontario, Canada: Pem Fountains, 1980), pp. 200–215.

81Kim Lighting, p. 5.

82*Ibid.,* p. 37.

83Jack Erbe, *Handbook for Designing Decorative Fountains* (Albuquerque, NM: Roman Fountains, Inc., 1974), p. 162.

84Micha, p. 220.

85Campbell, pp. 35–39.

86*Ibid.,* p. 108.

87Erbe, p. 69.

88W. M. Hobbs, Ltd. *Architectural Fountains,* Untitled Pamphlet (Atlanta, GA: W. M. Hobbs, Ltd., No date), p. 2.

89Campbell, p. 108.

90*Ibid.,* p. 109.

91Erbe, p. 105.

92McCulley, p. 493.

93Erbe, p. 98.

94Watkins, Figure 2–1, p. 33.

95*Ibid.*

96*Ibid.,* p. 38.

97*Ibid.,* Figure 2–4, p. 41.

98*Ibid.*

99Erbe, p. 92.

100Campbell, p. 110.

101Erbe, p. 75.

102Kim Lighting, Inc., p. 39.

103Campbell, p. 110.

104Erbe, p. 88.

105*Ibid.,* p. 90.

106Miller, p. 36–37.

107Kim Lighting, Inc. p. 23.

108Watson, p. 427.

109Roland E. Palmquist, *Guide to the 1981 Electrical Code* (Indianapolis, IN: Theodore Audel & Co., 1981), p. 607.

110*Ibid.,* pp. 608–609.

111Kim Lighting, Inc., p. 39.

112Palmquist, p. 608.

113Kim Lighting, Inc., p. 40.

114*Ibid.,* pp. 39–40.

115*Ibid.,* p. 40.

116Erbe, p. 33.

117*Ibid.*

118*Ibid.*

119Personal Interview with Technical Staff, Kim Lighting, Inc., City of Industry, CA: 15 May 1983.

120Horace Williams King and Ernest F. Brater, *Handbook of Hydraulics: For the Solution of Hydrostatic and Fluid-Flow Problems.* 5th ed (New York, NY: McGraw-Hill Book Co.), 1963, pp. 5–1 to 5–2.

121King and Brater, p. 5–1.

122Jim Leckie et. al., *Other Homes and Garbage: Designs for Self-Sufficient Living* (San Francisco, CA: Sierra Club Books, 1975), Table 3–2, p. 63.

123King and Brater, pp. 5–8, 5–9.

124*Ibid.,* Table 5–3, pp. 5–46.

125Jonas M. K. Dake, *Essentials of Engineering Hydraulics* (New York, NY: Wiley-Interscience, 1972), p. 153.

[126]Campbell, p. 100; Kim Lighting, Inc. p. 37.

[127]McCulley, p. 483.

[128]Kim Lighting, Inc., p. 37.

[129]*Ibid.*, p. 34.

[130]Personal Interview with Technical Staff of PEM Fountain Co., Ontario, Canada, 12 July 1983.

[131]Kim Lighting, Inc., p. 37.

[132]*Ibid.*

[133]*Ibid.*, p. 39.

[134]Watkins, p. 336.

[135]*Ibid.*, p. 335.

[136]*Ibid.*, p. 318.

[137]*Ibid.*, p. 319.

[138]*Ibid.*, p. 312.

[139]*Ibid.*, p. 313.

[140]*Ibid.*, p. 310.

[141]*Ibid.*, p. 311.

[142]*Ibid.*, p. 308.

[143]*Ibid.*, p. 309.

[144]*Ibid.*, p. 306.

[145]*Ibid.*, p. 307.

# ACKNOWLEDGMENTS

Many thanks to my friends, colleagues, and educators. Without their support and professional encouragement, this book would not have been possible.

Special thanks to:
Barbara Summers Aurand, Jo Ann Kornmann, Anna Tyson, James R. Lemon, J. Parks Hammond, Jack Douglas, Harry Porter, Allen Stovall, Richard Rosine, Don Girouard, and Margaret Summers.

Thanks a lot, wherever you are.

Technical assistance was received from the following companies: Acme Brick Company, Oklahoma City, Oklahoma; Cold Springs Granite Company, Cold Springs, Minnesota; Glen-Gery Corporation, Shoemakersville, Pennsylvania; Laticrete International Inc., Bethany, Connecticut; Kim Lighting, City of Industry, California; Sonneborne Building Products Division of ConTech Inc., Minneapolis, Minnesota; PEM Fountain Company, Ontario, Canada; and Robinson Iron, Alexander City, Alabama.

# BIBLIOGRAPHY

Bergwanger, Carl and Sarker, A. Farque. "Effect of Temperature and Age on Thermal Expansion and Modulus of Elasticity of Concrete," in *Behavior of Concrete Under Temperature Extremes.* Detroit, MI, Pub. #SP-39, American Concrete Institute, 1973.

Campbell, Craig S. *Water in Landscape Architecture.* New York: Van Nostrand Reinhold Co., 1978.

*Concrete Topics.* "Designing Concrete for Special Uses," Bulletin of Kaiser Cement and Gypsum Corporation, No. 15, 1965.

_____, "Factors Influencing Temperature of Concrete — Means of Attaining Low Temperature Concrete," Bulletin of Kaiser Cement and Gypsum Corporation, No. 11, 1965.

Dake, Jonas M. K. *Essentials of Engineering Hydraulics.* New York, NY: Wiley-Interscience, 1972.

Erbe, Jack. *Handbook for Designing Decorative Fountains.* Albuquerque, NM: Roman Fountains, Inc. 1974.

*General Electric Technical Bulletin.* "Silicone Construction Sealants," Waterford, NY: General Electric Corporation, January 1973.

*Hastings Technical Bulletin.* "Brick Paver Specifications," Lake Success, NY: Hasting Pavement Company, Inc., 1983.

Hobbs, W. M. Ltd. *Architectural Fountains,* Untitled Pamphlet, Atlanta, GA: (no date).

Keegan, Kent and Keegan, Pamela Jacobs. *Swimming Pools.* Passaic, NJ: Creative Homeowner Press, 1981.

Kim Lighting, Inc. *Architectural Fountain Equipment.* Brochure P1, City of Industry, CA: 1981.

_____, Personal Interview with Technical Aid Staff, City of Industry, CA: 15 May 1983.

King, Horace Williams and Brater, Ernest F. *Handbook of Hydraulics: For the Solution of Hydrostatic and Fluid-Flow Problems.* 5th ed., New York, NY: McGraw-Hill Co., 1963.

L & M Surco Mfg., Inc. *A Complete Product Line for Installing Grouting, Sealing and Cleaning Ceramic Tile, Slate and Clay Products.* Pamphlet Sweet's 6–81, South River, NJ: L & M Surco, June 1981.

Landphair, Harlow C. and Klatt, Fred Jr. *Landscape Architecture Construction.* NY: Elsevier North Holland, Inc. 1979.

Laticrete International, Inc., *Ceramics and Mosaics: Tile and Veneer,* Pamphlet 230.3–230.6, Bethany, CT: 1982.

_____, Personal Interview with Henry C., Technical Aid Staff, Bethany, CT: 17 May 1983.

_____, Personal Interview with Technical Aid Staff, Bethany, CT: 15 May 1983.

_____, *The Laticrete System,* Brochure Corbett 70M, Bethany, CT: 1982.

Leckie, Jim, et. al. *Other Homes and Garbage: Designs for Self-Sufficient Living.* San Francisco, CA: Sierra Club Books, 1975.

Letter and Drawings Received from J. Scott Howell, Vice President, General Manager of Robinson Iron Works, Alexander City, AL: 27 May 1983.

McCulley, E. Byron. "Waterpools and Fountains," *Handbook of Landscape Architectural Construction,* Ed. Jot D. Carpenter, McLean, VA: The Landscape Architecture Foundation, 1976.

Micha, Peter. *Pem Equipment.* 15th ed., Ontario, Canada: Pem Fountains, 1980.

Miller, Nelson, "Pouring Life into a Landscape: Water Gardens," *The Construction Specifier,* April 1983.

Mindness, Sidney and Young, Jay Francis. *Concrete.* New York: Prentice-Hall, 1981.

*1983 Handbook for Ceramic Tile Installation.* Conference for 1982/83 Handbook for Ceramic Tile Installation, Princeton, NJ: Tile Council of America, Inc., 1982.

*1982 Annual Book of A.S.T.M. Standards.* Chemical-Resistant Materials; Vitrified Clay, Concrete Fiber-Cement Products; Mortars; Masonry," ed. XVI, Philadelphia, PA: American Society for Testing and Materials, 1982.

_____, "Soil and Rock; Building Stones," ed. XIX, Philadelphia, PA: American Society for Testing and Materials, 1982.

Palmquist, Roland E. *Guide to the 1981 National Electrical Code.* Indianapolis, IN, Theodore Audel & Co., 1981.

Pem Fountain Co. Personal Interview with Technical Staff, Ontario, Canada, 12 July 1983.

Perkins, Philip H. *Swimming Pools.* 2nd ed. Essex, England: Applied Science Publishers Ltd., 1978.

Porter, L.C. "Some Surface Treatments Increase Concrete Durability," in *Durability of Concrete.* Detroit, MI: American Concrete Institute, 1975.

*Technical Notes on Brick and Tile Construction.* "Floors and Pavements," No. 14, Washington, D.C.: Structural Clay Products Inst., June 1962.

_____, "Portland Cement-Lime Mortars for Brick Masonry," No. 8, McLean, VA: September 1972.

_____, "Reinforced Brick Masonry Swimming Pools," Bulletin of Structural Clay Products, No. 17K, August 1967.

_____, "Standard Specification for Portland Cement-Lime Mortar for Brick Masonry," Bulletin of Structural Clay Products, No. 8A, Oct.–Nov., 1972.

Uniroyal-U.S. Rubber Waterproof Rubber Surfaces. Pamphlet 3619, Mishawaka, IN, Uniroyal (no date).

Watkins, James A. *Turf Irrigation Manual: The Complete Guide to Turf and Landscape Sprinkler Systems.* ed. H. Gene Johnson, 3rd ed., Dallas, TX: Telsco Industries, 1978.

Watson, Don A. *Construction Materials and Processes,* 2nd ed., New York, NY: McGraw-Hill, Inc. 1978.

# APPENDIX

## Table A-1[134]

PRESSURE LOSS

STANDARD PLUMBING VALVES and TUBE FITTINGS

APPROXIMATE EQUIVALENT FEET COPPER WATER TUBING

| | Nominal Tube Size: Inches | | | | | | | | | | | | |
|---|---|---|---|---|---|---|---|---|---|---|---|---|---|
| | 1/2 | 3/4 | 1 | 1-1/4 | 1-1/2 | 2 | 2-1/2 | 3 | 4 | 6 | 8 | 10 | 12 |
| TYPE APPURTENANCE | Base Footage Equivalents: Caution: Use only with conversion multiplying factors for correct types of Tubing | | | | | | | | | | | | |
| IPS Gate Valve, Full Open | 0.3 | 0.5 | 0.9 | 0.9 | 1.1 | 1.7 | 2.4 | 2.5 | 3.4 | 4.8 | 6.4 | 7.8 | 9.6 |
| IPS Straight Globe Valve, Full Open | 7.8 | 13.5 | 22.0 | 22.8 | 28.7 | 43.3 | 62.3 | 64.3 | 87.8 | 125.4 | 167.3 | 204.4 | 250.3 |
| IPS Angle Globe Valve, Full Open | 3.2 | 5.8 | 9.4 | 9.7 | 12.3 | 18.5 | 26.6 | 27.4 | 37.5 | 53.5 | 71.4 | 87.2 | 106.8 |
| IPS Conventional Check Valve, Full Open[1] | 3.0 | 5.4 | 8.7 | 9.0 | 11.4 | 17.2 | 24.7 | 25.6 | 34.9 | 49.8 | 66.4 | 81.2 | 99.4 |
| Corporation Cock, Full Open | 6.7 | 6.4 | 7.3 | 8.2 | 8.4 | 9.2 | — | — | — | — | — | — | — |
| Curb Stop, Full Open | 3.4 | 4.4 | 4.2 | 3.9 | 4.8 | 5.2 | — | — | — | — | — | — | — |
| Straight Meter Cock, Full Open | 3.3 | 4.4 | 4.4 | — | — | — | — | — | — | — | — | — | — |
| Angle Meter Cock, Full Open | 6.6 | 8.7 | 8.7 | — | — | — | — | — | — | — | — | — | — |
| Stop and Waste Cocks, Full Open | 6.6 | 6.6 | — | — | — | — | — | — | — | — | — | — | — |
| Wrought Tube Fittings: | | | | | | | | | | | | | |
| 90° Ell | 1.0 | 1.3 | 1.5 | 2.0 | 2.5 | 3.5 | 4.0 | 5.0 | 7.0 | 10.0 | 15.1 | — | — |
| 45° Ell | 0.6 | 0.8 | 1.0 | 1.2 | 1.5 | 2.0 | 2.5 | 3.0 | 4.0 | 6.0 | 7.9 | — | — |
| 90° Street Ell | | | | | | | | | | | | | |
| Run of Straight Tee | 0.3 | 0.4 | 0.5 | 0.6 | 0.8 | 1.0 | 1.3 | 1.5 | 2.0 | 3.0 | 4.0 | — | — |
| Branch of Straight Tee | 1.5 | 2.0 | 2.5 | 3.0 | 3.5 | 5.0 | 6.0 | 7.5 | 10.5 | 15.0 | 19.8 | — | — |
| Cast Fittings: | | | | | | | | | | | | | |
| 90° Ell | 1.0 | 2.0 | 4.0 | 5.0 | 8.0 | 11.0 | 14.0 | 18.0 | 28.0 | 52.0 | 68.4 | 85.9 | 102.3 |
| 45° Ell | 0.6 | 1.0 | 2.0 | 2.0 | 3.0 | 5.0 | 8.0 | 11.0 | 17.0 | 28.0 | 36.6 | 46.3 | 55.0 |
| 90° Street Ell | | | | | | | | | | | | | |
| Run of Straight Tee | 0.5 | 0.5 | 0.5 | 1.0 | 1.0 | 2.0 | 2.0 | 2.0 | 2.0 | 3.0 | 4.0 | 5.0 | 5.9 |
| Branch of Straight Tee | 2.0 | 3.0 | 5.0 | 7.0 | 9.0 | 12.0 | 16.0 | 20.0 | 37.0 | 61.0 | 80.3 | 100.9 | 120.2 |
| Straight Coupling | 0.3 | 0.4 | 0.5 | 0.6 | 0.8 | 1.0 | 1.3 | 1.5 | 2.0 | 3.0 | 4.0 | 5.0 | 5.9 |
| Reducing Bushing or Coupling:[3] | | | | | | | | | | | | | |
| Reduced 1 Standard[2] Size | — | 1.9 | 2.0 | 1.3 | 0.9 | 3.9 | 2.8 | 2.0 | 8.5 | 27.8 | 18.5 | 13.2 | 10.4 |
| Reduced 2 Standard[2] Sizes | — | — | 12.0 | 8.7 | 5.9 | 10.9 | 17.5 | 12.5 | 25.0 | 111.6 | 152.0 | 88.1 | 62.3 |
| Increasing Bushing or Coupling:[4] | | | | | | | | | | | | | |
| Increased 1 Standard[2] Size | 0.4 | 0.5 | 0.4 | 0.4 | 1.0 | 1.0 | 0.9 | 2.3 | 5.1 | 5.1 | 4.5 | 4.3 | — |
| Increased 2 Standard[2] Sizes | 0.9 | 1.0 | 1.1 | 1.6 | 2.2 | 2.3 | 3.6 | 6.8 | 9.4 | 7.8 | 11.4 | — | — |
| Ordinary Entrance | 0.9 | 1.3 | 1.8 | 2.3 | 2.8 | 3.9 | 5.0 | 6.2 | 8.6 | 13.7 | 18.9 | 24.1 | 29.9 |

[1] Check valve with less than 0.5 psi loss should not be used. See explanation in text.

[2] Standard sizes are those used in this table.

[3] Calculate loss with larger pipe.

[4] Calculate loss with smaller pipe.

| | Multiplying Factors to Convert Base Footage Equivalents to Footage Equivalents for Specific Tubes | | | | | | | | | | | | |
|---|---|---|---|---|---|---|---|---|---|---|---|---|---|
| | Nominal Pipe Size: inches | | | | | | | | | | | | |
| TYPE COPPER TUBE | 1/2 | 3/4 | 1 | 1-1/4 | 1-1/2 | 2 | 2-1/2 | 3 | 4 | 6 | 8 | 10 | 12 |
| Type K | 1.00 | 1.00 | 1.00 | 1.00 | 1.00 | 1.00 | 1.00 | 1.00 | 1.00 | 1.00 | 1.00 | 1.00 | 1.00 |
| Type L | 1.18 | 1.29 | 1.16 | 1.08 | 1.08 | 1.07 | 1.06 | 1.07 | 1.06 | 1.09 | 1.09 | 1.09 | 1.11 |
| Type M | 1.45 | 1.51 | 1.33 | 1.19 | 1.16 | 1.13 | 1.13 | 1.13 | 1.10 | 1.12 | 1.14 | 1.14 | 1.14 |

Courtesy of Weather-Matic Irrigation Division/Telsco Industries

# Table A-2 [135]

PRESSURE LOSS
## STANDARD PLUMBING VALVES and FITTINGS
APPROXIMATE EQUIVALENT FEET OF PIPING

| TYPE APPURTENANCE | 1/2 | 3/4 | 1 | 1-1/4 | 1-1/2 | 2 | 2-1/2 | 3 | 4 | 6 | 8 | 10 | 12 |
|---|---|---|---|---|---|---|---|---|---|---|---|---|---|
| | Nominal Pipe Size: inches | | | | | | | | | | | | |
| | Base Footage Equivalents: CAUTION: Use only with conversion multiplying factors for correct kind of pipe | | | | | | | | | | | | |
| Gate Valve | 0.7 | 0.9 | 1.1 | 1.5 | 1.7 | 2.2 | 2.7 | 3.3 | 4.4 | 6.6 | 8.6 | 10.9 | 12.9 |
| Straight Globe Valve | 17.6 | 23.3 | 29.7 | 39.1 | 45.6 | 58.6 | 70.0 | 86.9 | 114.1 | 171.8 | 226.1 | 283.9 | 338.2 |
| Angle Globe Valve | 7.5 | 10.0 | 12.7 | 16.7 | 19.5 | 25.0 | 29.8 | 37.1 | 48.7 | 73.3 | 96.4 | 121.1 | 144.3 |
| Conventional Check Valve[1] | 7.0 | 9.3 | 11.8 | 15.5 | 18.1 | 23.3 | 27.8 | 34.5 | 45.3 | 68.2 | 89.8 | 112.7 | 134.3 |
| Corporation Cock | 14.2 | 10.1 | 9.0 | 12.9 | 12.2 | 11.3 | — | — | — | — | — | — | — |
| Curb Stop | 7.3 | 7.0 | 5.2 | 6.2 | 7.1 | 6.5 | — | — | — | — | — | — | — |
| Straight Meter Cock | 7.0 | 6.9 | 5.4 | — | — | — | — | — | — | — | — | — | — |
| Angle Meter Cock | 14.0 | 13.8 | 10.8 | — | — | — | — | — | — | — | — | — | — |
| Stop and Waste Cock | 14.0 | 10.3 | — | — | — | — | — | — | — | — | — | — | — |
| 90° Ell | 1.6 | 2.1 | 2.6 | 3.5 | 4.0 | 5.2 | 6.2 | 7.7 | 10.1 | 15.2 | 20.0 | 25.1 | 29.9 |
| 45° Ell | 0.8 | 1.1 | 1.4 | 1.8 | 2.2 | 2.8 | 3.3 | 4.1 | 5.4 | 8.1 | 10.6 | 13.4 | 15.9 |
| 90° Street Ell | 2.6 | 3.4 | 4.4 | 5.8 | 6.7 | 8.6 | 10.3 | 12.8 | 16.8 | 25.3 | 33.3 | 41.8 | 49.7 |
| Run of Straight Tee | 1.0 | 1.4 | 1.8 | 2.3 | 2.7 | 3.5 | 4.1 | 5.1 | 6.7 | 10.1 | 13.3 | 16.7 | 19.9 |
| Branch of Straight Tee | 3.1 | 4.1 | 5.3 | 6.9 | 8.1 | 10.3 | 12.4 | 15.3 | 20.1 | 30.3 | 39.9 | 50.1 | 59.7 |
| Reducing Bushing or Coupling[3] | | | | | | | | | | | | | |
|   Reduced 1 Standard[2] Size | — | 1.6 | 1.5 | 2.5 | 0.7 | 3.5 | 1.7 | 4.0 | 8.1 | 32.1 | 19.8 | 15.2 | 10.4 |
|   Reduced 2 Standard[2] Size | — | — | 7.7 | 10.5 | 7.8 | 8.9 | 12.4 | 13.6 | 32.5 | 123.2 | 175.2 | 102.1 | 68.3 |
| Increasing Bushing or Coupling[4] | | | | | | | | | | | | | |
|   Increased 1 Standard[2] Size | 0.4 | 0.5 | 0.7 | 0.3 | 1.0 | 0.7 | 1.4 | 2.2 | 5.5 | 5.2 | 5.0 | 4.4 | — |
|   Increased 2 Standard[2] Sizes | 0.7 | 1.2 | 1.3 | 1.6 | 2.1 | 2.6 | 4.2 | 7.5 | 10.5 | 12.2 | 12.1 | — | — |
| Ordinary Entrance | 1.1 | 1.5 | 1.9 | 2.7 | 3.2 | 4.3 | 5.4 | 6.8 | 9.5 | 15.3 | 20.9 | 27.6 | 33.7 |

[1] Check valve with less than 0.5 psi loss should not be used. See explanation text.
[2] Standard sizes are those used in this table.
[3] Calculate loss with larger pipe.
[4] Calculate loss with smaller pipe.

| KIND OF PIPING | 1/2 | 3/4 | 1 | 1-1/4 | 1-1/2 | 2 | 2-1/2 | 3 | 4 | 6 | 8 | 10 | 12 |
|---|---|---|---|---|---|---|---|---|---|---|---|---|---|
| | Multiplying Factors To Convert Base Footage Equivalents To Footage Equivalents for Specific Pipes — Nominal Pipe Size: inches | | | | | | | | | | | | |
| **Controlled OD Thermoplastic** | | | | | | | | | | | | | |
|   SDR 11 Pipe | 1.42 | 1.09 | 1.01 | 0.84 | 0.78 | 0.69 | — | 0.67 | 0.61 | 0.54 | — | — | — |
|   SDR 13.5 Pipe | 1.96 | 1.51 | 1.44 | 1.19 | 1.10 | 0.97 | 1.04 | 0.94 | 0.85 | 0.76 | — | — | — |
|   SDR 17 Pipe | — | 1.80 | 1.71 | 1.42 | 1.30 | 1.16 | 1.25 | 1.13 | 1.02 | 0.91 | 0.87 | 0.84 | 0.82 |
|   SDR 21 Pipe | — | 1.84 | 1.92 | 1.61 | 1.48 | 1.31 | 1.41 | 1.28 | 1.16 | 1.04 | 0.99 | 0.95 | 0.93 |
|   SDR 26 Pipe | — | — | 1.97 | 1.77 | 1.63 | 1.45 | 1.56 | 1.42 | 1.29 | 1.15 | 1.10 | 1.06 | 1.04 |
|   SDR 32.5 Pipe | — | — | — | — | — | 1.57 | 1.69 | 1.54 | 1.40 | 1.26 | 1.19 | 1.15 | 1.13 |
|   Schedule 40 Pipe | 0.97 | 1.01 | 1.03 | 1.06 | 1.07 | 1.08 | 1.08 | 1.09 | 1.10 | 1.11 | 1.11 | 1.11 | 1.11 |
|   Schedule 80 Pipe | 0.50 | 0.60 | 0.65 | 0.72 | 0.74 | 0.78 | 0.79 | 0.81 | 0.84 | 0.85 | 0.88 | 0.87 | 0.87 |
|   SDR 26 PVC Tubing | 0.29 | 0.55 | 0.70 | 0.56 | — | — | — | — | — | — | — | — | — |
|   PE SDR 7.3 Tubing | 0.19 | 0.26 | 0.27 | 0.19 | 0.18 | 0.22 | — | — | — | — | — | — | — |
|   PE SDR 9 Tubing | 0.28 | 0.37 | 0.39 | 0.27 | 0.29 | 0.31 | — | — | — | — | — | — | — |
| **Controlled ID PE Pipe** | 1.00 | 1.00 | 1.00 | 1.00 | 1.00 | 1.00 | 1.00 | 1.00 | 1.00 | 1.00 | — | — | — |
| **Schedule 40 Galvanized Steel Pipe** | | | | | | | | | | | | | |
|   Valves | 0.54 | 0.54 | 0.54 | 0.54 | 0.54 | 0.54 | 0.54 | 0.54 | 0.54 | 0.54 | 0.54 | 0.54 | 0.54 |
|   Galvanized Fitting | 1.00 | 1.00 | 1.00 | 1.00 | 1.00 | 1.00 | 1.00 | 1.00 | 1.00 | 1.00 | 1.00 | 1.00 | 1.00 |
| **Asbestos-Cement Pipe** | | | | | | | | | | | | | |
|   Valves | | | | | | | | 0.90 | 0.97 | 0.84 | 0.92 | 0.92 | 0.91 |
|   Non-rusting or non-deteriorating Fittings | | | | | | | | 0.70 | 0.67 | 0.56 | 0.54 | 0.54 | 0.50 |
|   Rusting or deteriorating Fittings | | | | | | | | 1.30 | 1.25 | 1.04 | 1.00 | 1.00 | 0.93 |
| **Cast Iron Pipe** | | | | | | | (2-1/4)[5] | | | | | | |
|   Valves | | | | | | 0.46 | 0.35 | 0.49 | 0.52 | 0.51 | 0.55 | 0.53 | 0.56 |
|   Fittings | | | | | | 0.65 | 0.64 | 0.62 | 0.65 | 0.61 | 0.60 | 0.58 | 0.57 |

[5] 2-1/4 in cast iron pipe; Equivalent of 2-1/4 in pipe represents pressure loss in 2-1/2 in valve.

Courtesy of Weather-Matic Irrigation Division/Telsco Industries

# Table A-3 [136]

## C = 140*

## PRESSURE LOSS
## TYPE "K" COPPER TUBE

Pipe Sizes: Nominal  Losses per 100 ft: lb/in²

| gpm | 1/2 in | 3/4 in | 1 in | 1-1/4 in | 1-1/2 in | 2 in |
|---|---|---|---|---|---|---|
| 1 | 1.15 | 0.213 | 0.052 | 0.018 | 0.008 | 0.002 |
| 2 | 4.14 | 0.767 | .188 | .063 | .027 | .007 |
| 3 | 8.76 | 1.62 | .398 | .134 | .057 | .015 |
| 4 | 14.91 | 2.77 | 0.677 | .227 | .098 | .025 |
| 5 | 22.53 | 4.18 | 1.02 | .344 | .148 | .038 |
| 6 | 31.57 | 5.86 | 1.43 | .482 | .207 | .053 |
| 7 | 41.98 | 7.79 | 1.91 | .640 | .275 | .071 |
| 8 | 53.75 | 9.97 | 2.44 | 0.820 | .352 | .090 |
| 9 | 66.83 | 12.40 | 3.03 | 1.02 | .438 | .112 |
| 10 | 81.22 | 15.07 | 3.69 | 1.24 | 0.532 | 0.137 |
| 11 | | 17.98 | 4.40 | 1.48 | .635 | .163 |
| 12 | | 21.12 | 5.17 | 1.74 | .746 | .191 |
| 13 | | 24.49 | 5.99 | 2.01 | .865 | .222 |
| 14 | | 28.09 | 6.87 | 2.31 | 0.992 | .254 |
| 15 | | 31.91 | 7.81 | 2.62 | 1.13 | .289 |
| 16 | | 35.96 | 8.80 | 2.96 | 1.27 | .326 |
| 17 | | 40.22 | 9.84 | 3.31 | 1.42 | .364 |
| 18 | 2-1/2 in | 44.71 | 10.94 | 3.68 | 1.58 | .405 |
| 19 | | 49.41 | 12.09 | 4.06 | 1.75 | .448 |
| 20 | 0.171 | 54.33 | 13.29 | 4.47 | 1.92 | 0.492 |
| 22 | .204 | 64.81 | 15.86 | 5.33 | 2.29 | .587 |
| 24 | .239 | 76.13 | 18.63 | 6.26 | 2.69 | .690 |
| 26 | .278 | 88.28 | 21.60 | 7.26 | 3.12 | .800 |
| 28 | .318 | 101.25 | 24.77 | 8.32 | 3.58 | 0.917 |
| 30 | .362 | 115.03 | 28.14 | 9.46 | 4.06 | 1.04 |
| 32 | .408 | | 31.71 | 10.66 | 4.58 | 1.17 |
| 34 | .456 | | 35.48 | 11.92 | 5.12 | 1.31 |
| 36 | .507 | 3 in | 39.43 | 13.25 | 5.69 | 1.46 |
| 38 | .560 | | 43.58 | 14.64 | 6.29 | 1.61 |
| 40 | 0.616 | 0.260 | 47.92 | 16.10 | 6.92 | 1.77 |
| 42 | .674 | .285 | 52.45 | 17.62 | 7.57 | 1.94 |
| 44 | .735 | .310 | 57.16 | 19.21 | 8.25 | 2.12 |
| 46 | .797 | .337 | 62.06 | 20.85 | 8.96 | 2.30 |
| 48 | .863 | .364 | 67.14 | 22.56 | 9.70 | 2.49 |
| 50 | 0.930 | .393 | 72.41 | 24.33 | 10.46 | 2.68 |
| 52 | 1.00 | .423 | | 26.16 | 11.24 | 2.88 |
| 54 | 1.07 | .453 | | 28.05 | 12.06 | 3.09 |
| 56 | 1.15 | .485 | 4 in | 30.01 | 12.90 | 3.31 |
| 58 | 1.22 | .517 | | 32.02 | 13.76 | 3.53 |
| 60 | 1.30 | 0.551 | 0.139 | 34.09 | 14.65 | 3.76 |
| 62 | 1.39 | .585 | .148 | 36.22 | 15.57 | 3.99 |
| 64 | 1.47 | .620 | .157 | 38.42 | 16.51 | 4.23 |
| 66 | 1.56 | .657 | .166 | 40.67 | 17.48 | 4.48 |
| 68 | 1.64 | .694 | .175 | 42.97 | 18.47 | 4.74 |
| 70 | 1.73 | .732 | .185 | 45.34 | 19.49 | 5.00 |
| 75 | 1.97 | .832 | .210 | 51.52 | 22.14 | 5.68 |
| 80 | 2.22 | 0.937 | .237 | 58.05 | 24.95 | 6.40 |
| 85 | 2.48 | 1.05 | .265 | | 27.91 | 7.16 |
| 90 | 2.76 | 1.17 | .294 | | 31.02 | 7.95 |
| 95 | 3.05 | 1.29 | .325 | | 34.28 | 8.79 |
| 100 | 3.35 | 1.42 | 0.358 | | 37.69 | 9.67 |

| gpm | 2 in | 2-1/2 in | 3 in | 4 in | 6 in | 8 in |
|---|---|---|---|---|---|---|
| 105 | 10.58 | 3.67 | 1.55 | 0.392 | 0.057 | 0.015 |
| 110 | 11.53 | 4.00 | 1.69 | .427 | .062 | .016 |
| 115 | 12.52 | 4.34 | 1.83 | .463 | .067 | .017 |
| 120 | 13.54 | 4.70 | 1.98 | .501 | .072 | .019 |
| 125 | 14.61 | 5.07 | 2.14 | .541 | .078 | .020 |
| 130 | 15.70 | 5.45 | 2.30 | .581 | .084 | .022 |
| 135 | 16.84 | 5.84 | 2.47 | .624 | .090 | .023 |
| 140 | 18.01 | 6.25 | 2.64 | .667 | .096 | .025 |
| 145 | 19.22 | 6.67 | 2.82 | .712 | .103 | .027 |
| 150 | 20.46 | 7.10 | 3.00 | 0.758 | 0.109 | 0.028 |
| 160 | 23.06 | 8.00 | 3.38 | .854 | .123 | .032 |
| 170 | | 8.95 | 3.78 | 0.955 | .138 | .036 |
| 180 | 10 in | 9.95 | 4.20 | 1.06 | .153 | .040 |
| 190 | | 11.00 | 4.64 | 1.17 | .169 | .044 |
| 200 | 0.016 | 12.09 | 5.11 | 1.29 | .186 | .048 |
| 210 | .018 | 13.23 | 5.59 | 1.41 | .204 | .053 |
| 220 | .020 | 14.42 | 6.09 | 1.54 | .222 | .057 |
| 230 | .021 | | 6.61 | 1.67 | .241 | .062 |
| 240 | .023 | | 7.16 | 1.81 | .261 | .067 |
| 250 | .025 | | 7.72 | 1.95 | 0.281 | 0.073 |
| 260 | .027 | | 8.30 | 2.10 | .303 | .078 |
| 270 | .029 | | 8.90 | 2.25 | .325 | .084 |
| 280 | .031 | 12 in | 9.52 | 2.40 | .347 | .090 |
| 290 | .033 | | 10.15 | 2.57 | .370 | .096 |
| 300 | 0.035 | 0.015 | 10.81 | 2.73 | .394 | .102 |
| 325 | .040 | .017 | | 3.17 | .457 | .118 |
| 350 | .046 | .019 | | 3.63 | .525 | .135 |
| 375 | .053 | .022 | | 4.13 | .596 | .154 |
| 400 | .059 | .025 | | 4.65 | .672 | .173 |
| 425 | .067 | .028 | | 5.20 | .751 | .194 |
| 450 | .074 | .031 | | 5.78 | .835 | .216 |
| 475 | .082 | .034 | | 6.39 | 0.923 | 0.238 |
| 500 | .090 | .037 | | 7.03 | 1.01 | .262 |
| 550 | .107 | .045 | | 8.38 | 1.21 | .313 |
| 600 | 0.126 | 0.052 | | | 1.42 | .367 |
| 650 | .146 | .061 | | | 1.65 | .426 |
| 700 | .167 | .070 | | | 1.89 | .488 |
| 800 | .214 | .089 | | | 2.42 | .625 |
| 900 | .267 | .111 | | | 3.01 | .777 |
| 1000 | .324 | .135 | | | 3.66 | 0.945 |
| 1100 | .386 | .161 | | | 4.36 | 1.13 |
| 1200 | .454 | .189 | | | 5.13 | 1.32 |
| 1300 | .526 | .219 | | | | 1.53 |
| 1400 | .604 | .251 | | | | 1.76 |
| 1500 | 0.686 | 0.285 | | | | 2.00 |
| 2000 | 1.17 | .486 | | | | 3.41 |
| 2500 | 1.76 | 0.734 | | | | |
| 3000 | 2.47 | 1.03 | | | | |
| 3500 | | 1.37 | | | | |
| 4000 | | 1.75 | | | | |
| 5000 | | | | | | |

*Note: 5% has been added to losses determined with a "C" factor of 140 as an allowance for aging.

Courtesy of Weather-Matic Irrigation Division/Telsco Industries

# Table A-4[137]

| Velocity ft/s | Nominal Pipe Size: inches | | | | | | | | | | | | | Velocity ft/s |
|---|---|---|---|---|---|---|---|---|---|---|---|---|---|---|
| | 1/2 | 3/4 | 1 | 1-1/4 | 1-1/2 | 2 | 2-1/2 | 3 | 4 | 6 | 8 | 10 | 12 | |
| | Flow: gpm* | | | | | | | | | | | | | |
| 1 | 0.7 | 1.4 | 2.4 | 3.8 | 5.4 | 9.4 | 14.5 | 20.7 | 36.4 | 80.7 | 140.8 | 218.6 | 313.4 | 1 |
| 2 | 1.4 | 2.7 | 4.8 | 7.6 | 10.7 | 18.8 | 29.0 | 41.4 | 72.8 | 161.4 | 281.5 | 437.1 | 626.8 | 2 |
| 3 | 2.0 | 4.1 | 7.3 | 11.4 | 16.1 | 28.2 | 43.5 | 62.1 | 109.3 | 242.0 | 422.3 | 655.7 | 940.2 | 3 |
| 4 | 2.7 | 5.4 | 9.7 | 15.2 | 21.5 | 37.6 | 58.1 | 82.7 | 145.7 | 322.7 | 563.1 | 874.3 | 1253.7 | 4 |
| 5 | 3.4 | 6.8 | 12.1 | 19.0 | 26.8 | 47.0 | 72.6 | 103.4 | 182.1 | 403.4 | 703.8 | 1092.8 | 1567.1 | 5 |
| 6 | 4.1 | 8.2 | 14.5 | 22.8 | 32.2 | 56.4 | 87.1 | 124.1 | 218.5 | 484.1 | 844.6 | 1311.4 | 1880.5 | 6 |
| 7 | 4.8 | 9.5 | 17.0 | 26.6 | 37.6 | 65.8 | 101.6 | 144.8 | 254.9 | 564.8 | 985.3 | 1530.0 | 2193.9 | 7 |
| 8 | 5.4 | 10.9 | 19.4 | 30.4 | 43.0 | 75.2 | 116.1 | 165.5 | 291.3 | 645.5 | 1126.1 | 1748.5 | 2507.3 | 8 |
| 9 | 6.1 | 12.2 | 21.8 | 34.1 | 48.3 | 84.6 | 130.6 | 186.2 | 327.8 | 726.1 | 1266.9 | 1967.1 | 2820.7 | 9 |
| 10 | 6.8 | 13.6 | 24.2 | 37.9 | 53.7 | 93.9 | 145.1 | 206.9 | 364.2 | 806.8 | 1407.6 | 2185.6 | 3134.1 | 10 |
| 11 | 7.5 | 14.9 | 26.7 | 41.7 | 59.1 | 103.3 | 159.7 | 227.6 | 400.6 | 887.5 | 1548.4 | 2404.2 | 3447.5 | 11 |
| 12 | 8.2 | 16.3 | 29.1 | 45.5 | 64.4 | 112.7 | 174.2 | 248.2 | 437.0 | 968.2 | 1689.2 | 2622.8 | 3761.0 | 12 |
| 13 | 8.8 | 17.7 | 31.5 | 49.3 | 69.8 | 122.1 | 188.7 | 268.9 | 473.4 | 1048.9 | 1829.9 | 2841.3 | 4074.4 | 13 |
| 14 | 9.5 | 19.0 | 33.9 | 53.1 | 75.2 | 131.5 | 203.2 | 289.6 | 509.8 | 1129.6 | 1970.7 | 3059.9 | 4387.8 | 14 |
| 15 | 10.2 | 20.4 | 36.4 | 56.9 | 80.5 | 140.9 | 217.7 | 310.3 | 546.3 | 1210.2 | 2111.5 | 3278.5 | 4701.2 | 15 |

*Flows calculated with factors in Table 16 may vary slightly due to rounding-off of factors.

## MULTIPLYING FACTORS TO CHANGE VALUE OF "C"
## C = 140 TO OTHER VALUES

| To determine PRESSURE LOSSES with values of "C", multiply Losses computed with "C" = 140 by following factors* | | | | | | | | | | | | | |
|---|---|---|---|---|---|---|---|---|---|---|---|---|---|
| Value of "C" | 160 | 150 | 140* | 130 | 120 | 110 | 100 | 90 | 80 | 70 | 60 | 50 | Value of "C" |
| Multiplier | 0.781 | 0.880 | 1.0 | 1.15 | 1.33 | 1.56 | 1.86 | 2.26 | 2.82 | 3.61 | 4.79 | 6.72 | Multiplier |

*CAUTION: Table 10 was constructed with "C" = 140 and 5% added to calculated losses to allow for aging; before using above multiplying factors, losses in Table must be reduced to correct value of "C" = 140 by dividing by 1.05.

## PRESSURE LOSS
## TYPE "K" COPPER TUBE
### SIZES NOT LISTED OPPOSITE PAGE

| To determine PRESSURE LOSSES of 1/4, 3/8, and 5/8 in tube, multiply losses of 1/2 in Type "K" by following factors: | | | |
|---|---|---|---|
| Nominal Size, in | 1/4 | 3/8 | 5/8 |
| | Multipliers | | |
| Type "K" | 14.31 | 3.73 | 0.355 |

| To determine PRESSURE LOSSES of 3-1/2 and 5 in tube, multiply losses of 4 in Type "K" by following factors: | | |
|---|---|---|
| Nominal Size, in | 3-1/2 | 5 |
| | Multipliers | |
| Type "K" | 1.89 | 0.343 |

Courtesy of Weather-Matic Irrigation Division/Telsco Industries

# Table A-5 [138]

Table losses same for all Controlled OD
SDR 32.5 thermoplastic pipe.

C = 150

## PRESSURE LOSS

## 125 psi PR SDR 32.5 PVC PIPE

Pipe Sizes: Nominal — Losses per 100 ft: lb/in$^2$

| gpm | 2 in[1] | 2-1/2 in[1] | 3 in | 4 in | 6 in |
|---|---|---|---|---|---|
| 5 | 0.018 | 0.007 | 0.003 | 0.001 | |
| 10 | .064 | .025 | .010 | .003 | |
| 15 | .135 | .053 | .020 | .006 | .001 |
| 20 | .230 | .090 | .034 | .010 | .002 |
| 25 | .348 | .136 | .052 | .015 | .002 |
| 30 | .487 | .190 | .073 | .021 | .003 |
| 35 | .648 | .253 | .097 | .028 | .004 |
| 40 | .829 | .324 | .124 | .036 | .005 |
| 42 | .907 | .355 | .136 | .040 | .006 |
| 44 | 0.989 | .387 | .148 | .043 | .007 |
| 46 | 1.07 | .420 | .161 | .047 | .007 |
| 48 | 1.16 | .454 | .174 | .051 | .008 |
| 50 | 1.25 | 0.490 | 0.187 | 0.055 | 0.008 |
| 52 | 1.35 | .527 | .202 | .059 | .009 |
| 54 | 1.44 | .565 | .216 | .063 | .010 |
| 56 | 1.55 | .604 | .231 | .067 | .010 |
| 58 | 1.65 | .645 | .247 | .072 | .011 |
| 60 | 1.76 | .687 | .263 | .077 | .012 |
| 62 | 1.87 | .730 | .279 | .081 | .012 |
| 64 | 1.98 | .774 | .296 | .086 | .013 |
| 66 | 2.09 | .819 | .313 | .091 | .014 |
| 68 | 2.21 | .866 | .331 | .097 | .015 |
| 70 | 2.33 | .913 | 0.349 | 0.102 | 0.015 |
| 72 | 2.46 | 0.962 | .368 | .107 | .016 |
| 74 | 2.59 | 1.01 | .387 | .113 | .017 |
| 76 | 2.72 | 1.06 | .407 | .119 | .018 |
| 78 | 2.85 | 1.12 | .427 | .125 | .019 |
| 80 | 2.99 | 1.17 | .447 | .131 | .020 |
| 85 | 3.34 | 1.31 | .500 | .146 | .022 |
| 90 | 3.72 | 1.45 | .556 | .162 | .025 |
| 95 | 4.11 | 1.61 | .615 | .179 | .027 |
| 100 | 4.52 | 1.77 | 0.676 | 0.197 | 0.030 |
| 105 | 4.94 | 1.93 | .740 | .216 | .033 |
| 110 | 5.39 | 2.11 | .806 | .235 | .036 |
| 115 | 5.85 | 2.29 | .875 | .255 | .039 |
| 120 | 6.33 | 2.48 | 0.947 | .276 | .042 |
| 125 | | 2.67 | 1.02 | .298 | .045 |
| 130 | | 2.87 | 1.10 | .321 | .049 |
| 135 | | 3.08 | 1.18 | .344 | .052 |
| 140 | | 3.29 | 1.26 | .368 | .056 |
| 145 | | 3.51 | 1.34 | .392 | .060 |
| 150 | | 3.74 | 1.43 | 0.418 | 0.063 |

| gpm | 2-1/2 in | 3 in | 4 in | 6 in | 8 in | 10 in | 12 in |
|---|---|---|---|---|---|---|---|
| 160 | 4.22 | 1.61 | 0.471 | 0.071 | 0.020 | 0.007 | 0.003 |
| 170 | 4.72 | 1.80 | .526 | .080 | .022 | .008 | .003 |
| 180 | 5.24 | 2.00 | .585 | .089 | .025 | .008 | .004 |
| 190 | | 2.22 | .647 | .098 | .027 | .009 | .004 |
| 200 | | 2.44 | .711 | .108 | .030 | .010 | .004 |
| 210 | | 2.67 | .778 | .118 | .033 | .011 | .005 |
| 220 | | 2.91 | .848 | .129 | .036 | .012 | .005 |
| 230 | | 3.16 | .921 | .140 | .039 | .013 | .006 |
| 240 | | 3.41 | 0.996 | .151 | .042 | .014 | .006 |
| 250 | | 3.68 | 1.07 | 0.163 | 0.045 | 0.015 | 0.007 |
| 260 | | 3.96 | 1.16 | .175 | .049 | .017 | .007 |
| 270 | | | 1.24 | .188 | .052 | .018 | .008 |
| 280 | | | 1.33 | .201 | .056 | .019 | .008 |
| 290 | | | 1.41 | .215 | .059 | .020 | .009 |
| 300 | | | 1.51 | .229 | .063 | .022 | .009 |
| 325 | | | 1.75 | .265 | .073 | .025 | .011 |
| 350 | | | 2.00 | .304 | .084 | .029 | .013 |
| 375 | | | 2.28 | .346 | .096 | .033 | .014 |
| 400 | | | 2.56 | 0.389 | 0.108 | 0.037 | 0.016 |
| 425 | | | 2.87 | .436 | .121 | .041 | .018 |
| 450 | | | 3.19 | .484 | .134 | .046 | .020 |
| 475 | | | | .535 | .148 | .051 | .022 |
| 500 | | | | .588 | .163 | .056 | .024 |
| 550 | | | | .702 | .194 | .067 | .029 |
| 600 | | | | .824 | .228 | .078 | .034 |
| 650 | | | | 0.956 | .265 | .091 | .040 |
| 700 | | | | 1.10 | .304 | .104 | .045 |
| 800 | | | | 1.40 | .389 | .133 | .058 |
| 900 | | | | 1.75 | .483 | .166 | .072 |
| 1000 | | | | 2.12 | 0.587 | 0.201 | 0.088 |
| 1100 | | | | | .701 | .240 | .105 |
| 1200 | | | | | .823 | .282 | .123 |
| 1300 | | | | | 0.954 | .327 | .143 |
| 1400 | | | | | 1.09 | .375 | .163 |
| 1500 | | | | | 1.24 | .426 | .186 |
| 2000 | | | | | | 0.726 | .316 |
| 2500 | | | | | | 1.10 | .478 |
| 3000 | | | | | | | 0.669 |
| 3500 | | | | | | | 0.890 |
| 4000 | | | | | | | |
| 4500 | | | | | | | |
| 5000 | | | | | | | |

[1] Not ASTM Standard pipe.

Courtesy of Weather-Matic Irrigation Division/Telsco Industries

188

# Table A-6 [139]

Table Velocity Flows same for all Controlled OD
SDR 32.5 thermoplastic pipe.

## VELOCITY FLOWS
## SDR 32.5 PVC PIPE

| Velocity ft/s | Nominal Pipe Sizes: inches | | | | | | | | Velocity ft/s |
|---|---|---|---|---|---|---|---|---|---|
| | 2[1] | 2-1/2[1] | 3 | 4 | 6 | 8 | 10 | 12 | |
| | Flow: gpm* | | | | | | | | |
| 1 | 11.9 | 17.6 | 26.1 | 43.3 | 93.9 | 159.1 | 247.2 | 347.8 | 1 |
| 2 | 23.9 | 35.1 | 52.2 | 86.5 | 187.8 | 318.3 | 494.3 | 695.5 | 2 |
| 3 | 35.8 | 52.7 | 78.2 | 129.8 | 281.7 | 477.4 | 741.5 | 1043.3 | 3 |
| 4 | 47.8 | 70.3 | 104.3 | 173.1 | 375.6 | 636.6 | 988.6 | 1391.1 | 4 |
| 5 | 59.7 | 87.8 | 130.4 | 216.3 | 469.4 | 795.7 | 1235.8 | 1738.8 | 5 |
| 6 | 71.7 | 105.4 | 156.5 | 259.6 | 563.3 | 954.9 | 1482.9 | 2086.6 | 6 |
| 7 | 83.6 | 123.0 | 182.6 | 302.9 | 657.2 | 1114.0 | 1730.1 | 2434.4 | 7 |
| 8 | 95.6 | 140.6 | 208.6 | 346.1 | 751.1 | 1273.2 | 1977.2 | 2782.1 | 8 |
| 9 | 107.5 | 158.1 | 234.7 | 389.4 | 845.0 | 1432.3 | 2224.4 | 3129.9 | 9 |
| 10 | 119.5 | 175.7 | 260.8 | 432.6 | 938.9 | 1591.5 | 2471.5 | 3477.7 | 10 |
| 11 | 131.4 | 193.3 | 286.9 | 475.9 | 1032.8 | 1750.6 | 2781.7 | 3825.4 | 11 |
| 12 | 143.3 | 210.8 | 313.0 | 519.2 | 1126.7 | 1909.8 | 2965.8 | 4173.2 | 12 |
| 13 | 155.3 | 228.4 | 339.0 | 562.4 | 1220.5 | 2068.9 | 3213.0 | 4521.0 | 13 |
| 14 | 167.2 | 246.0 | 365.1 | 605.7 | 1314.4 | 2228.1 | 3460.2 | 4868.7 | 14 |
| 15 | 179.2 | 263.5 | 391.2 | 649.0 | 1408.3 | 2387.2 | 3707.3 | 5216.5 | 15 |

*Flows calculated with factors in Table 16 may vary slightly due to rounding-off of factors.

[1] Not ASTM standard pipe.

## MULTIPLYING FACTORS TO CHANGE VALUE OF "C"
## C = 150 TO OTHER VALUES

| To determine PRESSURE LOSSES with other values of "C", multiply losses computed with "C" = 150 by following factors: | | | | | | | | | | | | |
|---|---|---|---|---|---|---|---|---|---|---|---|---|
| Value of "C" | 160 | 150 | 140 | 130 | 120 | 110 | 100 | 90 | 80 | 70 | 60 | 50 | Value of "C" |
| Multiplier | 0.887 | 1.0 | 1.14 | 1.30 | 1.51 | 1.77 | 2.12 | 2.57 | 3.20 | 4.10 | 5.45 | 7.63 | Multiplier |

## PRESSURE LOSS
## SDR 32.5 PVC PIPE
### SIZES NOT LISTED OPPOSITE PAGE

| To determine PRESSURE LOSSES in 3-1/2 and 5 in SDR 32.5 PVC pipe, multiply losses of 4 in SDR 32.5 by following factors: | | |
|---|---|---|
| Nominal Size, in | 3-1/2[a] | 5[a] |
| | Multipliers | |
| SDR 32.5 | 1.78 | 0.355 |

[a] Determine availability before designing systems with these sizes.

Courtesy of Weather-Matic Irrigation Division/Telsco Industries

# Table A-7 [140]

Table losses same for all controlled OD
SDR 26 thermoplastic pipe.

C = 150

## PRESSURE LOSS
### 160 psi PR SDR 26 PVC PIPE

| Pipe Sizes: Nominal | | | | | | | | | | | | Losses per 100 ft: lb/in² | |
| gpm | 1/2 in [1] | 3/4 in [1] | 1 in | 1-1/4 in | 1-1/2 in | 2 in | gpm | 2 in | 2-1/2 in | 3 in | 4 in | 6 in | 8 in |
|---|---|---|---|---|---|---|---|---|---|---|---|---|---|
| 1 | 0.248 | 0.067 | 0.019 | 0.005 | 0.003 | 0.001 | 105 | 5.35 | 2.10 | 0.802 | .235 | .036 | .010 |
| 2 | 0.896 | .243 | .070 | .021 | .011 | .004 | 110 | 5.84 | 2.28 | 0.874 | .256 | .039 | .011 |
| 3 | 1.90 | .515 | .148 | .044 | .022 | .007 | 115 | 6.34 | 2.48 | 0.949 | .278 | .042 | .012 |
| 4 | 3.23 | 0.876 | .253 | .074 | .038 | .013 | 120 | 6.86 | 2.68 | 1.03 | .300 | .046 | .013 |
| 5 | 4.88 | 1.32 | .382 | .112 | .057 | .019 | 125 | | 2.89 | 1.11 | .324 | .049 | .014 |
| 6 | 6.84 | 1.86 | .535 | .157 | .081 | .027 | 130 | | 3.11 | 1.19 | .348 | .053 | .015 |
| 7 | 9.09 | 2.47 | .711 | .209 | .107 | .036 | 135 | | 3.34 | 1.28 | .373 | .057 | .016 |
| 8 | 11.64 | 3.16 | 0.911 | .267 | .137 | .046 | 140 | | 3.57 | 1.37 | .399 | .061 | .017 |
| 9 | 14.48 | 3.93 | 1.13 | .332 | .171 | .057 | 145 | | 3.81 | 1.46 | .426 | .065 | .018 |
| 10 | 17.59 | 4.77 | 1.38 | 0.404 | 0.207 | 0.069 | 150 | | 4.05 | 1.55 | 0.454 | 0.069 | .019 |
| 11 | 20.98 | 5.69 | 1.64 | .481 | .247 | .082 | 160 | | 4.57 | 1.75 | .511 | .078 | .022 |
| 12 | 24.65 | 6.69 | 1.93 | .565 | .290 | .097 | 170 | | 5.11 | 1.96 | .572 | .087 | .024 |
| 13 | | 7.75 | 2.24 | .656 | .337 | .112 | 180 | 10 in | | 2.17 | .636 | .097 | .027 |
| 14 | | 8.89 | 2.56 | .752 | .386 | .129 | 190 | | | 2.40 | .703 | .107 | .030 |
| 15 | | 10.11 | 2.91 | .854 | .439 | .146 | 200 | 0.011 | | 2.64 | .773 | .118 | .033 |
| 16 | | 11.39 | 3.28 | 0.963 | .494 | .165 | 210 | .012 | | 2.89 | .846 | .129 | .036 |
| 17 | | 12.74 | 3.67 | 1.08 | .553 | .184 | 220 | .013 | | 3.15 | 0.922 | .140 | .039 |
| 18 | | 14.16 | 4.08 | 1.20 | .615 | .205 | 230 | .014 | | 3.42 | 1.00 | .152 | .042 |
| 19 | | 15.65 | 4.51 | 1.32 | .679 | .227 | 240 | .016 | | 3.70 | 1.08 | .165 | .046 |
| 20 | | 17.21 | 4.96 | 1.45 | .747 | .249 | 250 | .017 | | 3.99 | 1.17 | 0.178 | 0.049 |
| 22 | | | 5.92 | 1.74 | 0.891 | 0.297 | 260 | .018 | | | 1.26 | .191 | .053 |
| 24 | | | 6.95 | 2.04 | 1.05 | .349 | 270 | .019 | | | 1.35 | .205 | .057 |
| 26 | 2-1/2 in | | 8.06 | 2.36 | 1.21 | .405 | 280 | .021 | 12 in | | 1.44 | .219 | .061 |
| 28 | | | 9.25 | 2.71 | 1.39 | .464 | 290 | .022 | | | 1.54 | .234 | .065 |
| 30 | 0.206 | | 10.51 | 3.08 | 1.58 | .527 | 300 | 0.024 | 0.010 | | 1.64 | .249 | .069 |
| 32 | .233 | | 11.84 | 3.47 | 1.78 | .594 | 325 | .027 | .012 | | 1.90 | .289 | .080 |
| 34 | .260 | | 13.24 | 3.88 | 1.99 | .665 | 350 | .031 | .014 | | 2.18 | .332 | .092 |
| 36 | .289 | 3 in | | 4.32 | 2.22 | .739 | 375 | .036 | .016 | | 2.47 | .377 | .104 |
| 38 | .320 | | | 4.77 | 2.45 | .817 | 400 | .040 | .018 | | 2.79 | .424 | .118 |
| 40 | .352 | 0.135 | | 5.24 | 2.69 | .898 | 425 | .045 | .020 | | 3.12 | .475 | .132 |
| 42 | .385 | .147 | | 5.74 | 2.95 | 0.983 | 450 | .050 | .022 | | | 0.528 | 0.146 |
| 44 | .419 | .161 | | 6.26 | 3.21 | 1.07 | 475 | .055 | .024 | | | .583 | .162 |
| 46 | .455 | .174 | 4 in | 6.79 | 3.49 | 1.16 | 500 | .061 | .027 | | | .641 | .178 |
| 48 | .493 | .189 | | 7.35 | 3.77 | 1.26 | 550 | .073 | .032 | | | .765 | .212 |
| 50 | 0.531 | 0.203 | 0.059 | 7.92 | 4.07 | 1.36 | 600 | 0.085 | 0.037 | | | 0.899 | .249 |
| 52 | .571 | .219 | .064 | 8.52 | 4.38 | 1.46 | 650 | .099 | .043 | | | 1.04 | .289 |
| 54 | .613 | .234 | .069 | 9.14 | 4.69 | 1.56 | 700 | .113 | .049 | | | 1.20 | .331 |
| 56 | .655 | .251 | .073 | 9.77 | 5.02 | 1.67 | 800 | .145 | .063 | | | 1.53 | .424 |
| 58 | .699 | .268 | .078 | | 5.35 | 1.79 | 900 | .180 | .079 | | | 1.90 | .527 |
| 60 | .744 | .285 | .083 | | 5.70 | 1.90 | 1000 | .219 | .096 | | | | .640 |
| 62 | .791 | .303 | .089 | | 6.06 | 2.02 | 1100 | .261 | .114 | | | | .764 |
| 64 | .839 | .321 | .094 | | 6.42 | 2.14 | 1200 | .307 | .134 | | | | 0.897 |
| 66 | .888 | .340 | .099 | | 6.80 | 2.27 | 1300 | .356 | .155 | | | | 1.04 |
| 68 | .938 | .359 | .105 | | 7.19 | 2.40 | 1400 | .408 | .178 | | | | 1.19 |
| 70 | 0.990 | 0.379 | 0.111 | | 7.58 | 2.53 | 1500 | .464 | .202 | | | | 1.36 |
| 75 | 1.12 | .430 | .126 | | 8.62 | 2.87 | 2000 | 0.790 | 0.344 | | | | |
| 80 | 1.27 | .485 | .142 | | | 3.24 | 2500 | 1.19 | .521 | | | | |
| 85 | 1.42 | .543 | .159 | | | 3.62 | 3000 | | .729 | | | | |
| 90 | 1.58 | .603 | .176 | | | 4.03 | 3500 | | 0.970 | | | | |
| 95 | 1.74 | .667 | .195 | | | 4.45 | 4000 | | | | | | |
| 100 | 1.92 | 0.733 | 0.214 | | | 4.89 | 5000 | | | | | | |

[1] 1/2 and 3/4 in SDR 26 not standard. For convenience, losses for 1/2 in SDR 13.5 and 3/4 in SDR 21 listed.

Courtesy of Weather-Matic Irrigation Division/Telsco Industries

# Table A-8[141]

Table Velocity Flows same for all
controlled OD SDR 26 thermoplastic pipe.

## VELOCITY FLOWS
## SDR 26 PVC PIPE

| Velocity ft/s | 1/2[1] | 3/4[2] | 1 | 1-1/4 | 1-1/2 | 2 | 2-1/2 | 3 | 4 | 6 | 8 | 10 | 12 | Velocity ft/s |
|---|---|---|---|---|---|---|---|---|---|---|---|---|---|---|
| | | | | | | | Flow: gpm[*] | | | | | | | |
| 1 | 1.2 | 2.0 | 3.4 | 5.6 | 7.4 | 11.6 | 17.0 | 25.2 | 41.8 | 90.6 | 153.6 | 238.7 | 335.7 | 1 |
| 2 | 2.4 | 4.1 | 6.8 | 11.2 | 14.7 | 23.1 | 34.0 | 50.4 | 83.6 | 181.2 | 307.2 | 477.3 | 671.5 | 2 |
| 3 | 3.6 | 6.1 | 10.1 | 16.8 | 22.1 | 34.7 | 51.0 | 75.7 | 125.5 | 271.8 | 460.8 | 716.0 | 1007.2 | 3 |
| 4 | 4.7 | 8.1 | 13.5 | 22.4 | 29.4 | 46.2 | 68.0 | 100.9 | 167.3 | 362.4 | 614.4 | 954.7 | 1342.9 | 4 |
| 5 | 5.9 | 10.1 | 16.9 | 28.0 | 36.8 | 57.8 | 85.0 | 126.1 | 209.1 | 453.1 | 768.0 | 1193.3 | 1678.7 | 5 |
| 6 | 7.1 | 12.2 | 20.3 | 33.6 | 44.2 | 69.4 | 102.0 | 151.3 | 250.9 | 543.7 | 921.6 | 1432.0 | 2014.4 | 6 |
| 7 | 8.3 | 14.2 | 23.7 | 39.2 | 51.5 | 80.9 | 119.0 | 176.6 | 292.7 | 634.3 | 1075.1 | 1670.7 | 2350.2 | 7 |
| 8 | 9.5 | 16.2 | 27.0 | 44.8 | 58.9 | 92.5 | 136.0 | 201.8 | 334.5 | 724.5 | 1228.7 | 1909.3 | 2685.9 | 8 |
| 9 | 10.7 | 18.2 | 30.4 | 50.4 | 66.2 | 104.0 | 153.0 | 227.0 | 376.3 | 815.5 | 1382.3 | 2148.0 | 3021.6 | 9 |
| 10 | 11.9 | 20.3 | 33.8 | 56.0 | 73.6 | 115.6 | 170.0 | 252.2 | 418.2 | 906.1 | 1535.9 | 2386.7 | 3357.3 | 10 |
| 11 | 13.0 | 22.3 | 37.2 | 61.6 | 81.0 | 127.2 | 187.0 | 277.5 | 460.0 | 996.7 | 1689.5 | 2625.3 | 3693.1 | 11 |
| 12 | 14.2 | 24.3 | 40.6 | 67.2 | 88.3 | 138.7 | 204.0 | 302.7 | 501.8 | 1087.3 | 1843.1 | 2864.0 | 4028.8 | 12 |
| 13 | 15.4 | 26.4 | 43.9 | 72.8 | 95.7 | 150.3 | 221.0 | 327.9 | 543.6 | 1178.0 | 1996.7 | 3102.7 | 4364.5 | 13 |
| 14 | 16.6 | 28.4 | 47.3 | 78.4 | 103.0 | 161.8 | 238.0 | 353.1 | 585.4 | 1268.6 | 2150.3 | 3341.4 | 4700.3 | 14 |
| 15 | 17.8 | 30.4 | 50.7 | 83.9 | 110.4 | 173.4 | 255.0 | 378.4 | 627.2 | 1359.2 | 2303.9 | 3580.0 | 5036.0 | 15 |

[*]Flows calculated with factors in Table 16 may vary slightly due to rounding-off of factors.
[1] Flows are for velocities in SDR 13.5 pipe.
[2] Flows are for velocities in SDR 21 pipe.

## MULTIPLYING FACTORS TO CHANGE VALUE OF "C"
## C = 150 TO OTHER VALUES

| To determine PRESSURE LOSSES with other values of "C", multiply losses computed with C = 150 by following factors: | | | | | | | | | | | | |
|---|---|---|---|---|---|---|---|---|---|---|---|---|
| Value of "C" | 160 | 150 | 140 | 130 | 120 | 110 | 100 | 90 | 80 | 70 | 60 | 50 | Value of "C" |
| Multiplier | 0.887 | 1.0 | 1.14 | 1.30 | 1.51 | 1.77 | 2.12 | 2.57 | 3.20 | 4.10 | 5.45 | 7.63 | Multiplier |

## PRESSURE LOSS
## SDR 26 PVC PIPE
### SIZES NOT LISTED OPPOSITE PAGE

| To determine PRESSURE LOSSES of 3-1/2 and 5 in SDR 26 PVC pipe, multiply Losses of 4 in SDR 26 PVC pipe by following factors: | | |
|---|---|---|
| Nominal Size, in | 3-1/2[a] | 5[a] |
| | Multiplier | |
| SDR 26 | 1.78 | 0.357 |

[a] Determine availability before designing systems with these sizes.

## PRESSURE LOSS
## SDR 26 PVC TUBING

| To determine PRESSURES of SDR 26 PVC TUBING, multiply Losses of 1 in SDR 26 PIPE by following factors: | | | | |
|---|---|---|---|---|
| Size, in | 1/2 | 3/4 | 1 | 1-1/4 | Size, in |
| SDR 26 PVC Tubing | 73.36 | 9.74 | 2.35 | 0.782 | SDR 26 PVC Tubing |

Courtesy of Weather-Matic Irrigation Division/Telsco Industries

# Table A-9[142]

Table Losses same for all
Controlled OD SDR 21 thermoplastic pipe.

C = 150

## PRESSURE LOSS
## 200 psi PR SDR 21 PVC PIPE

| Pipe Sizes: Nominal | | | | | | | | | | | Losses per 100 ft: lb/in² | |
|---|---|---|---|---|---|---|---|---|---|---|---|---|
| gpm | 1/2 in[1] | 3/4 in | 1 in | 1-1/4 in | 1-1/2 in | 2 in | gpm | 2 in | 2-1/2 in | 3 in | 4 in | 6 in | 8 in |
| 1 | 0.248 | 0.067 | 0.020 | 0.006 | 0.003 | 0.001 | 105 | 5.92 | 2.32 | 0.885 | 0.260 | 0.040 | 0.011 |
| 2 | 0.896 | .243 | .072 | .023 | .012 | .004 | 110 | 6.45 | 2.53 | 0.964 | .284 | .043 | .012 |
| 3 | 1.90 | .515 | .152 | .048 | .025 | .008 | 115 | | 2.74 | 1.05 | .308 | .047 | .013 |
| 4 | 3.23 | 0.876 | .259 | .082 | .042 | .014 | 120 | | 2.97 | 1.13 | .333 | .051 | .014 |
| 5 | 4.88 | 1.32 | .391 | .123 | .063 | .021 | 125 | | 3.20 | 1.22 | .359 | .055 | .015 |
| 6 | 6.84 | 1.86 | .548 | .173 | .089 | .030 | 130 | | 3.44 | 1.31 | .386 | .059 | .016 |
| 7 | 9.09 | 2.47 | .729 | 230 | .118 | .039 | 135 | | 3.69 | 1.41 | .414 | .063 | .017 |
| 8 | 11.64 | 3.16 | 0.934 | .294 | .151 | .051 | 140 | | 3.95 | 1.51 | .443 | .068 | .019 |
| 9 | 14.48 | 3.93 | 1.16 | .366 | .188 | .063 | 145 | | 4.21 | 1.61 | .473 | .072 | .020 |
| 10 | 17.59 | 4.77 | 1.41 | 0.445 | 0.228 | 0.076 | 150 | | 4.48 | 1.71 | 0.503 | 0.077 | 0.021 |
| 11 | 20.98 | 5.69 | 1.68 | .531 | .272 | .091 | 160 | | 5.05 | 1.93 | .567 | .086 | .024 |
| 12 | 24.65 | 6.69 | 1.98 | .623 | .320 | .107 | 170 | | | 2.16 | .634 | .097 | .027 |
| 13 | | 7.75 | 2.29 | .723 | .371 | .124 | 180 | 10 in | | 2.40 | .705 | .108 | .030 |
| 14 | | 8.89 | 2.63 | 829 | .425 | .142 | 190 | | | 2.65 | .779 | .119 | .033 |
| 15 | | 10.11 | 2.99 | 0.942 | .483 | .162 | 200 | 0.012 | | 2.91 | .857 | .131 | .036 |
| 16 | | 11.39 | 3.37 | 1.06 | .544 | .182 | 210 | .014 | | 3.19 | 0.938 | .143 | .040 |
| 17 | | 12.74 | 3.77 | 1.19 | .609 | .204 | 220 | .015 | | 3.48 | 1.02 | .156 | .043 |
| 18 | 2-1/2 in | 14.16 | 4.19 | 1.32 | .677 | .226 | 230 | .016 | | 3.77 | 1.11 | .169 | .047 |
| 19 | | 15.65 | 4.63 | 1.46 | .748 | .250 | 240 | .017 | | 4.08 | 1.20 | .183 | .051 |
| 20 | 0.108 | 17.21 | 5.09 | 1.60 | 0.823 | 0.275 | 250 | .019 | | | 1.29 | 0.197 | 0.055 |
| 22 | .129 | | 6.07 | 1.91 | 0.981 | .328 | 260 | .020 | | | 1.39 | .212 | .059 |
| 24 | .151 | | 7.13 | 2.25 | 1.15 | .386 | 270 | .022 | | | 1.49 | 228 | .063 |
| 26 | .175 | | 8.27 | 2.61 | 1.34 | .447 | 280 | .023 | 12 in | | 1.60 | .244 | .067 |
| 28 | .201 | | 9.48 | 2.99 | 1.53 | .513 | 290 | .025 | | | 1.70 | .260 | .072 |
| 30 | .228 | | 10.77 | 3.40 | 1.74 | .583 | 300 | 0.026 | 0.011 | | 1.81 | .277 | .076 |
| 32 | .257 | | 12.14 | 3.83 | 1.96 | .657 | 325 | .030 | .013 | | 2.10 | .321 | .089 |
| 34 | .288 | | 13.58 | 4.28 | 2.20 | .735 | 350 | .035 | .015 | | 2.41 | .368 | .102 |
| 36 | .320 | 3 in | | 4.76 | 2.44 | .816 | 375 | .040 | .017 | | 2.74 | .418 | .116 |
| 38 | .354 | | | 5.26 | 2.70 | .902 | 400 | .045 | .019 | | 3.09 | .471 | .130 |
| 40 | 0.389 | 0.148 | | 5.78 | 2.97 | 0.992 | 425 | .050 | .022 | | | .527 | .146 |
| 42 | .426 | .162 | | 6.33 | 3.25 | 1.09 | 450 | .055 | .024 | | | 0.586 | 0.162 |
| 44 | .424 | .177 | | 6.90 | 3.54 | 1.18 | 475 | .061 | .027 | | | .647 | .179 |
| 46 | .504 | .192 | | 7.49 | 3.84 | 1.28 | 500 | 0.067 | 0.029 | | | .712 | .197 |
| 48 | .545 | .208 | | 8.10 | 4.15 | 1.39 | 550 | .080 | .035 | | | .849 | .235 |
| 50 | .588 | .224 | | 8.74 | 4.48 | 1.50 | 600 | .094 | .041 | | | 0.997 | .276 |
| 52 | .632 | .241 | | 9.39 | 4.82 | 1.61 | 650 | .110 | .048 | | | 1.16 | .320 |
| 54 | .677 | .259 | | 10.07 | 5.17 | 1.73 | 700 | .126 | .055 | | | 1.33 | .367 |
| 56 | .725 | .277 | 4 in | | 5.53 | 1.85 | 800 | .161 | .070 | | | 1.70 | .470 |
| 58 | .773 | .295 | | | 5.90 | 1.97 | 900 | .200 | .087 | | | | .584 |
| 60 | 0.823 | 0.314 | 0.092 | | 6.28 | 2.10 | 1000 | 0.243 | 0.106 | | | | .710 |
| 62 | .875 | .334 | .098 | | 6.67 | 2.23 | 1100 | .290 | .126 | | | | .846 |
| 64 | .928 | .354 | .104 | | 7.07 | 2.37 | 1200 | .340 | .148 | | | | 0.994 |
| 66 | 0.982 | .375 | .110 | | 7.49 | 2.51 | 1300 | .395 | .172 | | | | 1.15 |
| 68 | 1.04 | .396 | .116 | | 7.91 | 2.65 | 1400 | .453 | .197 | | | | 1.32 |
| 70 | 1.09 | .418 | .123 | | 8.35 | 2.79 | 1500 | .514 | .224 | | | | 1.50 |
| 75 | 1.24 | .475 | .140 | | | 3.17 | 2000 | 0.876 | .382 | | | | |
| 80 | 1.40 | .535 | .157 | | | 3.58 | 2500 | 1.32 | .577 | | | | |
| 85 | 1.57 | .599 | .176 | | | 4.00 | 3000 | | 0.809 | | | | |
| 90 | 1.74 | .665 | .196 | | | 4.45 | 3500 | | 1.08 | | | | |
| 95 | 1.93 | .735 | .216 | | | 4.92 | 4000 | | | | | | |
| 100 | 2.12 | 0.808 | 0.238 | | | 5.40 | 5000 | | | | | | |

[1] 1/2 in SDR 21 not standard. For convenience, losses for SDR 13.5 listed.

Courtesy of Weather-Matic Irrigation Division/Telsco Industries

# Table A-10[143]

Table Velocity Flows same for all
Controlled OD SDR 21 thermoplastic pipe

## VELOCITY FLOWS
## SDR 21 PVC PIPE

| Velocity ft/s | 1/2[1] | 3/4 | 1 | 1-1/4 | 1-1/2 | 2 | 2-1/2 | 3 | 4 | 6 | 8 | 10 | 12 | Velocity ft/s |
|---|---|---|---|---|---|---|---|---|---|---|---|---|---|---|
| | | | | | | Flow: gpm* | | | | | | | | |
| 1 | 1.2 | 2.0 | 3.3 | 5.4 | 7.1 | 11.1 | 16.3 | 24.2 | 40.1 | 86.8 | 147.3 | 228.8 | 321.8 | 1 |
| 2 | 2.4 | 4.1 | 6.7 | 10.8 | 14.1 | 22.2 | 32.6 | 48.5 | 80.1 | 173.6 | 294.5 | 457.5 | 643.6 | 2 |
| 3 | 3.6 | 6.1 | 10.0 | 16.1 | 21.2 | 33.3 | 48.9 | 72.7 | 120.2 | 260.4 | 441.8 | 686.3 | 965.3 | 3 |
| 4 | 4.7 | 8.1 | 13.4 | 21.5 | 28.3 | 44.4 | 65.2 | 96.9 | 160.3 | 347.2 | 589.0 | 915.1 | 1287.1 | 4 |
| 5 | 5.9 | 10.1 | 16.7 | 26.9 | 35.4 | 55.5 | 81.5 | 121.1 | 200.4 | 434.1 | 736.3 | 1143.8 | 1608.9 | 5 |
| 6 | 7.1 | 12.2 | 20.1 | 32.3 | 42.4 | 66.6 | 97.8 | 145.4 | 240.4 | 520.9 | 883.6 | 1372.6 | 1930.7 | 6 |
| 7 | 8.3 | 14.2 | 23.4 | 37.6 | 49.5 | 77.7 | 114.2 | 169.6 | 280.5 | 607.7 | 1030.8 | 1601.4 | 2252.4 | 7 |
| 8 | 9.5 | 16.2 | 26.8 | 43.0 | 56.6 | 88.8 | 130.5 | 193.8 | 320.6 | 694.5 | 1178.1 | 1830.1 | 2574.2 | 8 |
| 9 | 10.7 | 18.2 | 30.1 | 48.4 | 63.7 | 99.9 | 146.8 | 218.1 | 360.7 | 781.3 | 1325.3 | 2058.9 | 2896.0 | 9 |
| 10 | 11.9 | 20.3 | 33.5 | 53.8 | 70.7 | 111.0 | 163.1 | 242.3 | 400.7 | 868.1 | 1472.6 | 2287.7 | 3217.8 | 10 |
| 11 | 13.0 | 22.3 | 36.8 | 59.1 | 77.8 | 122.1 | 179.4 | 266.5 | 440.8 | 954.9 | 1619.9 | 2516.4 | 3539.6 | 11 |
| 12 | 14.2 | 24.3 | 40.1 | 64.5 | 84.9 | 133.1 | 195.7 | 290.7 | 480.9 | 1041.7 | 1767.1 | 2745.2 | 3861.3 | 12 |
| 13 | 15.4 | 26.4 | 43.5 | 69.9 | 92.0 | 144.2 | 212.0 | 315.0 | 521.0 | 1128.5 | 1914.4 | 2974.0 | 4183.1 | 13 |
| 14 | 16.6 | 28.4 | 46.8 | 75.3 | 99.0 | 155.3 | 228.3 | 339.2 | 561.0 | 1215.4 | 2061.6 | 3202.7 | 4504.9 | 14 |
| 15 | 17.8 | 30.4 | 50.2 | 80.6 | 106.1 | 166.4 | 244.6 | 363.4 | 601.1 | 1302.2 | 2208.9 | 3431.5 | 4826.7 | 15 |

*Flows calculated with factors in Table 16 may vary slightly due to rounding off of factors.
[1]Flows for velocities in SDR 13.5 pipe.

## MULTIPLYING FACTORS TO CHANGE VALUE OF "C"
## C = 150 TO OTHER VALUES

| | To determine PRESSURE LOSSES with other values of "C", multiply Losses computed with C = 150 by following factors: | | | | | | | | | | | | |
|---|---|---|---|---|---|---|---|---|---|---|---|---|---|
| Value of "C" | ·160 | 150 | 140 | 130 | 120 | 110 | 100 | 90 | 80 | 70 | 60 | 50 | Value of "C" |
| Multiplier | 0.887 | 1.0 | 1.14 | 1.30 | 1.51 | 1.77 | 2.12 | 2.57 | 3.20 | 4.10 | 5.45 | 7.63 | Multiplier |

## PRESSURE LOSS
## SDR 21 PVC PIPE
### SIZES NOT LISTED OPPOSITE PAGE

| To determine PRESSURE LOSSES of 3-1/2 and 5 in SDR 21 PVC pipe, multiply LOSSES of 4 in SDR 21 by following factors: | | |
|---|---|---|
| Nominal Size, in | 3-1/2[a] | 5[a] |
| | Multiplier | |
| SDR 21 | 1.78 | 0.357 |
| SDR 17 | 2.02 | 0.406 |

[a] Determine availability before designing systems with these sizes.

## PRESSURE LOSS
## SDR 17 PVC PIPE

| | To determine PRESSURE LOSSES of SDR 17 PVC pipe, multiply losses of same size SDR 21 by following factors: | | | | | | | | | | | | |
|---|---|---|---|---|---|---|---|---|---|---|---|---|---|
| Size, in | 3/4 | 1 | 1-1/4 | 1-1/2 | 2 | 2-1/2 | 3 | 4 | 6 | 8 | 10 | 12 | Size, in |
| | Multipliers | | | | | | | | | | | | |
| SDR17 | 1.02 | 1.13 | 1.13 | 1.14 | 1.13 | 1.13 | 1.14 | 1.14 | 1.14 | 1.14 | 1.14 | 1.14 | SDR17 |

Courtesy of Weather-Matic Irrigation Division/Telsco Industries

# Table A-11[144]

Table Losses Same for all Controlled OD
SDR 13.5 thermoplastic pipe.  For PE pipe,
convert losses to equivalent of C = 140

C = 150

## PRESSURE LOSS
## 315 psi PR SDR 13.5 PVC PIPE

| Pipe Sizes: Nominal | | | | | | | | | | Losses per 100 ft: lb/in$^2$ | |
|---|---|---|---|---|---|---|---|---|---|---|---|
| gpm | 1/2 in | 3/4 in | 1 in | 1-1/4 in | 1-1/2 in | 2 in | gpm | 2-1/2 in | 3 in | 4 in | 6 in |
| 1 | 0.248 | 0.082 | 0.027 | 0.008 | 0.004 | 0.001 | 105 | 3.15 | 1.21 | 0.356 | 0.054 |
| 2 | 0.896 | .296 | .096 | .031 | .016 | .005 | 110 | 3.44 | 1.32 | .388 | .059 |
| 3 | 1.90 | 0.626 | .204 | .065 | .033 | .011 | 115 | 3.73 | 1.43 | .421 | .064 |
| 4 | 3.23 | 1.07 | .347 | .110 | .057 | .019 | 120 | 4.04 | 1.55 | .455 | .069 |
| 5 | 4.88 | 1.61 | .524 | .116 | .086 | .029 | 125 | 4.35 | 1.67 | .491 | .075 |
| 6 | 6.84 | 2.26 | .734 | .233 | .120 | .040 | 130 | 4.68 | 1.79 | .528 | .081 |
| 7 | 9.09 | 3.00 | 0.976 | .310 | .159 | .053 | 135 | 5.02 | 1.92 | .566 | .086 |
| 8 | 11.64 | 3.84 | 1.25 | .397 | .204 | .068 | 140 | 5.37 | 2.06 | .606 | .092 |
| 9 | 14.48 | 4.78 | 1.55 | .493 | .254 | .085 | 145 | 5.73 | 2.19 | .646 | .099 |
| 10 | 17.59 | 5.81 | 1.89 | 0.599 | 0.308 | 0.103 | 150 | 6.10 | 2.34 | 0.688 | 0.105 |
| 11 | 20.98 | 6.93 | 2.25 | .715 | .368 | .123 | 160 | | 2.63 | .775 | .118 |
| 12 | 24.65 | 8.14 | 2.65 | .840 | .432 | .144 | 170 | | 2.95 | .867 | .132 |
| 13 | | 9.44 | 3.07 | 0.974 | .501 | .167 | 180 | | 3.27 | 0.964 | .147 |
| 14 | | 10.82 | 3.52 | 1.12 | .575 | .192 | 190 | | 3.62 | 1.07 | .163 |
| 15 | | 12.30 | 4.00 | 1.27 | .653 | .218 | 200 | | 3.98 | 1.17 | .179 |
| 16 | | 13.86 | 4.51 | 1.43 | .736 | .246 | 210 | | 4.35 | 1.28 | .196 |
| 17 | | 15.50 | 5.04 | 1.60 | .823 | .275 | 220 | | 4.75 | 1.40 | .213 |
| 18 | | 17.23 | 5.60 | 1.78 | 0.915 | .305 | 230 | | | 1.52 | .231 |
| 19 | | 19.04 | 6.19 | 1.96 | 1.01 | .338 | 240 | | | 1.64 | .250 |
| 20 | | 20.94 | 6.81 | 2.16 | 1.11 | 0.371 | 250 | | | 1.77 | 0.270 |
| 22 | | | 8.12 | 2.58 | 1.33 | .443 | 260 | | | 1.90 | .290 |
| 24 | | | 9.54 | 3.03 | 1.56 | .520 | 270 | | | 2.04 | .311 |
| 26 | | | 11.06 | 3.51 | 1.81 | .603 | 280 | | | 2.18 | .333 |
| 28 | 2-1/2 in | | 12.69 | 4.03 | 2.07 | .692 | 290 | | | 2.33 | .355 |
| 30 | 0.311 | | 14.42 | 4.57 | 2.35 | .786 | 300 | | | 2.48 | .378 |
| 32 | .350 | | | 5.15 | 2.65 | .886 | 325 | | | 2.88 | .439 |
| 34 | .391 | | | 5.77 | 2.97 | 0.991 | 350 | | | 3.30 | .503 |
| 36 | .435 | 3 in | | 6.41 | 3.30 | 1.10 | 375 | | | 3.75 | .572 |
| 38 | .481 | | | 7.08 | 3.64 | 1.22 | 400 | | | | .644 |
| 40 | .529 | 0.203 | | 7.79 | 4.01 | 1.34 | 425 | | | | .721 |
| 42 | .579 | .222 | | 8.52 | 4.39 | 1.46 | 450 | | | | .801 |
| 44 | .631 | .242 | | 9.29 | 4.78 | 1.60 | 475 | | | | .885 |
| 46 | .685 | .262 | 4 in | 10.09 | 5.19 | 1.73 | 500 | | | | 0.973 |
| 48 | .741 | .284 | | 10.91 | 5.61 | 1.88 | 550 | | | | 1.16 |
| 50 | 0.799 | 0.306 | 0.090 | | 6.05 | 2.02 | 600 | | | | 1.36 |
| 52 | .859 | .329 | .097 | | 6.51 | 2.17 | 650 | | | | 1.58 |
| 54 | .921 | .353 | .104 | | 6.98 | 2.33 | 700 | | | | 1.81 |
| 56 | 0.985 | .378 | .111 | | 7.47 | 2.49 | 800 | | | | 2.32 |
| 58 | 1.05 | .403 | .119 | | 7.97 | 2.66 | 900 | | | | |
| 60 | 1.12 | .429 | .126 | | 8.48 | 2.83 | 1000 | | | | |
| 62 | 1.19 | .456 | .134 | | 9.01 | 3.01 | 1100 | | | | |
| 64 | 1.26 | .483 | .142 | | | 3.19 | 1200 | | | | |
| 66 | 1.34 | .512 | .151 | | | 3.38 | 1300 | | | | |
| 68 | 1.41 | .541 | .159 | | | 3.57 | 1400 | | | | |
| 70 | 1.49 | 0.571 | 0.168 | | | 3.77 | 1500 | | | | |
| 75 | 1.69 | .648 | .191 | | | 4.28 | 2000 | | | | |
| 80 | 1.91 | .730, | .215 | | | 4.82 | 2500 | | | | |
| 85 | 2.13 | .817 | .241 | | | 5.40 | 3000 | | | | |
| 90 | 2.37 | 0.908 | .267 | | | 6.00 | 3500 | | | | |
| 95 | 2.62 | 1.00 | .296 | | | 6.63 | 4000 | | | | |
| 100 | 2.88 | 1.10 | 0.325 | | | 7.29 | 5000 | | | | |

Courtesy of Weather-Matic Irrigation Division/Telsco Industries

# Table A-12[145]

Table VELOCITY FLOWS same for all
Controlled OD SDR 13.5 thermoplastic pipe.

## VELOCITY FLOWS
## SDR13.5 PVC PIPE

| Velocity ft/s | Nominal Pipe Size inches | | | | | | | | | | Velocity ft/s |
|---|---|---|---|---|---|---|---|---|---|---|---|
| | 1/2 | 3/4 | 1 | 1.1 4 | 1.1 2 | 2 | 2.1 2 | 3 | 4 | 6 | |
| | Flow gpm* | | | | | | | | | | |
| 1 | 1.2 | 1.9 | 3.0 | 4.8 | 6.3 | 9.8 | 14.4 | 21.3 | 35.2 | 76.3 | 1 |
| 2 | 2.4 | 3.7 | 5.9 | 9.5 | 12.5 | 19.6 | 28.7 | 42.6 | 70.5 | 152.7 | 2 |
| 3 | 3.6 | 5.6 | 8.9 | 14.3 | 18.8 | 25.4 | 43.1 | 64.0 | 105.7 | 229.0 | 3 |
| 4 | 4.7 | 7.5 | 11.9 | 19.0 | 25.0 | 39.2 | 57.5 | 85.3 | 140.9 | 305.3 | 4 |
| 5 | 5.9 | 9.3 | 14.8 | 23.8 | 31.3 | 49.1 | 71.9 | 106.6 | 176.2 | 381.7 | 5 |
| 6 | 7.1 | 11.2 | 17.8 | 28.5 | 37.5 | 58.9 | 86.2 | 127.9 | 211.4 | 458.0 | 6 |
| 7 | 8.3 | 13.1 | 20.8 | 33.3 | 43.8 | 68.7 | 100.6 | 149.2 | 246.7 | 534.3 | 7 |
| 8 | 9.5 | 15.0 | 23.7 | 38.1 | 50.0 | 78.5 | 115.0 | 170.5 | 281.9 | 610.6 | 8 |
| 9 | 10.7 | 16.8 | 26.7 | 42.8 | 56.3 | 88.3 | 129.3 | 191.9 | 317.1 | 687.0 | 9 |
| 10 | 11.9 | 18.7 | 29.7 | 47.6 | 62.5 | 98.1 | 143.7 | 213.2 | 352.4 | 763.3 | 10 |
| 11 | 13.0 | 20.6 | 32.6 | 52.3 | 68.8 | 107.9 | 158.1 | 234.5 | 387.6 | 839.6 | 11 |
| 12 | 14.2 | 22.4 | 35.6 | 57.1 | 75.0 | 117.7 | 172.5 | 255.8 | 422.8 | 916.0 | 12 |
| 13 | 15.4 | 24.3 | 38.6 | 61.8 | 81.3 | 127.5 | 186.8 | 277.1 | 458.1 | 992.3 | 13 |
| 14 | 16.6 | 26.2 | 41.5 | 66.6 | 87.5 | 137.4 | 201.2 | 298.5 | 493.3 | 1068.6 | 14 |
| 15 | 17.8 | 28.0 | 44.5 | 71.4 | 93.8 | 147.2 | 215.6 | 319.8 | 528.6 | 1145.0 | 15 |

*Flows calculated with factors in Table 16 may vary slightly due to rounding off of factors.

## MULTIPLYING FACTORS TO CHANGE VALUE OF "C"
## C = 150 TO OTHER VALUES

| To determine PRESSURE LOSSES with other values of "C", multiply Losses computed with C = 150 by following factors: | | | | | | | | | | | | |
|---|---|---|---|---|---|---|---|---|---|---|---|---|
| Value of "C" | 160 | 150 | 140 | 130 | 120 | 110 | 100 | 90 | 80 | 70 | 60 | 50 | Value of "C" |
| Multiplier | 0.887 | 1.0 | 1.14 | 1.30 | 1.51 | 1.77 | 2.12 | 2.57 | 3.20 | 4.10 | 5.45 | 7.63 | Multiplier |

## PRESSURE LOSS
## SDR 13.5 PVC PIPE
### SIZES NOT LISTED OPPOSITE PAGE

| To determine PRESSURE LOSSES of 1/8, 1/4 and 3/8 in SDR 13.5 PVC pipe, multiply Losses of 1/2 in SDR 13.5 by following factors: | | | |
|---|---|---|---|
| Nominal Size, in | 1/8 | 1/4 | 3/8 |
| | Multipliers | | |
| SDR 13.5 | 109.8 | 14.80 | 3.60 |

| To determine PRESSURE LOSSES of 3-1/2 and 5 in SDR 13.5 PVC pipe, multiply Losses of 4 in SDR 13.5 by following factors: | | |
|---|---|---|
| Nominal Size, in | 3-1/2[a] | 5[a] |
| | Multipliers | |
| SDR 13.5 | 1.78 | 0.357 |

(a) Determine availability before designing systems with these sizes.

Courtesy of Weather-Matic Irrigation Division/Telsco Industries

## CONVERSION FACTORS

| | |
|---|---|
| Feet head (ft. hd.) x .433 | = Pounds per square inch (P.S.I.) |
| Pounds per square inch x 2.31 | = Feet head |
| U.S. gallons per minute x .1337 | = Cubic feet per minute |
| Cubic feet per minute x 7.48 | = U.S. gallons per minute |
| U.S. gallon x 8.336 | = Pounds |
| Horse power (H.P.) x 746 | = Watts |
| Horse power x .746 | = Kilowatts |
| Circumference of circle x .3183 | = Diameter of circle |
| Diameter of circle x 3.1416 | = Circumference of circle |
| Diameter of circle squared x .7854 | = Area of circle |

Cubic feet per second $= \dfrac{\text{Gallons per minute}}{449}$

Velocity in feet per second $= \dfrac{.408 \times \text{U.S. g.p.m.}}{\text{Diam. of pipe squared}}$ or $\dfrac{.32 \times \text{g.p.m.}}{\text{Pipe area}}$

| | |
|---|---|
| Cubic foot of water | = 62 pounds |
| Cubic foot of water | = 7.48 gallons |

### METRIC CONVERSIONS

| | |
|---|---|
| 1 inch | = 2.54 cm |
| 1 foot | = 30.48 cm = .3048 m |
| 1 yard | = 91.44 cm = .91444 m |
| 1 gallon | = 3.785 4 L |

## SPECIFICATION SUMMARY

| Material | Grade, Specification or Product Source |
|---|---|
| *In Situ Concrete* | 4,000 psi concrete @ 28 days. Air-entrained admix 4½ to 1½ percent ASTM C260. ¾ inch maximum diameter aggregate. Water cement ratio of 6 gallons per sack of concrete maximum. |
| *Precast Concrete* | 7,000 to 12,000 psi concrete as manufactured by a precaster with a minimum of 5 years experience. |
| *Concrete Accessories* *Waterstops* | PVC or vinyl waterstop as manufactured by Harbour Town Plastics, Inc., W.R. Grace & Company or Greenstreak Plastic Products. Waterstop to meet Corps of Engineers specifications CRD-C572-74. |
| *Joint Sealants* | Join sealants as manufactured by the Sonneborn Building Products Division. |
| *Backer Rods* | Closed cell backer rod as manufactured by the Sonneborn Building Products Division. Material to meet ASTM D-1622-75. |
| *Snap Ties* | Stainless steel or galvanized ties as manufactured by the Burke Company. |
| *Concrete Paint* for Submerged Applications | Ramuc enamel by Koppers Chemicals and Coatings or equal. |
| *Gunite* | 5,000 to 9,000 psi gunite @ 28 days. Water cement ratio of .33 to .35 by weight. Gunite contractor to have a minimum of 5 years experience. |
| *Tile* | Vitreous, frostproof or certified for exterior use by the tile manufacturer. Tile to meet ANSI A137.1. |
| *Brick* | Grade 'SW' solid core facing brick meeting ASTM C216. Grade 'SX' paving brick meeting ASTM C-902-79A. Facing brick to have a full mortar joint behind the masonry unit. |
| *Granite* | 19,000 psi granite meeting ASTM C170. |
| *Sandstone* | Type II quartzitic sandstone, or type III quartzite meeting ASTM C616. |
| *Limestone* | Statuary or select grade limestone. |
| *Slate* | Exterior grade slate meeting ASTM C629. |
| *Marble* | Grades 'A' and 'S' Marble meeting ASTM C503. Some marble types are not suitable for submersed applications. |
| *Masonry Accessories* *Joint Reinforcing and Ties* | Galvanized or stainless steel ties as manufactured by Dur-O-Wal Inc. |

## SPECIFICATION SUMMARY

| Material | Grade, Specification or Product Source |
| --- | --- |
| *Masonry Mortar* | Type 'M' mortar. Use where high strength and good bonding is required. |
| | Type 'S' mortar. Use where higher bonding and lower strength than type 'M' mortar is required. |
| | Type '8510' admix by Laticrete International Inc. Use where high strength and good bonding of full-size masonry units are required. |
| | Type '3710' admix by Laticrete International Inc. Use for thick bed installations of tile, brick splits and stone veneers. |
| | Type '4237' admix by Laticrete International Inc. Use for thin bed installations of tile, brick splits and stone veneers. |
| *Copper* | 110 cold rolled copper soldered with ASTM B-32 50 percent lead and 50 percent tin solder. Attach to substrate with copper or copper alloy fastener. |
| *Brass* | Cast or sheet metal consisting of 70 to 85 percent copper and 15 to 30 percent zinc. (Brass and cartridge brass) Weld with brass rod. |
| *Bronze* | Cast or sheet metal consisting of 90 percent copper and 10 percent zinc, or 96 percent copper, 3 percent silicon, and 1 percentage managanese (commercial bronze or silicon bronze). Weld with bronze rod. |
| *Cast Iron* | Class 30 gray iron meeting ASTM A48. Weld with nicle welding rod according to AWS standards. |
| *High Strength Steel* | Corten, Mayari-r or Dynalloy steel. Weld according to AWS standards. |
| *Stainless Steel* | Type 302, 316 or 304 stainless steel. Weld according to AWS standards. |
| *Aluminum* | Type 5005, 5050 or 5052 aluminum. Weld with an inert-gas shielded arc welder. |
| *Wood* | Redwood or pressure treated pine. Pine to be treated in accordance with AWPA standards. |
| *Fiberglas* | Polyester resin coated fiberglas mat or woven rovings. Mat to weigh a minimum of ¾ to 1½ ounces per square foot. Finished tensile strength to be 50,000 psi. Material to be surface treated with gel coat. |
| *Acrylic* | Lucite or Korad sheets, or colored molded acrylic meeting ASTM D1003, D1044, D1499 and/or ANSI 297.1a 1977. Solvent welded or one piece molded. |

## SPECIFICATION SUMMARY

| Material | Grade, Specification or Product Source |
|---|---|
| *Waterproof Membranes* | |
| *Surface applied* | High density polyethylene, chlorinated polyethylene alloy reinforced, EPDM, butyl and/or PVC. Material to be high in U.V. and ozone resistance. Linings as manufactured by Palco Linings, Inc., Schlegel Lining Technology, Inc. or equal. Splice as per manufacturers recommendations. |
| *Sandwich application* | Liquid or sheet membranes as manufactured by Laticrete International, Inc. or Sonneborn Building Products Division. |
| *Balancing Valve and valves* | *Gate valve* — brass or bronze valve by Nibco or equal. Use when low pressure loss through valve is required and infrequent valve operation is anticipated. |
| | *Glove valve* — brass or bronze valve by Nibco or equal. Use where high pressure loss is allowable. |
| | *Husky valve* — brass and neoprene valve by Nibco or equal. Use when balancing valve is closer than two diameters from the nozzle base. Check availability before specifying. |
| | *Electric solenoid valves* — brass or PVC valve as manufactured by Hydro-rain. |
| *Pumps* | *Small submersible* — nylon or polypropylene pump as manufactured by Little Giant Pump Company or equal. U.L. listed for underwater applications only. |
| | *Submersible wastewater pumps* — cast iron and stainless steel pump as manufactured by Peabody Barnes. |
| | Submersible — brass and stainless steel pumps as supplied by Kim Lighting, Roman Fountains or Flair Fountains. |
| | *Dry centrifugal pump* — cast iron, brass or bronze pump assemblies as supplied by Kim Lighting, Roman Fountains or Flair Fountains. |
| *Fountain Mechanical Supplies* | Supplied by Pem Fountains, Kim Lighting, Roman Fountains and Flair Fountains. |
| *Brass Conduit* | Brass or copper alloy conduit as supplied by Pem Fountains, Flair Fountains or Everdure. |
| *Corrosion Protection Tape for Pipe and Conduit* | Tape and tape primer as manufactured by 3M Company. |

# INDEX